MEXICAN AMERICANS

ETHNIC GROUPS IN AMERICAN LIFE SERIES

Milton M. Gordon, *editor*

MEXICAN

Second Edition

AMERICANS

JOAN W. MOORE

University of Wisconsin, Milwaukee

with

HARRY PACHON

Contributing Author
Michigan State University

PRENTICE-HALL, INC., ENGLEWOOD CLIFFS, NEW JERSEY

Library of Congress Cataloging in Publication Data

MOORE, JOAN W
  Mexican Americans.

  (Prentice-Hall ethnic groups in American life series)
  Includes bibliographical references and index.
  1. Mexican Americans—Southwest, New. 2. Southwest,
New—History. I. Pachon, Harry, joint author. II. Ti-
tle.
F790.M5M6 1976   301.45′16′872079   75–29456
ISBN 0–13–579516–8
ISBN 0–13–579508–7 pbk.

10 9 8

Printed in the United States of America

PRENTICE-HALL INTERNATIONAL, INC. *London*
PRENTICE-HALL OF AUSTRALIA, PTY. LTD., *Sydney*
PRENTICE-HALL OF CANADA, LTD., *Toronto*
PRENTICE-HALL OF INDIA PRIVATE LTD., *New Delhi*
PRENTICE-HALL OF JAPAN, INC., *Tokyo*
PRENTICE-HALL OF SOUTHEAST ASIA (PTE.) LTD., *Singapore*

Contents

CHAPTER EIGHT

Foreword

As the United States, with its racially and ethnically variegated population, moves through the 1970s, the myths of the melting pot and complete assimilation recede farther and farther into the distance both in this country and abroad. Contrary to the expectations and pronouncements of many social scientists, industrialization and urbanization have not reduced the salience of ethnicity in the modern world, nor is there substantial evidence that ethnicity as a critical issue subsides because it happens to exist within the borders of a particular social system: capitalist, socialist, communist, or some mixture in between. The stubborn persistence of the racial and ethnic factor as a source of ethnic communality, and the conflict of ethnic collectivities as interest groups seeking by various means their (frequently previously withheld) fair share of material and status rewards make it all the more imperative that the resources of the sociologist, the political scientist, the historian, the psychologist, the anthropologist, and other practitioners of the art and science of understanding human behavior be brought to bear on the problem. Such application should produce both the theoretical knowledge and the practical measures that would help create a state of affairs where the positive potentialities of ethnic pluralism can be effectively realized while the negative results of unlimited ethnic conflict can be minimized and kept within tolerable bounds.

Thus, the ethnic problem before the American people today is what shape the new pluralism shall take. Is it to be cultural pluralism, with its emphasis on a broad kaleidoscope of ethnic patterns and peoples reaching to the point of conscious promotion of sustained bilingualism? Or is structural pluralism, with its social separation in primary group relationships, to be the dominant mode, with differing cultural heritages to be recognized and maintained by symbolic appropriations and reinterpretations of one's ethnic past? What form and resolution will the political contests take, brought on by the black revolt and newly-emphasized ethnic consciousness and sense of pride among Mexican Americans, Puerto Rican Americans, American Indians, and Oriental Americans, together with the probably consequent revival of collective consciousness among the traditional white ethnic groups of European ancestral origin?

The issues around which this new pluralism will form have such names as affirmative action, de jure and de facto segregation, school busing to achieve racial integration, cultural nationalism, community control of local institutions, and breakdown of racial and ethnic barriers to housing, ethnic voting, and confrontation politics; and they are all intimately related to the overriding question of how present-day America deals with the problems of inflation, unemployment, and recession, which fall with particularly heavy impact on its racial minorities.

In order to make the best decisions on these issues, the American of the 1970s needs to be well informed on the history, contributions, and current problems of the racial and ethnic groups that make up the American people, and how the issues highlighted above are affected by, and in turn affect, the nature of the emerging pluralism. The books in this series are designed to provide this information in a scholarly, yet highly accessible, manner. Each book on a particular ethnic group (and we include the white Protestants as such a sociologically definable entity) is written by an expert in the field of intergroup relations and the social life of the group about which he writes. In many cases the author derives ethnically himself or herself from that group. I hope that the publication of this series will aid substantially in the process of enabling Americans to understand more fully what it means to live in a multiethnic society and, concomitantly, what we must do in the future to eliminate the corrosive and devastating phenomena of prejudice and discrimination and to ensure that a pluralistic society can at the same time fulfill its promised destiny of being truly "one nation indivisible."

MILTON M. GORDON

Preface

This book attempts to develop a complete yet compact description of the Mexican American experience in the United States. The present diversity of this huge and growing minority is a consequence of their history. I emphasize the historical background of Mexican Americans in their region of traditional concentration—the Border States of the American Southwest. Much of this history is unfamiliar to most Americans, yet it is critical in understanding the wide variations in modern Chicano life.

This second edition includes comprehensive surveys of Chicano history, immigration, demographic material, settlement patterns, employment and income, educational status, family and community patterns, language and culture, and recent political developments. Because certain American institutions are critical in Mexican American life, there is particular attention to the educational and law enforcement systems in the Southwest.

All of the most recent demographic information is summarized with particular attention to recent research in education. This edition contains much new material on the growing demand for equality in both education and civil rights.

It is my hope that the interpretations in this book will serve to sustain a yet more intensive interest among both Mexican American scholars and Anglo scholars. I am convinced that increased understanding of Mexican Americans (and of any minority population) can best be reached in the process of mutual interaction—and mutual research. Both members of the minority itself and those outside the minority must participate.

Three groups of Mexican Americans and Anglos interacted to develop the perspectives of this book. First was a group of academic colleagues and students, Chicano and Anglo. Some of these persons worked at one time or another with the Mexican American Study Project at the University of California at Los Angeles or were associated with the author at the University of California, Riverside, and the University of Southern California. Next were groups of Mexican Americans throughout the Southwest who generously interacted with the author in their own communities.

Their contributions were the mature insights that come only after a lifetime of attempting to cope with Anglo institutions in the Southwest. During the past five years, in which I have participated more actively with community groups, this relationship has become more significant. And third, there were approximately 2,500 Mexican Americans who responded to surveys conducted by U.C.L.A. in Los Angeles and San Antonio, by Operation SER in Albuquerque, and by the Chicano Pinto Research Project at U.S.C.

These are the academic and community colleagues, students, informants, and respondents (in the process of interaction) who helped create this story of the Mexican American experience. Particular gratitude is due Leo Grebler for his extraordinary qualities as director of the U.C.L.A. Mexican American Study Project, and also for his willingness to comment on portions of this volume and to make available important data from the project.

Finally, I wish to thank Harry Pachon, who contributed chapter eight, which deals with politics and the Mexican American experience. In addition his comments on other parts of the manuscript were helpful and are appreciated.

JOAN W. MOORE

MEXICAN AMERICANS

As do most American ethnic or minority groups, Mexican Americans must live with some prevailing and popular ideas about themselves. These ideas are important because they are clues to the social realities for people who must live, comfortably or not, inside a larger society. The traits of a group as perceived by outsiders are often an artifact of its place inside the larger society and of its meaning for the larger society. The word for this kind of popular notion is "stereotype."

A stereotype is a set of assumptions permitting the classification of individuals into groups. These "beliefs" therefore "support, justify, and determine the character of interracial relationships."[1] But one of the most important general conclusions to be made in this book is that the American Mexican population probably is more diverse in social composition than any immigrant minority group in American history. Therefore, no minority less deserves simple stereotyping, whether it appears in the popular press or in scholarly books. And yet the Chicanos have been stereotyped quickly and haphazardly.

Anglo American settlers began to meet Mexicans early in the nineteenth century, and the racial myths appeared at once. There were differences in attitudes, temperament, and behavior that were supposed to be genetic, although it is hard now to imagine the normal mixture of Spanish and Indian as any kind of distinct "race." But in the nineteenth century the Anglo Americans of the Southwest had no doubts.[2] When

Mexican Americans in American Life

---

[1] Alfred R. Lindesmith and Anselm L. Strauss, *Social Psychology* (New York: Dryden Press, 1950), p. 396.

[2] Genetic diversity specifically rules out race as a factor in the analysis of distinctive Mexican American patterns of health and health care, for example. See A. Taher Moustafa and Gertrude Weiss, *Health Status and Practices of Mexican Americans*, Advance Report 11 (University of California, Los Angeles: Mexican-American Study Project, 1968). Definition of the group in racial terms persists, despite denial and suppression. Increasingly, paralleling the emphasis on Black identity, Mexican Americans appear to be consciously confronting their own feelings about being partially Indian. The paradox comes to the surface when a hazel-eyed, pale-skinned man talks about his "Indianness" and a dark-skinned, Indian-featured man talks about his "whiteness." Both "whiteness" and "Indianness" have acquired many dimensions of meaning for Chicanos, on the basis of interaction within the group and between Anglos and Mexicans legally, and in normal social contacts. As recently as 1930, the U.S. Census counted Mexicans as a separate, nonwhite race. (See Chapter Eight for some recent political results of the "race" issue in the development of *Chicanismo*.)

the new southwestern territories were absorbed into the United States, these alleged racial qualities were used to explain the social status quo— a division of labor in which the Mexicans were most often on the bottom.

There are very few educated Americans who argue today that there are any *innate* differences in abilities or character between races. Racial explanations for Mexican American patterns of conduct are even less popular. However, cultural stereotypes are now quite acceptable, and cultural stereotypes are useful in the justification of a position in society (thus, "The Irish are always drunken; it is part of their culture" or "The Italian cultural tradition allows organized crime on the Mafia pattern"). The majority can give itself a rationale for differential treatment of the Irish and the Italians, in spite of the fact that our knowledge of the cultural factors that affect the behavior of any ethnic group is never complete, never quite up to date, and never applicable to all new and changing situations. Even basic information on cultural patterns is difficult to assemble. Often individual members of an ethnic group are unreliable informants about the total subculture because their knowledge may be limited or difficult to articulate. No single family of any cultural group is likely to be a representative family. This is particularly true in the complex and highly differentiated society of modern America.

We must then discover what Americans have thought of Mexicans and of Mexican Americans in terms of racial and cultural stereotypes. We must also determine how these conceptions, in turn, have been adapted to the actual roles of Mexicans in the society and in the economy of the American Southwest.

This inquiry will demand some discussion of the long literary tradition dealing with the encounter between Mexican and Anglo. As sources, this encounter has produced reminiscences, official government reports, novels, essays, and academic history. There is also some modern interview survey data on how Mexican Americans are seen by other people and how they see themselves.

MEXICANS AS ANGLOS SEE THEM

The first encounters between Mexicans and Americans occurred when the Southwest was still Mexican soil. These first encounters were very important because they fixed the first image of Mexicans that Americans had. Americans came to Texas as colonists with Stephen Austin. They came to what is now New Mexico as traders on the Santa Fe trail; to California with the clipper ships from New England; to wilderness areas as explorers; and as soldiers and irregular fighters. In 1836, after a short period of colonization, the Texas American settlers overthrew by violence the Mexican government in Texas.

Whatever their role, Anglos did not hesitate to record their scorn for what they felt to be a backward people in a backward land. They attributed the backwardness to *innate* Mexican traits, one of which was thought to be laziness. "To the early writers the Mexican was just plain lazy and deserved to lose out, as he surely would, to the energetic, productive Northerner."[3] During the Mexican war of 1846–1848 simple hatred crept in. Americans began to call the Mexicans "yellow-belly greasers" and to develop the idea that Mexicans by race were naturally cowards. The belief in the cowardice of Mexicans is commemorated most strikingly in the simplified popular Anglo mythology about the defense of the Alamo. There, during the Texas revolution, overwhelming numbers of cowardly Mexican troops were defied by a small, brave band of Texas rebels. The enormous significance of this event, both in Texas history and in modern relations between Texas Anglos and Mexican Americans, is not in the least affected by the fact that inside the Alamo there were Mexicans fighting with the Americans. The Alamo is a Texas shrine and a standing monument to the Texas belief that Mexicans at heart are a very cowardly people. A second alleged trait is that Mexicans are by nature corrupt. This impression was strengthened by the bloodless conquest of New Mexico; the Anglo legend of the conquest of New Mexico involved Mexican corruption and Mexican cowardice. The Anglo settlers felt simply that a people too cowardly to fight would willingly sell the state of New Mexico. From the guerrilla warfare of this period and later years comes yet a third related image—that the Mexican is unbelievably cruel when he has the upper hand in battle.

But a very different set of images was also appearing during these early years of contact. Such early explorers as John C. Fremont and Major Zebulon Pike met extraordinarily gracious receptions from the Mexicans and reported their contacts with great enthusiasm. Those Mexicans living in what is now California (the *californios*) particularly, were portrayed as living an idealistically pleasurable existence full of warmth, charm, grace, and gaiety. A "great capacity for life enjoyment" was seen to characterize Mexican culture.

Thus certain elements in the Mexican stereotype—positive as well as negative—were established very early. These images were forged on the frontier rather than in the crowded cities of the East and Midwest; they

[3] Cecil Robinson, *With the Ears of Strangers: The Mexican in American Literature* (Tucson: University of Arizona Press, 1963), p. 33. This book is an exhaustive analysis of the portrayal of Mexican Americans in literature from the earliest contact between Mexicans and Americans through the present.

were established in contacts first on Mexican soil and then in the violent context of the Texas rebellion and the Mexican war of 1848. Because the first contact was made on Mexican soil, Americans were exposed to a full range of social classes, from aristocrat to peon. They encountered cultural styles that ranged from the aristocratic to the primitive. Further, American settlers met Mexicans not only in organized battle but also just as they met the many tribes of southwestern Indians as clever opponents in an almost endless and violent guerrilla warfare.

Although the exposure to upper-class as well as lower-class life meant that the image of "the Mexican" could acquire some social depth, it also meant that the Anglo absorbed the strong Mexican upper-class ideas of race. The upper classes believed themselves to be of "pure blood," pure Spanish untainted by any mixture of Indian blood. Anglos very early began to assume that the aristocratic people and the elaborate fiestas of *rancho* life were "Spanish," whereas the lower classes were "Mexican." Thus the American conquest was imposed on a society that was the result of a former Spanish conquest and of racial mixture—and racial stereotypes. Anglo acceptance of the already existing prejudices of Spanish America had very important consequences for Mexican Americans.

In later decades the benevolent stereotypes became elaborated. A highly romantic popular literature appeared, which reiterated early themes about aristocratic California life. It is best exemplified by Helen Hunt Jackson's *Ramona*, published in 1884, which depicted *rancho* owners as cultivated, gentle, and exploited. Throughout the twentieth century, American writers continued the benevolent stereotypes whether they wrote about the Mexican Americans of Texas as did Tom Lea and J. Frank Dobie or the poor wage earners of Monterey, California, as did John Steinbeck. The strongly folkloric themes of these latter writers appealed to thousands of readers; explicit in these works of fact and fiction is a very real admiration for the Mexican of Cannery Row (Monterey) or the Kineños of the King Ranch (in Texas). The appeal is romantic; it follows a theme, still strong in American literature about the American Indian, of an unspoiled, close to nature, strong, unchanging peasant who follows the simple life without neurotic complications.[4] In the end however, he must fall prey to a more sophisticated and exploiting society.

Without overstressing the point, we can see that these racial or cul-

---

[4] See Leslie Fiedler, *Waiting for the End* (New York: Stein and Day, 1964). Fiedler discusses the ambivalence in American literature about portrayals of Indians and Blacks. Alternately they represent a lost Eden of strength and innocence and a hell of uncontrolled cruelty and lustfulness. He suggests that such ambivalence permits Americans to project their own unwanted impulses on the members of minorities, and suggests a psychological function of racial stereotypes.

tural stereotypes have certain important social functions, just as in ordinary husband-and-wife relations it may be useful for both parties to play stereotyped roles. Thus a harassed and anxious man may find it enormously comforting to come home to a woman who plays the role of a weak, simple-minded, excessively "feminine" housewife. With such a wife, the husband can maintain an image of himself as "strong" in a highly competitive world.

In general, the enormous demands for achievement in American society may have facilitated the creation of certain stereotypes about subordinate minority groups. To follow this idea out for a moment: the American cultural ideals of achievement are both demanding and guilt-provoking. Americans are supposed to work hard, build, be constructive. The other side of the coin is that they must do so despite human costs. "You can't make an omelet without breaking eggs," the proverb runs. If the eggs must be broken, Americans must cope with the psychic consequences. One way of coping has been to project ego-alien impulses onto visible subpopulations such as the Mexicans. (Ego-alien impulses are so unacceptable to the ego-ideal that their very existence cannot be acknowledged by the individual.) Thus Mexicans became mythically lazy, warm, and possibly savage. In addition, the myth serves to justify their low status in the American West.

On the conscious cultural level, a related logic demands that Mexicans be defined as indolent and accepting. The new Anglo American settlers established ranches and towns and brought in a network of essential administrative and professional services to a wilderness. But another group of people, the Mexicans, did not participate in this work and they did not share in its rewards. For the Anglo Americans the moral equation had to be completed—Mexicans are poor *because* they are unwilling to suffer hard work and boredom. Moreover (so the argument runs), they are quite content with their status; they even prefer the life of the casual laborer and don't really mind poverty. Thus the comfortable Anglo Protestant moral equation of vice and punishment, hard work and material reward can remain intact. Poverty becomes a just return for laziness rather than a reminder of social injustices.

The American Southwest has changed quickly, and Mexicans have been caught up in the changes. But a new generation of writers persists in interpreting what has happened in the light of past stereotypes. John Steinbeck himself provides a hint of this kind of interpretation; when he returns to Monterey in 1960, he is saddened to discover that the "field of love" has become a used car lot.[5] Steinbeck finds his noble Mexican

[5] John Steinbeck, *Travels with Charley* (New York: Bantam Books, 1962), pp. 198–203.

peasants swallowed by an encroaching urban environment that destroys both land and people. Exposure to the vices of materialistic America will spoil those happy people, the Mexican Americans. Modern romanticism owes much to such visions. The most important legacy of this romanticism is the use of the concept "Mexican culture." We will discuss Mexican culture in some detail in Chapter Seven, noting only for the moment that the liberal who glorifies this selective view of the Mexican heritage shares much (from a functional point of view) with the unromantic conservative who argued that the Mexican Americans were "unassimilable" and lobbied doggedly against Mexican immigration during the 1930s.

The present equivocality of the concept "Mexican culture" is one American symptom of the endless struggle inside all societies that are undergoing rapid change. Values change in all societies. Cultural priorities shift. The search for new meanings and new institutional forms for these meanings was characteristic of American society (and particularly of American young people) in the late 1960s and early 1970s. Such a search inevitably draws on the resources available in the society, including its highest ideals and variant ideals from the subcultures. A quite new and important notion in American society is that the oppressed are ennobled by injury and thus morally *superior* to the majority. This, along with the notion that the poor can be "spoiled" by materialism, is a significant part of the "new romanticism." It represents a significant continuity with the old romantic legacy; at the present time it means a great interest in the "soul" cultures, Mexican included. There are virtues in this interest; it allows general social norms to be reexamined and possibly some past wrongs to be righted. It also presents some dangers. Witness this warning from a noted psychologist: "Even a remorseful majority . . . must be watchful lest it persist unconsciously in habitual patterns."[6] When "cultural differences" are also associated with poverty and discrimination, members of the dominant system who claim to "respect" and "appreciate" these cultural differences must do so very self-consciously lest they slip into a new kind of paternalism, a psychological exploitation that helps perpetuate the poverty and separation.

MEXICAN AMERICANS AS THEY SEE THEMSELVES

What do Mexicans themselves think of all this? There has, in fact, been a long history of exploration of Mexican American identity on the

---

[6]Erik Erikson, *Identity: Youth and Crisis* (New York: W. W. Norton & Company, 1968), p. 305.

part of Mexican and Chicano intellectuals.[7] It is a constant theme in the new Chicano literature. It is echoed endlessly on the popular level. And as we shall show later (Chapter Eight), issues about identity are a major focus of some new types of political activity among Chicanos. Until recently, however, there has been little confrontation with the cultural and racial stereotypes held and promulgated by Anglos, despite much intragroup irritation and attempts to redefine these images. Chicanos are now succeeding in redefining themselves in the movies, and in television and radio as part of the new sensitivity of media producers to racial pressure groups. "Jose Jimenez" (Bill Dana) was the last important American dialect comedian and even "Jose" was formally withdrawn by his creator in 1969. But as late as 1969 Tomás Martinez could still find eleven major advertisers who portrayed Chicanos as lazy, dirty, and shiftless.[8] (The best example of a classic American movie with a stereotypical Mexican villain is *The Treasure of Sierra Madre*. Recent television versions of this film have virtually eliminated the Mexican bandit chief so that the movie is acceptable to audiences in the Southwest. In other areas of the United States, longer portions of the villain are allowed to remain.)

One possible reason for the survival of stereotypes in television advertising is suggested by the survey methods of the major television rating services. Both A.C. Nielsen and the American Research Bureau select their diary-keeping sample households from telephone directories, a practice that tends to exclude minority responses to television programming. For reasons not known, low-income persons have a disproportionate number of unlisted telephones in some large Southwestern cities and, of course, a great many low-income homes have no telephone service at all.[9] At this time several Chicano groups both inside the media industries and outside from the community are monitoring television, newspaper, and other media presentations of Mexican stereotypes. This monitoring also includes Chicano employment and the enforcement of recent rulings from the Federal Communications Commission that television stations must devote a certain portion of access time to programs of special interest to minorities.

We should also know to just what extent Mexican Americans think of themselves and their fellows as a distinctive group or "a people." Identifying persons as "Mexican American" *is* important to the larger society. What about Mexicans themselves? First we may note that Mexican Ameri-

---

[7] Both traditions are summarized in Ralph C. Guzman, "The Function of Ideology in the Process of Political Socialization" (Unpublished ms.). See also Octavio Paz, *The Labyrinth of Solitude* (New York: Grove Press, 1961).

[8] Tomás Martinez, "Advertising and Racism: The Case of the Mexican-American," *El Grito* 2 (Summer 1969): 3–13.

[9] *New York Times*, February 19, 1974, p. 48.

cans who are asked what they want to be called by Anglos usually do not want to be called just "American." Most people interviewed in recent surveys in Los Angeles, San Antonio, and Albuquerque wanted to be called "Mexican," "Mexican American," "Spanish American," "Latin American," or "Chicano." In short, they see themselves as a distinctive people, rather than as a people or stock fully merged with an all-encompassing American identity. The name they prefer varies from city to city. In 1965–1966, Mexican Americans in San Antonio most wanted to be called "Latin Americans." In Los Angeles most wanted to be called "Mexican" or "Mexican American." In Albuquerque most wanted to be called "Spanish American." And it appears that some of these preferences are shifting over time.

Each variant has a special historical root and special historical meanings. Contemporary youth movements take the term *Chicano* (a contraction of *Mexicano*) as their term of self-reference. (Formerly this term was almost entirely an in-group word and implied lack of sophistication. This very quality, formerly depreciated, is now exalted as "soul.") Even now the other names prevail despite the Chicano movement—especially among older people. Self-designations can be a rapidly changing aspect of ethnic ideology. In this book we will settle on "Mexican American," "Chicano," and "Mexican" as useful terms, to be used as if they were interchangeable. This is not in any way to depreciate the attachments to the other names.

But to what extent do Mexican Americans see themselves as Anglos have tended to see them—as lazy, volatile, exhibiting a special warmth and love of life, and so on? There is evidence that Chicanos accept many self-deprecatory stereotypes as well as the positive features.[10] Although the survey data are very limited, they also show, interestingly, that Mexican Americans are quite aware of varying degrees of discrimination in Los Angeles, San Antonio, and Albuquerque.

A new and rather exciting accompaniment to this process of self-definition and self-awareness is beginning to appear in the form of a new literature. These new novels, poems, and essays by Mexican Americans are highly autobiographical and most were written in the impetus of the

---

[10] Survey data for Los Angeles and San Antonio are from the Mexican-American Study Project, University of California, at Los Angeles, household surveys conducted in 1965–1966. See Leo Grebler, John W. Moore, and Ralph Guzman, *The Mexican American People* (New York: Free Press, 1970), for description of samples and data. Data from Albuquerque are from samples drawn by Operation SER, 1506 3rd Street, Santa Monica, California. Recent data and some interesting changes over time are reported by Biliana Ambrecht and Harry Pachon, "Continuity and Change in a Mexican American Community: East Los Angeles 1965–1972," prepared for delivery to the American Political Science Association, 1973.

Chicano movement. The new novelists are preoccupied by their need to "find" themselves and to "define" their heritage and their people, as are the poets and the essayists. Perhaps the best-known work is *Yo Soy Joaquin*, a lyric and moving epic poem by Rodolfo (Corky) Gonzalez.[11] Gonzalez is also an important political leader. (See Chapter Eight.) His long evocation of Mexican history is a tribute to the endurance of the Mexican people and defines (if such a lackluster word is appropriate) the Chicano as a many and various person with an unconquerable appetite for freedom. *Yo Soy Joaquin* is very popular, often reprinted, has been made into a film, and is an important document of *Chicanismo*.

Much of the same compelling need to define the elements of the Chicano heritage appears in two of the most recent novels.[12] Richard Vasquez describes the slow and painful adaptation of a *campesino* (peasant) family to life in Los Angeles. Edmund Villasenor sees the loss of old virtues in accommodation to Anglo values. His hero returns to a simple but comprehensible life in village Mexico. And in an engaging story of a boy's growth into the best elements of two cultures, Ernesto Galarza has written an autobiography of his youth in Mexico in the time of the Revolution and his immigration to Sacramento, California.[13]

But it is Oscar Acosta who describes the Mexican American as an urban person, doomed to live in Anglo cities and face Anglo discrimination. Acosta's two books (one an autobiography and one a novel) picture Chicanos as people who can achieve nothing except in full battle against a destructive Anglo society. Acosta seems to define Chicanos as good people foredoomed to lose against a hypocritical system no matter how much they want to accept the values of the Anglo schools, the courts, and the Roman Catholic church. Because Acosta is a successful student, an accomplished criminal lawyer, and a former Baptist missionary, his attack is important and convincing. *The Autobiography of a Brown Buffalo* is a perceptive look at a Chicano childhood and coming of age—the story of an outsider forced to fight for acceptance and then to realize the hypocrisy of that acceptance.[14] *The Revolt of the Cockroach People* continues his story in fictional form.[15] Throughout the intense political activity of 1968–1970 in East Los Angeles, Acosta continues to sharpen

[11] Rodolfo Gonzalez, *Yo Soy Joaquin (I Am Joaquin)* (New York: Bantam Books, 1972).

[12] Richard Vasquez, *Chicano* (Garden City, N.Y.: Doubleday & Company, 1970). Edmund Villasenor, *Macho* (New York: Bantam Books, 1973).

[13] Ernesto Galarza, *Barrio Boy* (New York: Ballantine Books, 1972).

[14] Oscar Z. Acosta, *The Autobiography of a Brown Buffalo* (San Francisco: Straight Arrow Books, 1972).

[15] Oscar Z. Acosta, *The Revolt of the Cockroach People* (San Francisco: Straight Arrow Books, 1973).

his definition of himself—a "Brown Buffalo" because he and his people are unwanted survivals of the West, doomed to be hunted to death like cockroaches. For Acosta there is no alternative but apartness, an active condition of being a minority, and fighting back with the sophisticated institutional weapons of the Anglo himself.

MEXICAN AMERICANS AS A NATIONAL MINORITY

In recent years Mexican Americans have been "discovered" by official institutions as yet another American minority. The discovery came slowly—and as a process of interaction between various elements in American society—Anglo, Chicano, and Black and other Latin Americans. Before this definition the idea of being a "minority" was hard to accept for many middle-class Mexican Americans, including political spokesmen, because it implied the relinquishment of special claims to regional prestige, and perhaps the hardest thing of all—accepting classification with other "disadvantaged" groups in the United States, especially the Blacks. The struggle for equity is continuous and difficult. As a minority among other minorities, the Chicanos have won some consideration from the mass media. The federal government has recognized the Mexican Americans as in need of affirmative action by the many agencies concerned with education, employment, housing, income, and health.

Even now elements of this new definition are still emerging. We will see something of the process later in this book. For the moment we have been concerned with Anglo American stereotypes about Chicanos— and the parallel process in the Chicano community of defining their own views of themselves.

The history of the Chicano minority is unlike that of any other American minority group. The only close parallel is with the American Indians, and even there we can find only a few similarities. Mexican Americans *became* a minority not by immigrating or being brought to this country as a subordinate people, but by being conquered. The early history of the Mexican Americans, beginning in the nineteenth century, is thus the history of how they became subordinate people. As we shall see, the process was somewhat different in each of the Border States—Texas, New Mexico, Arizona, and California. This early history, with its very important variations from state to state, set the stage for the large-scale immigration from Mexico in the twentieth century; and it influenced the economic, social, and politcal roles Mexican Americans were able to play.

It is almost impossible to write a coherent history of any American minority. History is normally written from documents, and in the past conquest period Mexicans become visible in them only occasionally, often in reaction against some interest or action of the larger society. Except in New Mexico, the Mexican minority has been obscure in the economic and social events of American history.[1] The Border States themselves have been ignored by American historians until very recently. It might even be argued that the sudden appearance

History: An American Minority Appears

of Mexican Americans in the national consciousness is only one aspect of the sudden appearance of the entire region in a more tightly interdependent nation.

EARLY HISTORY
OF THE MEXICANS: TO 1900

The history of this minority begins when the Border States passed into the control of the United States. This happened through rebellion (in Texas), after warfare between Mexico and the United States (Texas

---

[1]See, for example, Juan Gomez-Quinones, 'Toward a Perspective on Chicano History" *Aztlan: Chicano Journal of the Social Sciences and the Arts* 2 (Fall 1971). The difficult problem of periodization is discussed by Rodolfo Alvarez in "The Psycho-Historical and Socioeconomic Development of the Chicano Community in the United States," *Social Science Quarterly* 53, no. 4 (March 1973): 920–942.

and New Mexico), and by purchase (Arizona and New Mexico). Between the Battle of San Jacinto in 1836 and the Gadsden Purchase of 1853, the United States acquired the present states of Texas and New Mexico and parts of Colorado, Arizona, Utah, Nevada, and California.

In all that vast stage at that time there were no more than a handful of actors. If we look at the approximate number of Mexicans in each state when it was first taken over, we can begin to understand something of the very diverse experience of Mexicans in each area. There were perhaps 5,000 Mexicans in Texas, 60,000 in New Mexico, no more than 1,000 in Arizona, and perhaps 7,500 along the length of California.[2] There were also some settlements in what is now modern Colorado, but they were small and isolated.

Generally the Mexican colonists had settled in a pattern resembling the ribs of a giant fan; they had entered the Southwest through mountain passes and river valleys. The "fan" their settlements formed stretched more than 2,000 miles along its northern edge, but in only a very few places did it extend more than 150 miles north of the Mexican border. These first Spanish settlers established small, tight, defensible clusters in strategic valléys, fertile river areas, and other typical frontier locations. Three factors nearly always dominated the choice of site: the availability of water, transportation resources, and protection from marauding Indians.

From the first years protection from Indians was essential. There might well have been as many as 120,000 Indians ranging through these territories. For most of the nineteenth century the Indians, particularly the successful Apache tribes, held much of this area by force, thereby helping to isolate and keep intact the existing Mexican Spanish institutions and settlements. Carey McWilliams writes, "From 1848 to 1887, the Anglo Americans were so preoccupied with the Indians that they had little time left to devote to the settlement of the region or the exploitation of its resources."[3] More important, the interminable ambushes, battles, and massacres made the Mexicans welcome the protection of the American troops, particularly in the territories of New Mexico and Arizona. But by 1886 the last of the Apache raiding parties either came under U.S. control or went across the border into Mexico. Then the Anglo American settlement of the Southwest could begin.

[2] See Carey McWilliams, *North from Mexico* (Philadelphia: J. B. Lippincott Company, 1949), p. 52; and U.S. Bureau of the Census, *Historical Statistics of the United States, Colonial Times to 1957* (Washington, D.C.: Government Printing Office, 1960). McWilliams' book remains the best general history available.

[3] McWilliams, *North from Mexico*, p. 53.

Texas

The frontier of original Mexican settlement in Texas ran n
north than the Nueces River, north and east of which the hostile Coman-
ches prevented further advance. There was considerable Mexican settlement even in the dangerous area between the Rio Grande and the Nueces
rivers, but most Mexicans (probably 80 percent) lived in the lower Rio
Grande valley and in the river cities, with El Paso the most westerly
town of any consequence. Such present-day south Texas counties as Starr,
Zapata, Cameron, and Hidalgo thus had thousands of early residents.
In west and south Texas the population grew rapidly from about 8,500
in 1850 to 50,000 in 1880 and 100,000 in 1910, in spite of the fear and
dislocation caused by the many wars, large and small. (During one episode
of the Cortina War in 1859, for example, a slice of lower Texas 150 miles
long and from 50 to 75 miles wide was invaded and devastated by Mexican horsemen.) Texas was also the only part of the border area that was
seriously involved in the Civil War.[4]

The economy of this area depended upon the large cattle ranch
but in an early form common in the Border States, which was based upon
the ownership of livestock rather than land. After the annexation of
Texas, the Anglos easily assumed the role of landowners (between 1840
and 1859 all Mexican-owned grants but one in Nueces County passed
into the hands of Anglo settlers).[5] Mexican *peones* were available for
labor on these ranches. Meanwhile, along the Rio Grande a series of
mercantile towns grew up (Brownsville, Dolores, Laredo, Rio Grande
City, Roma) to handle the commercial needs of this area. Although all
these river towns had some Anglo residents and some Europeans, most
were almost entirely Mexican. Here early appeared some Mexican middle-
class elements, which were to be important in the future as the valley of
the Rio Grande became more Anglicized. The change came very slowly;
as late as 1903 Brownsville held only 7,000 persons, mostly Mexican. At
that time Corpus Christi was not yet a deep water port and numbered
only 4,500 persons.[6] To a large degree the Mexicans of the Rio Grande
valley and the river towns were still dominant numerically.

[4]For a description of Cortina and the state of semi-war in south Texas, 1855–1875,
see Tom Lea, *The King Ranch*, vol. 1 (Boston: Little, Brown and Company, 1957),
and Rodolfo Acuna, *Occupied America: The Chicano's Struggle Toward Liberation* (San
Francisco: Canfield Press, 1972).

[5]Paul S. Taylor, *An American-Mexican Frontier* (Chapel Hill: University of
North Carolina Press, 1934), p. 294.

[6] Arthur J. Rubel, *Across the Tracks. Mexican-Americans in a Texas City*
(Austin: University of Texas Press, 1966), pp. 34–35.

However, the large cattle and sheep ranches of south and east Texas were very soon fenced, following the invention of barbed wire in 1875. Enclosure was of major importance because cutting a fairly unrestricted cattle range into small pieces tended to freeze out a large number of small and medium-sized cattle and sheep ranchers, including both Mexicans and Anglos who owned livestock but little or no land. A few years later cotton plantations slowly moved into south Texas from east Texas, continuing a movement toward the west and cheap new land that was long characteristic of cotton culture. However, cotton required a great deal of hand labor and this time there were no Black slaves to follow the new plantings westward. The resulting demand for cheap Mexican labor to cultivate cotton, either as wage laborers or as tenants, was so great that it fixed, very nearly in its modern form, the economic fate of the Mexican immigrant and the Mexican old settler in Texas. A few Mexicans would succeed in achieving ownership of the land they worked, but not many.

By 1890 the cotton culture of the deep South was well established in Nueces County. The attractive prices for good cotton land, the high profits in "brushing out" and cultivating former pastureland, and the availability of cheap labor from across the border doomed all but a few of the old cattle ranches in south Texas in a very few years. By 1900 the Mexican laborer in both rural and urban Texas had become defined as an inferior person and as a member of a distinctive race entitled to neither political, educational, nor social equality. Remnants of Mexican equality survived only to a limited extent in some of the commercial towns of the Rio Grande valley where Mexicans remained in the majority.

New Mexico

The Texas pattern of economic subordination of Mexicans extended west into the grain and ranching area of eastern New Mexico, an area that is still called "Little Texas." As large cattlemen began to enclose their land and to push out Mexican and Anglo sheep ranchers, enough friction was generated to produce the famous Lincoln County wars from 1869 to 1881.[7] Some Mexicans did retain their holdings, although serious overgrazing in nearly all areas of New Mexico had damaged this form of economic enterprise well before 1900.

New Mexico entered the period of Anglo settlement with its share of Mexican colonization centered in three types of inhabited areas: mili-

---

[7]Nancie L. González, *The Spanish Americans of New Mexico: A Distinctive Heritage*, Advance Report 9 (University of California, Los Angeles: Mexican-American Study Project, 1967).

tary and administrative towns (such as Sante Fe and Albuquerque), large ranches, and a considerable number of small villages. Most of the villages depended heavily on agriculture and livestock ranching. Isolation and continual warfare with the Indians meant that Anglo inroads came very slowly; in 1848 there were about 60,000 persons in the territory and virtually all of them were Mexican. Most, in fact, lived either within a 50-mile radius of Santa Fe or on the headwaters of the Rio Grande and Pecos rivers.[8] Unlike those in the borderlands of Texas, New Mexico's Spanish-speaking residents had a full range of class structure and a well-established ruling group, able in every respect and interested in retaining political power. The territorial legislature was thus dominated by "Spanish Americans" (actually members of no more than twenty prominent families) from its establishment until statehood in 1912. For sixty-four years an alliance between the wealthy Spanish and certain Anglo interests in banking, ranching, and railroading effectively controlled New Mexican political and economic life through the infamous "Sante Fe Ring." Federal land policies designed to "open up the West" were vital to the operations of this group.

New Mexicans lived for the most part a considerable distance from the border and were not greatly disturbed by the endemic border warfare and raids that characterized south Texas. Not until the coming of the railroads was movement throughout the territory easy in any direction, and not until 1886 was it easy to pass back and forth across the border because very large stretches of this area were held by Apache raiders.

Nonetheless, economic changes were swiftly breaking down this small and curiously isolated Mexican society. By 1900 overgrazing and erosion, the consolidation of larger ranches, the fraudulent transfer of old land grant territories to logging, railroads, and other exploitative interests, the steady division of lands among heirs, and the rapid withdrawal of grazing land to various types of federal use forced many, perhaps most, small herders and farmers into wage labor. By 1910, only 30 percent of the pre-conquest landowners held their original land. At the same time some immigration coming west from Texas swelled the labor pool and tended to reduce wage rates. Thus, long before the turn of the century, the New Mexican villager was fighting a slow but losing battle against pauperization. The full effect would not be felt for several generations, but the decline of sheepherding was obvious. This primary and traditional activity of New Mexicans was disappearing and with it a form of social organization many years old.

New Mexico was slow to develop discrimination against and isola-

---

[8] González, *Spanish Americans of New Mexico*, p. 29.

tion of the Mexican minority. As Nancie González writes, "Inter-marriage between Anglo men and Mexican women was apparently quite common, and not restricted to any particular social class. Business and commercial mergers between Anglos and Mexicans occurred frequently, and in politics, coalitions of Anglos and Mexicans worked together in each of the major parties."[9] But there is evidence that this tolerant mood began to change by 1900 as, inevitably, more and more American settlers and important American mining, ranching, and transportation interests flowed into New Mexico. Railroad lines had opened the territory quite effectively by 1881. The new railroads allowed dozens of isolated company towns to exploit the considerable mineral resources of New Mexico with Mexican labor. The new markets for wool, meat, and hides opened by the railroads accelerated the consolidation of larger and more efficient ranches. Continuous enclosure slowly destroyed the smaller sheepherders and the smaller cattlemen. Thus the very forces that spelled economic opportunity to large Anglo enterprises were forcing a considerable portion of Mexicans into the status of a dependent minority.

Arizona

In Arizona settlement began north from the Mexican state of Sonora in the seventeenth and eighteenth centuries with a chain of missions that opened the valleys of the San Miguel, Altar, Santa Cruz, and San Pedro Rivers. Some colonization followed, mostly in the form of large estates. But these estates were subject to continuous raids from Indians. Thus, when in 1751 troops from Mexico were withdrawn for a time, Apache raiders laid waste to the entire province, an area covering nearly all of modern Arizona. A military stalemate was just barely restored in succeeding years and then slowly the Indians gained the upper hand again until by 1856 nearly all Arizona colonists lived (for safety) in the fortified city of Tucson.

In Arizona the shift to Anglo domination was less painful than elsewhere because there were so few resident Mexicans. By the 1880s the final collapse of Indian resistance coincided very closely with the beginning of large-scale mining and the building of the railroads. The few Mexicans in Arizona were heavily involved in marketing functions and were too few to feed the endless appetite for cheap wage labor. Thousands more were imported through the labor markets of the border towns of Laredo and El Paso. Thus the familiar pattern of transition to wage labor

---

9 The Santa Fe Ring was an alliance of Mexican and Anglo interests that dominated the economic and political life of New Mexico for a period after the Civil War.

appeared very early in Arizona—and with it the dreary succession of lynchings, unsolved murders, and vigilante actions against a working-class population of what was defined as a different race.

Arizona settlement patterns are notable for the large number of isolated mining towns, nearly all of them with a large majority of Mexicans. Some Mexicans were natives; some were imported. Some probably followed the mines as they were opened and closed by a single company in different areas. These company towns appear in large numbers in the 1880s, nearly always extremely isolated places as Tubac, Miami, San Manuel, Mammoth, Walker, Dewey, Morenci, Duquesne, Metcalf, Ajo, Bluebell, and scores of others. Some are still in existence; others are ghost towns. Miners' enclaves also provided the original impetus for many larger Arizona towns, such as Bisbee, Prescott, and Douglas. Typically the mining towns were totally isolated from the normal American society of the time. Many were too small or too dominated by a single employer to provide any but the most rudimentary public services. From the beginning there was rigid separation by occupation, which meant segregation of the Mexicans from the Anglos, with such additional forms of segregation as "Mexican" shopping hours in the company store.

Copper was Arizona's single most important mineral product, and its exploitation expanded rapidly with the nation's needs for electrical equipment. There was also some cattle ranching in Arizona, and some cotton farming, but ranching and agriculture were hazardous and very expensive enterprises in a country so arid. Generally both were conducted on a grand scale by large companies. A territory so dominated by a few economic interests was also dominated politically by the same interests. It could not have been otherwise in a remote western territory. Territorial governments have been summarized as "poor government by a remote Congress which was not responsible to the inhabitants; limited appropriations mainly for military posts, the Indian service, roadbuilding, and mail routes; and inadequate and frequently corrupt administration."[10]

California

California was the most westerly province in the great fan of original Mexican settlement—so far west, in fact, that its principal economic partner was not Mexico but New England, via the clipper ships of the nineteenth century. Here during the Mexican hegemony a handful of *rancheros* held an enormous area, separated almost completely from Mexi-

[10] From an unpublished manuscript prepared by Paul Fisher for the Mexican-American Study Project (Los Angeles: University of California, October 1967).

can centers of control.[11] Mexico generally ignored its westernmost province and even failed (beyond an occasional shipment of felons) to settle it in any substantial numbers. Most of the resident Mexican population approved of the idea of annexation by the United States. Mexico was weak; there were endless petty quarrels with Mexican officials; there were serious troubles with Indians in Southern California but no help from Mexico and the ranchers were long accustomed to trade with the United States. Thus the "Bear Flag" rebellion of 1846 was welcomed, as was the succeeding military occupation by U.S. troops.

The early occupation was amiable enough, but meanwhile gold was discovered in the interior, and suddenly northern California was being "settled" at tremendous speed by Anglo miners; at least 100,000 miners were arriving each year. Massive immigrations of Sonorans from Mexico and Chileans (13,000 Latin Americans in 1849 alone) complicated the problem. The Anglo miner of midwestern or southern origin felt that "a greaser is a greaser" even if he owned 35,000 acres of land and was pure Castilian. In the mines, remote from any law, Mexicans were taxed, lynched, robbed, and expelled in an endless series of incidents. Many of the Mexicans and Chileans then drifted into California towns and formed a substantial group of landless laborers. The mining troubles were an early and a bad precedent for American Mexican relations in California.

Very soon the gold mines became less profitable and the new arrivals turned to agriculture, squatting on the Mexican grants in large numbers and filling California courts with endless and complicated title litigation.[12] Many of the Mexican grants had been of dubious legality from the beginning, and others were often "floated" (or extended) in court to cover all nearby improvements and available sources of water. There was considerable violence in some northern counties between squatters and owners. At one time 1,000 armed squatters near Healdsburg ambushed surveyors, the Mexican owners, and a sheriff's posse with complete impartiality. Within a few years, the *californios* (Mexicans living in what is now California) had lost nearly all economic power in northern California. Not all the land claims were decided against them, but the steady and growing influence of Anglo settlers left them in the position of a small, tightly knit group of overextended landlords, barely able to hold

[11]This account is based substantially on Leonard Pitt, *The Decline of the Californios: A Social History of the Spanish-Speaking Californians, 1846–1890* (Berkeley and Los Angeles: University of California Press, 1966).

[12] State reports in 1849 showed that 200 California families owned 14 million acres of California in parcels ranging from 4,500 acres to about 50,000 acres. Against this concentration, the American white settler invoked the Jacksonian idea that a few men of immoderate wealth and special privilege wasted the land and denied industry its due. Pitt, *Decline of the Californios*, p. 87.

their lands, and hated by most of the community. Although California became a state in 1850 and the government was more decentralized, more powerful, and more responsive than in either Arizona or New Mexico, the land troubles in northern California were beyond the capacity of government on any level to resolve.

In southern California the situation was completely different. There were very few important changes for nearly a generation after the Gold Rush. Mexican *rancheros* owned the land; the Indians did the work; the Anglo settlers were few and unimportant. Most of arable southern California was owned by no more than fifty men and their immediate families, including a group of about a dozen Mexicanized Yankees. The availability of both Indian labor and cheap land worked against the development of a Mexican lower class, either on ranches or in towns. Nor was there yet a large number of immigrants; no economic enterprise in southern California needed any appreciable quantity of wage labor, although a few Mexicans worked in the "dry" gold mines of southern California. (The railroads before 1875 used Chinese and Indians for laborers.) Southern California also was spared the Anglo squatter because northern California offered a more humid climate and family-sized farms. The squatters found arid southern California unattractive.

Although the ranchers shared power in local and state government and their economic base held firm after 1850, this generation watched uneasily as racial tension grew noticeably. Los Angeles was inhabited by an explosive combination of lower-class Mexicans, Anglos, Indians, and Chinese, and it soon became almost impossible to maintain even a façade of racial harmony in an era of strong anti-Catholicism, nativism, and frequent violent crime. Even the state became less tolerant: taxes were imposed upon land; laws were no longer published in Spanish; in 1855 a law was passed forbidding school instruction in Spanish.

The *rancheros* responded by pressing hard for the separation of southern California from northern California (along a line near San Luis Obispo) but this effort was doomed when the local issue became entangled with national questions of sectionalism and slavery. The final blow, however, was economic. In 1862 a devastating flood was followed by two years of extreme drought. This disaster very nearly destroyed California's Mexican wealth at its source. Mortgages, legal fees, taxes, and low cattle prices completed the ruin. According to Leonard Pitt, before the catastrophe of the 1860s practically all land parcels worth more than $10,000 were held by old families, mostly Mexican. By 1870 these same families held barely one quarter of these large parcels.[13] Politi-

13 Pitt, *Decline of the Californios*, p. 248.

cally the erosion was reflected by the gradual disappearance of *californios* from public life; by the early 1880s there were no longer any Spanish names in the public offices of southern California.

The final blow (as in all the Border States) was the arrival of the railroad, which reached as far west as San Francisco in 1869. In 1876 the railroad was completed to Los Angeles from northern California; the next year, a line to Los Angeles from the East was finished. In 1887 alone the two new railroads brought in more than 120,000 Anglo American settlers. There were by that year only 12,000 Mexicans in all southern California. Thus, almost in one year, the Mexican majority became a local minority. A fierce land boom after the arrival of the railroads ended most of what remained of Mexican ownership of the great ranches and transferred the land to the not-too-gentle management of financiers, railroad developers, town planners, cooperative colonizers, and irrigation companies.

This was roughly the state of the Mexican Americans in the border states of 1900. In general, their first massive contact with Anglo settlement (normally settlers brought in large numbers by the new railroads) coincided with their subordination, even if it did not immediately cause it. Everywhere except in New Mexico, this charter-member minority (a minority status acquired by conquest rather than immigration) was by 1900 hopelessly inundated by the tide of Anglo immigration, reduced to landless labor, and made politically and economically impotent. Socially the long-settled charter-members had become "Mexicans" indistinguishable from the new immigrants from Mexico. Perhaps more important, by now all Mexicans, whatever their isolation from other Mexican communities, had in common a heritage of racial conflict. Only in New Mexico did the Mexicans retain numerical plurality and some degree of control in political affairs.

LATER HISTORY OF THE MEXICANS:
AFTER 1900
TO THE GREAT DEPRESSION

By 1900 the basic Mexican settlements were well established. In nearly every city where there would be a sizable urban Mexican population, its rudiments had appeared by the turn of the century. After 1900 the history of Mexican Americans is inextricably bound with the movement of the Border States into fuller articulation with the rest of the American society and economy.

Agricultural Technology

The first great force changing the Southwest was that of agricultural technology. The age of cattle in these states came and went rather quickly, destroyed by overexpansion both of herds and of land holdings, by competition from more efficient ranchers, and by droughts and severe winters. After the arrival of the railroads, ranching was followed by a boom in dry-farming (farming without irrigation), which ended disastrously in a series of great droughts throughout the West after 1885. An immediate result of these droughts was the realization in Congress that the key to large-scale settlement of the Border States would be water. Thus the Reclamation Act of 1902 authorized a series of expensive reservoirs designed to provide irrigation water for certain areas. Irrigated farming is intensive farming—highly capitalized, with heavy labor requirements, year-round production, and crop specialization. No poor farmer or homesteader could possibly own or maintain such land. An acre of lettuce required more than 125 man-hours of labor per crop and an acre of strawberries more than 500 man-hours.[14] Melons, grapes, citrus fruit, sugar beets, cotton, vegetables: all required the initial investment for irrigated land and then the costs of brush grubbing, deep plowing, leveling, extensive planting and, in the case of citrus, a long wait for a first crop.

As a result, the demand for cheap Mexican labor grew at a rapid pace. With the arrival of factory farms came further work: crating, packing, processing, and shipping. These new irrigated farms—and the work on them—were to dominate the conditions of life of the Mexican minority in the Border States as decisively as the working patterns of coal mining once dominated wage labor in Appalachia.

Cotton continued to move steadily westward from Texas and then, suddenly, with the coming of irrigation it spread into the Mesilla Valley of New Mexico (1910–1920); into the Gila and Salt river valleys of Arizona (1908–1909); into the Imperial Valley of southern California (1910); and into the San Joaquin Valley of central California (1920). Mexicans followed in every case as migratory workers or as seasonal workers who lived nearby. It was a pattern repeated in hundreds of towns in five large states, including a good portion of eastern Colorado. But the migratory labor story is too well known to repeat in detail here; it was—and is—a pattern of low earnings, miserable health and housing conditions, child labor, and virtually no contact with the Anglo world beyond the labor

[14] Lawrence Leslie Waters, "Transient Mexican Agricultural Labor," *Southwest Social and Political Science Quarterly* 22 (June 1941): 49–66.

agent (or smuggler) and the grower, together with a squalid "Mextown" somewhere near the fields.

The railroads also needed cheap labor—so much, in fact, that most of the Mexican laborers who entered the United States in the first two decades of the century may have worked on them. Because much railroad work is seasonal and many workers left to remain in towns newly opened by the railroads, recruitment of labor was continual. In sum, "since 1880 Mexicans have made up 70 percent of the section crews and 90 percent of the extra gangs on the principal western lines which regularly employ [in 1930] between 35,000 and 50,000 workmen in these categories. In 1930 the Santa Fe reported that it was then employing 14,000 Mexicans; the Rock Island, 3,000; the Great Northern, 1,500; and the Southern Pacific, 10,000."[15] Typically, Mexicans were assembled in El Paso and then sent out on six month work contracts. (In 1908 some 16,000 Mexicans were recruited in this one Texas city.) Section hands and extra crews lived on the rails or in boxcars. Where these boxcars settled for a while, a small colony of Mexicans appeared. There were soon hundreds of these remote shantytowns scattered throughout the Border States, West, and Midwest.

For the Border States this steady flow of labor was vital, and legislative and political pressure made sure it kept arriving. Sugar beet recruiters from other states (notably Colorado) so angered Texans that the Texas Emigrant Agent Law of 1929 made this type of recruiting illegal. (It was still done illegally at the rate of about 60,000 Mexicans a year.) The theft of workers was common, as was the practice of selling the same work crew more than once. "Crews of imported Mexicans [in 1915] were marched through the streets of San Antonio under armed guard in broad daylight and, in Gonzales County, workers who attempted to break their contracts were chained to posts and guarded by men with shotguns," reports Mc-Williams.[16] Many, if not most, of these workers were smuggled across the border. Thus Texas served as the main reservoir of cheap wage labor for sugar beet harvesting in the North, the central states, and the West; interurban electric railway construction and fruit picking in California, cotton harvesting in Arizona, and wage labor in the tanneries, meat packing plants, and steel mills of Chicago. Mexicans appeared in the automobile factories in Detroit, the steel mills of Ohio and Pennsylvania, the mines and smelters of Arizona and Colorado, and in railroad maintenance everywhere.

In Texas and elsewhere an important by-product of this traffic in labor soon appeared. It became customary to employ "reliable" Mexicans to hire and transport this vast flow. Slowly, an upper working class began

15 McWilliams, *North from Mexico*, p. 168.
16 McWilliams, *North from Mexico*, p. 179.

to appear, based on the need for straw-bosses, foremen, and labor recruiters. In the fields themselves the workers sometimes moved into more
skilled work: operating vehicles or equipment, handling processing
machinery and even clerical tasks. The older communities in the Border
States also supplied an array of small ethnic services: all the restaurants,
rooming houses, small retail stores, and personal services required by a
flow of workers.

Public Land

The second great force, particularly apparent in New Mexico, was the
pattern of public land usage. Timbercutting, overgrazing, and incautious
dry-farming by a flood of Anglo homesteaders threatened the land itself.
Accordingly, the allocation of land for national forests began in New
Mexico as early as 1892, and many small villages found themselves cut
off from grazing lands used for generations. Ultimately an eighth of the
land in New Mexico passed into restricted usage. Other large grants were
made to railroad companies, amounting to 20 million acres in California
alone. Still other tracts were restricted to aid education, forming land
grant colleges. In Arizona the same process stifled even the beginnings
of self-sufficiency for small stock operators and small farmers.

Conflict

The third important force shaping Mexican American life after 1900
was the almost unending racial and international conflict in the Border
States of both the United States and Mexico. The northern Mexican
provinces traditionally spawned revolutions, and inevitably some of the
conflict spilled over the border, particularly into the New Mexico and
Texas borderlands. By 1911 there was internal turmoil in Mexico. Without going into the details of the strange German effort to involve Mexico
in her 1917–1918 war against the United States (by reviving an old Mexican dream of "recovering her lost provinces") it can be said that between
1908 and 1925 the Texas border was in nearly continuous conflict. Mexico
itself had had relative peace only during the thirty-five-year regime of
Porfírio Díaz. After downfall of that regime in 1911 a full-scale revolution
developed, with fighting so continuous, so chaotic, and so violent that
the "Mexican government" (when it existed) could neither control border
raids into the United States nor protect the lives and property of its own
citizens from American reprisals.

El Paso provides one example of the strategic importance of the
border for relations between the two countries at this time. It was a cen-

ter for arms shipment to all partisans in the Mexican revolution, just as it shipped refugees and contract laborers to all corners of the Border States. A full-scale American "Punitive Expedition," commanded by General John J. Pershing, entered Mexico in 1916. *Villista* raids (raids by followers of the Northern Mexican revolutionary, General Pancho Villa) on Columbus, N.M., Nogales, Ariz., and four towns in Texas (Dryden, Eagle Pass, Glen Springs, and Boquillas), prompted the invasion.

On the domestic scene, the years before and just after World War I brought a great deal of labor conflict involving Mexicans in the United States. Some of these strikes and protests were extremely violent, although neither frequent nor coordinated enough to destroy the Anglos' belief in "Mexican docility." Of course it is not difficult to imagine that during the period of international conflict between the United States and Mexico, Mexican laborers in the Border States should have acted with circumspection. Nonetheless, in Ventura in 1903 more than a thousand Mexican and Japanese sugar beet workers went on strike. In 1913, a particularly ugly strike-connected riot at Wheatland, California attracted national attention. Soon after, in 1915, three unions of Mexican miners, numbering about 5,000 men, went on strike at the Clifton, Morenci, and Metcalf mines in Arizona. Also in 1915, Arizona miners struck the mines at Ray. At Bisbee there was a violent strike in 1917. In 1920 Mexican workers struck the Los Angeles urban railway. In later years the strikes in the fields and mines of the Border States were both more numerous and more sophisticated. The earlier ones were significant, however, because Mexicans were generally denied normal channels of political expression in any of the Border States except New Mexico. The alien, of course, had no voice, but the settled and native-born were also efficiently disenfranchised, either by means of the poll tax and the open primary (as in Texas) or by simply being overwhelmed in numbers and by political manipulation (as in California).[17]

Mexicans soon became a topic of controversy within the legislatures of the Border States and in Congress as well. The Mexican labor pool continued to grow. More federal irrigation projects, particularly in Arizona, and the rapid extension of fruit farming, cotton, and intensive year-round

17 The idea may seem strange to a modern "progressive" or liberal, but the political reformers of the Populist and Progressive age were strongly anti-minority and anti-alien. Thus their ideas for political reform had very little direct effect on Mexicans in the United States. The Populists in Texas made no effort whatever to reach the Mexicans in Texas, and in 1913 the California Progressives worked in the state legislature to pass a child labor law, old age pensions, and oddly, an alien land bill to deprive 331 Japanese farm owners of their land. The latent Progressive hostility to Mexicans became evident when Senator Albert Beveridge led a bloc of Progressives in Congress in opposing Arizona and New Mexico statehood, because they felt the large Mexican population of these territories was unfit for full citizenship.

truck crops into California kept the supply of labor always slightly less than the demand. The massive and irresponsible manipulation of this politically voiceless minority depended on the domination of state legislatures by the big agricultural, railroad, and mining interests.

However, World War I had begun to change things for the Mexican laborer and to remove him from complete economic dependence on these three industries. Urbanization was speeded up, and the wartime industries provided high wages for a few years to some Mexican Americans who learned skilled trades. The resultant loss of workers in agriculture was filled temporarily by more Mexican immigrants, but this immigration could not last forever. By the early 1920s some important signs of strain appeared: Congress was considering restrictionist legislation.

It was in the testimony on the quota legislation considered in 1924 and 1925 that the political implications of the changing situation in the Border States became evident and the political power of the big economic interests was challenged. The growers had always believed that—since their workers vanished from *their* sight at the end of the work season— Mexicans went "home to Mexico." ("The Mexican is a 'homer.' Like the pigeon he goes back to roost," a farm lobbyist told Congress.[18]) But the cities had evidence that this was not so: city taxpayers throughout the Border States were becoming aware of how much these "homing pigeons" were costing to support when they were unable to find agriculture work. In 1925, Riverside, California, spent 90 percent of its welfare budget on Mexican cases, and much larger Los Angeles spent 28 percent of its 1927 charitable funds on Mexicans, who were only 7 percent of the population.[19] The hearings in Congress accurately reflected new realities in the Border States, and the changed political significance of the Mexican minority. Within the decade the strains were to produce massive deportations, detailed in the next chapter.

It took some time for the changing situation to work its way into the conscious imagery relating to Mexican Americans. For generations, Mexicans had been seen as a necessary part of the Border States' extractive industries, yet as primarily alien and locked forever into a relationship to the land that could be either romantic or sordid depending on the observer's point of view. But by 1920, Mexicans were exhibiting many of the desires shown by other and earlier immigrant groups: they wanted economic security; they liked (or were forced) to live in urban areas, and whenever possible their children went to school and abandoned agricultural labor. Just as the development of the northern Black ghettos went

---

[18] Carey McWilliams, *Factories in the Field: The Story of Migratory Farm Labor in California* (Boston, Mass.: Little, Brown and Company, 1939), p. 127.

[19] McWilliams, *Factories in the Field*, pp. 148–49.

largely unnoticed, however, so the urbanized Mexican (whether new-comer to the city or charter member) was at the time largely invisible. Sometimes the swift spread of urban areas enveloped small colonies of Mexicans, whose actual style of life was relatively unaffected by the process. Sometimes the rapid urbanization meant the development of slums near the city's center and a new, though generally ignored, "urban problem." The full measure of these changes can probably never be traced because of the inadequacy of data—particularly of census returns—for the years involved. Nonetheless, all the most important forces affecting the Border States during these years tended to push Mexicans into the cities—and to make the image of the Mexican as a rural farm laborer less valid.

THE EMERGING MEXICAN MINORITY: THE DEPRESSION AND AFTER

The deepening agricultural depression of the 1920s was followed by the Great Depression. The resulting stagnation hurt Mexicans as much as any other minority group dependent upon wage labor. In the cities, the burden of Mexican welfare cases became increasingly onerous. Few Border State cities were prepared to handle any substantial amount of social welfare during the early years of the Depression. Many were particularly vulnerable to the economic stresses of the Depression because they lacked a well-diversified economic base. Although the cities had grown rapidly in the years preceding the Depression, they were simply not large enough nor financially strong enough to cope with massive relief loads. Throughout the area, and also in the Midwest, cities began to implement the suggestion that the growers had made during the Congressional debates of the previous decades—that the Mexicans be "repatriated."[20] Thus the Mexicans may have been the group most severely and most directly hit by the economic problems of the Border State cities.

Things were not much better in agriculture. In Texas, cotton became so unprofitable that vast areas of the Texas Panhandle and west Texas turned from cotton to cattle, reversing a historic process. Falling prices hurt the small farmers substantially and the Mexican small farmers among them, accelerating their collapse in the long competition with larger, more efficient mechanized farms. There were further complications. The famous Dust Bowl migrations into the Border States, particularly into California, and the movement of many urban workers, both Anglo and Mexican, to agriculture (sometimes under pressure from

---

[20] A valuable unpublished manuscript and documents on the Los Angeles repatriations of the 1930s were supplied by Ronald López.

urban relief agencies) drastically cut down the amount of agricultural work available to the unskilled ethnic. Half of California's farm labor in 1934 was native white: no more than a third of the field workers were Mexican.[21] Wage rates fell drastically, as did farm prices. Isolated areas that depended upon a single crop or product (south Texas on cotton farming, the San Joaquin valley of California on citrus fruit, southern Arizona on copper mining) were seriously damaged when employment was sharply cut down. The persons most severely affected were the unskilled and the relatively immobile or unadaptable. Many of these were Mexicans. In New Mexico (a state that suffered severely) a group of New Deal surveys revealed just how much the agricultural problems of New Mexico had pushed the Hispano *rancheros* into wage labor. Unfortunately, there was suddenly almost no wage labor available. Nancie González summarizes one of the findings of an important study by the Department of Agriculture in the Tewa Basin of New Mexico:

> In 11 Spanish-American villages containing 1,202 families, an average of 1,110 men went out of the villages to work for some part of each year prior to 1930. In 1934, only 157 men out of 1,202 families had found outside work. When this situation occurred, they tried to fall back upon the more traditional sources of income—farming and sheepherding—and then discovered that changes in the ecological balance, new laws, and competition with modern techniques made it impossible to support the existing population.[22]

Federal programs took up some of the slack, most spectacularly in New Mexico, where a *majority* of the Spanish Americans were directly dependent upon the federal government. Foreclosures and tax sales removed still another large portion of the indigenous landowners. In general the response of the New Mexicans to the extreme economic deprivation of the Depression was twofold. They joined the migratory labor army following the crops throughout the Border States, and their families moved into nearby cities to reduce the risk of starvation. The effects of increasing urbanization began to be apparent in these years. We learn in New Mexico for example, that in the village of San Geronimo, 15 miles southwest of Las Vegas, more than one third of its fifty-eight houses were deserted before 1940.[23] In yet other areas of the Border States the story of rural depopulation was repeated, if less spectacularly.

Several other factors worked to complete the economic decline of the Spanish Americans in New Mexico. First, many Anglo Texans and

[21] McWilliams, *Factories in the Field*, p. 305.
[22] González, *Spanish Americans*, p. 88.
[23] González, *Spanish Americans*, p. 90.

others from southern states emigrated into the eastern plains area of the state. Second, there was heavy immigration of Mexican nationals into the mines and fields of New Mexico, and these workers competed for jobs with the older residents. Third, there was a striking volume of Anglo American immigration into New Mexico from other parts of the nation after the 1920s. Inevitably the Anglo newcomers (particularly those from Texas and the other southern states) confused the older charter-member residents with the new immigrants from Mexico. As Nancie González points out, a considerable amount of racial discrimination followed, an attitude quite new in New Mexico. At this time begins an intensified effort by the native inhabitants to distinguish themselves from the new immigrants. Hence the important distinction between "Spanish American" and "Mexican."[24]

It was during the years of the Great Depression that the New Deal and the Democratic party won the undying allegiance of Mexican Americans. More important, however, during the Depression the attitudes of both business and labor toward Mexicans (and minorities in general) reversed completely. Business opinion stopped claiming that the Mexicans were a necessary source of labor. On the other hand, labor interests stopped blaming immigrant Mexicans for the prevailing low wages and made some organizational gains among them. Nevertheless, despite symbolic gains, it seems probable that the New Deal efforts to provide a minimum of economic security for impoverished segments of the population affected Mexican Americans only peripherally, mainly when Mexicans left rural areas for industrial employment in the cities.[25]

The gradual improvement in economic conditions between the end of the Great Depression and the beginning of World War II left the newly urbanized Mexicans in a much better position. The cities offered superior education, even if it was often segregated. Cities offered a greater variety of work opportunities and much greater contact with Anglo society and its varied institutions and agencies. Most important, it was becoming increasingly clear that Mexicans were to be permanently on the scene, and this acknowledgment that Mexicans were here to stay was important, even if they were seen as unacculturated and nearly unassimilable. As Thomas Carter notes, during the 1930s educators in the Border States began to set themselves the task of acculturation rather than simply evading their responsibility for educating Mexican Americans.[26]

In Los Angeles and San Diego this consciousness of a new minority

24 González, *Spanish Americans*, chap. 8.
25 Fisher, see footnote 10 above.
26 From an unpublished manuscript prepared by Thomas P. Carter for the Mexican-American Study Project (Los Angeles: University of California, October, 1967).

was exacerbated and made urgent as a consequence of the famous "zoot suit" riots and "pachuco" disturbances of the early 1940s. As with the race upheavals of the 1960s among Blacks, the disturbances discredited all former assumptions about the minority, nearly destroyed an older generation of Mexican spokesmen by revealing their impotence, and ended forever the convenient myth in such cities as Los Angeles that the real Mexican leaders centered around the Mexican consul. The riots in Los Angeles (publicized nationally as instigated by the Mexican youth gangs) left a residue of deep bitterness and shame in the Mexican community. It was to be years before the full story of the riots, with the racist activities of servicemen and policemen, became widely known and before they came to be generally acknowledged as race riots.[27]

World War II offered Mexican Americans new opportunities. Between 300,000 and 500,000 men served in the armed forces and thus saw both the United States outside their isolated five-state ghetto and also significant parts of the rest of the world—where Mexicans had never been considered an inferior people. Many others learned skilled trades in the defense employment boom and changed residence permanently. In New Mexico perhaps a fifth of the rural population of Mexican origin may have left the state.[28] By 1950 the Border States were even more completely urbanized than the rest of the United States. Mexican leaders frequently trace the beginnings of general self-awareness to the social changes brought on by the war. By this time a steady and accelerating migration from Texas to California had begun. Slowly, also, the choice of entering immigrants from Mexico shifted from Texas to California and from rural areas to cities. The exchange of information, the broadening of experience, the increasing ethnic awareness, all meant a shift away from areas of more restricted economic and social opportunity.

Large-scale importation of cheap Mexican labor in the form of *braceros* began once more during World War II. This new wave of agricultural immigration, tailored to the needs of the growers, had less overall impact on the Mexican Americans than had the earlier immigration, largely because in fact most of the *braceros* did "go home" to Mexico when the agricultural season was finished. Furthermore, there was some degree of governmental supervision over their living standards, which had some indirect beneficial effects on Mexican Americans living in some of the more discriminatory towns in Texas. However, when the war ended, both legal and illegal immigration began again on a large and increasing

---

[27] See McWilliams, *North from Mexico*, for an account of the riots and other problems of Mexican Americans in Los Angeles.

[28] William W. Winnie, Jr., "The Hispanic Peoples of New Mexico" (Master's thesis, University of Florida, 1955), p. 97. Cited in González, *Spanish Americans*, p. 89.

scale. And this time the widespread opposition to cheap labor and the declining power of Border State agricultural interests combined to produce the second great deportation of Mexicans—"Operation Wetback." This time the question was not indigence but illegality. In five years there were 3.8 million deportations of Mexicans (only 63,515 under formal proceedings), although it was common knowledge that many if not most deportees returned to the United States, perhaps to be deported again and yet again.[29]

It is also from the World War II era that most of the signs of Mexican American minority self-consciousness date. A more aggressive political style characterizes the organizations formed at the time; on many local scenes there were protests against some of the more flagrant acts of discrimination practiced in the Border States. Very slowly, the results of decades of isolation had become obvious to the Mexican Americans, and increasing efforts were made to change the situation within the context of the American political and legal systems. (See details in Chapter Eight.)

But as indicated in the first chapter, neither ethnic self-consciousness nor Anglo recognition of Mexican problems is as yet fully developed. From the minority side, there is continued diversity in outlook and self-conception, the product of generations of isolation from other Mexican Americans as well as from the larger society. Isolation bred diversity, and a history of racial conflict and impoverishment increased the isolation. The gradual emergence of Mexican Americans as an American minority is the end result of a century and a half of contact.

[29] These deportations are also discussed in the next chapter as part of the history of immigration from Mexico. For details, see Leo Grebler, *Mexican Immigration to the United States: The Record and Its Implications*, Advance Report 2 (University of California, Los Angeles: Mexican-American Study Project, 1966).

Mexican American life was shaped by the land in which they settled. In many ways the geographic, economic, social, and demographic peculiarities of the American Southwest were decisive factors. Mexican American life was also shaped by the manner in which they entered the Southwest: patterns of immigration determined to a very large extent when Mexicans would enter and who would enter. Who, then, were the immigrants? When did they enter the United States? How was immigration controlled? How will patterns of immigration change in the future?

THE BORDER STATES: BACKGROUND FOR A MINORITY

The Origins of Diversity

Any group entering the American Southwest[1] in the late nineteenth century would have faced a peculiar situation. Paradigms of assimilation and acculturation derived from American contacts with immigrants in the East and Midwest simply are not relevant. Some of the peculiarities of the Border States tended to result in dispersal and isolation of the Spanish-speaking populations, particularly the immigrants. Other and perhaps weaker factors tended to push the immigrants from Mexico and the "charter member" Mexicans into a common pattern.

Geography and Economy

Among the peculiarities that tended to scatter enclaves of Mexicans, the vast spaces of the Border States may have been decisive. Even today the two most concentrated areas of Mexican American population in the United States are more than a thousand miles apart, separated not only by

---

[1] The phrase "American Southwest" is used as a convenience and because of its identification in the American mind with the old "Spanish Southwest." Terms for this region are various and often confusing. Texas is a major center of Mexican American population and yet is a true part of the deep South. California, Arizona, and New Mexico belong to the West. Again, New Mexico, Arizona, and Colorado are Mountain states. Colorado is not properly a southwestern state, although its early population of Mexican Americans means that it is generally included in any figures covering the entire Southwest. Accordingly the term "Southwest" will be used throughout to refer to the five states of California, Arizona, New Mexico, Texas, and Colorado. The term "Border States" will include California, Arizona, New Mexico, and Texas—all states sharing the Mexican border.

sheer distance but by massive mountain ranges and desert lands hundreds of miles in width. Only a few highways and railroads connect these areas today. Before 1880 there was no east-west through passage whatever. It was inevitable that the small settlements, beginning in the latter part of the sixteenth century and continuing throughout the seventeenth and eighteenth centuries, would be effectively isolated: from each other, from the centers of population in Mexico, from the weak U.S. territorial governments—and even today, from the federal government in Washington.

The Border States also offer Mexican Americans comparatively easy access to the homeland. We shall discuss control of the border later in this chapter; but despite increasing administrative control it is normal and natural today that all manner of intercourse should occur easily across the border. By contrast the American Black cannot easily return home; his ties with Africa have been all but severed. European and Asian immigrants are far from home. But most Chicanos still live within a short driving distance of Mexico.

Still another peculiar condition affecting the Border States is their economic climate.[2] The economic development of these states lagged behind that of the rest of the United States—and, in fact, thus retained until very recent years their reliance on agriculture and mining. This is an economy heavily oriented toward the exploitation of natural resources and required much capital (which had to be imported from the East) and vast quantities of cheap and unskilled labor. There were few European settlers in these states in the nineteenth century. Accordingly a succession of non-Europeans served as cheap labor, coming either as temporary contract laborers or as immigrants. Thus Mexicans were recruited in large numbers following the Chinese (until 1882), Japanese (until 1907), Filipino, and even Hindu workers as the chief supply of labor. The housing and control of such workers, in gangs or in groups of families, meant the construction of labor camps and cheap housing near work sites but nearly always remote physically, socially, and politically from southwestern life. A pattern of workers' enclaves, of pockets of isolation—the direct result of the economy of the Border States—was firmly established and has left many traces.

The Border States were much more slowly urbanized than the rest of the United States. In 1900, 70 percent of the population of the American Southwest was rural, a proportion considerably higher than in the East or the Midwest. By 1940 the proportion of urban and rural residents

---

[2] This account of the social, political, and economic milieu of the Border States draws heavily upon Leo Grebler, Joan W. Moore, and Ralph Guzman, *The Mexican American People* (New York: Free Press, 1970), Chap. 4.

approached equality, and, surprisingly, since that date the process of urbanization throughout the Border States has rushed ahead of that in the United States as a whole, although quite unevenly within the area. Thus the Mexican American population was caught up quite late in one of the most significant national trends of this century.

Politics

The Border States were also very slow to reach political maturity. All except Texas and California were territories for many years, and New Mexico and Arizona did not attain statehood until 1912. (The recency of these events is suggested by the fact that Arizona's first senator, Carl Hayden, still served in the U.S. Senate as recently as the mid-1960s.) Throughout the Border States political organization was late and relatively unstructured by what the East and Midwest define as normal political party activities. There was never much opportunity for any ethnic group to duplicate the success of Irish, Italian, and Jewish immigrants in the urban areas of the East in influencing the objectives of local or state government. Moreover, party organization in these states is generally moribund between elections. At no time has there been any counterpart of the urban ward system so characteristic of eastern cities. Thus there was no training ground for the political game, no recruiting process for ethnic leadership as there had been for some other American ethnic groups. The heritage for Mexicans has been delayed entry into politics, and a parochialism and a sense of ineffectuality in organizational and political activity.

Furthermore, as indicated in the previous chapter, state governments in the Border States were for many years dominated by a relatively few economic interests.[3] The railroads, the powerful mining companies, the owners of the big "factory farms" and the big land development companies controlled Border State governments for many years and are today a powerful influence. In the past, however, such an alliance between business and politics meant that a politically unsophisticated minority group could be easily manipulated. The late formal structuring of state and local government also has had unfortunate effects on Border State law enforcement. All too often the weak and undermanned local authorities became the arm of private interests, for example, in labor disputes. In recent years the well-known Texas Rangers have been used in labor-management disputes and local political controversy involving Mexican

[3] This account uses material prepared by Paul Fisher for the Mexican-American Study Project (Los Angeles: University of California, November, 1967).

Americans, an action quite in keeping with their historical record of violence against Chicanos.[4]

Internal Diversity

The Border States also present a remarkable and often bewildering social and economic diversity. Local social systems differ considerably and the effect of a wide range of opportunity and of toleration for Mexicans has been enormous. In California, a relatively rich and well-developed state, the variation from city to city ranges from the relatively open and industrialized society of San Francisco and Oakland to the social system of the nearby San Joaquin Valley, in whose large cities the Mexican minority is still quite rigidly segregated. Albuquerque is a world apart from the nearby isolated villages in the northern valleys of New Mexico in terms of Mexican American life. Then, as an extreme range from either, the life of the Texas border cities of El Paso, Laredo, and the string of cities from Brownsville to McAllen is conditioned by the presence of nearby Mexico. In 1970 the percentage of Mexican Americans in El Paso was 45 percent; in Laredo, 74 percent; in the Brownsville-Harlingen-San Benito metropolitan area, 65 percent. Many smaller towns along the Rio Grande are almost all Mexican.

A few indicators of the range of social acceptance, economic opportunity, and governmental concern will be sufficient—income, political participation, and educational achievement. The median annual income of Mexican American families in the San Francisco-Oakland Standard Metropolitan Statistical Area (SMSA) in 1970 was $7,361. (Though very high for Mexicans, this was still below the Anglo median.) This is an area that is highly developed economically and reasonably open to its minorities. By contrast, the median family income of Mexican Americans for the same year in the Brownsville-Harlingen-San Benito SMSA (a Texas border area) was $3,396.

Political participation is more difficult to appraise, but the most casual inspection shows that Mexicans living in Texas have a very small political voice, especially in local affairs. Many remained completely disfranchised up to 1966, the year the poll tax was abolished. In New Mexico, by contrast, the Mexicans carry an important tradition of political activity, supplying state legislators and even U.S. senators with fair regularity. Until World War II the "Spanish" population of New Mexico actually outnumbered the Anglo residents. In New Mexico a large num-

---

[4]See John Shockley's account of the role of the Rangers in Crystal City, Texas, *Chicano Revolt in a Texas Town* (Notre Dame, Ind.: University of Notre Dame Press, 1973).

ber of small cities and a dispersal of political power to rural areas tended to work in favor of the minority group.

Access to education is yet another important index of the comparative ability of existing agencies of government to meet the needs of a minority population. In general, the Mexican American minority is shockingly undereducated, but the range in educational attainment is also impressive. The median years of school completed in 1970 by Spanish-surname persons over twenty-five years of age varies from 9.7 years in California to 6.7 years in Texas. It is not likely that this wide range in educational achievement reflects any important difference in ambition or ability between the two groups of Mexican Americans. The difference, rather, is the ability or the desire of the school system to teach Mexican Americans. (See Chapter Five.)

Population Characteristics

Demographic factors have also worked to create a peculiar climate in the Border States: it is possible they have significantly increased a climate of racial intolerance. First, through most of this century these four states have had a higher proportion of native whites (as compared with foreign-born whites) than the rest of the United States. This was true at each census date from 1910 to 1960. Texas and New Mexico tended to have the highest percentages of native whites.

The second demographic reality in the Border States is that Mexican Americans share their minority status with several non-European groups. In all Border States, except Texas and California, there have always been large numbers of American Indians. In Arizona's first census in 1870, Indians outnumbered whites four to one. There are also very large numbers of Orientals. In California, to illustrate this point, the nonwhite population in 1910 was 5.0 percent, of whom only 0.9 percent were Blacks; 0.7 percent were Indian, and 3.4 percent were Orientals. By 1970 the nonwhites had grown to 10.0 percent, of whom most were Blacks (7.0 percent), only a few (0.4 percent) Indian, and a considerable number still Oriental (2.6 percent). In later years the Mexican Americans increasingly found themselves sharing the bottom of the economic ladder with Black Americans and Indians. The growth of California's present Black population began only during World War II, and although the proportion of Blacks in the Texas population has been declining, Texas was still 12.5 percent Black in 1970. These demographic factors are important, first because the Anglo population of the Border States has faced *several* racial minorities (contact that preconditioned their relations with Mexican Americans), and second because the minorities themselves have frequently and increasingly been placed in competitive relations with each other.

Yet another factor in the Border States populations has been important to Mexican Americans. This predominantly Roman Catholic minority confronted an Anglo population that was substantially more Protestant than in most other parts of the nation. Of the non-Catholics, an extraordinary proportion, particularly in Texas, are oriented toward fundamentalist Protestantism. No other American religious group would be so likely to be hostile to the Catholic church, with its hierarchy, ritualism, and priestly control. (As it happened, this stereotype of the Catholic church was not very accurate in the Border States, as we shall detail in Chapter Five.)

This uncongenial combination of population elements produced antagonism very early in the region's history, as we discussed in the previous chapter. No other part of the United States saw such prolonged intergroup violence as did the Border States from 1848 to 1925. Even the relationship between Blacks and whites in the South offers less conflict. The extent of the violence—cattle raids, border looting expeditions, expulsions, deportations, lynchings, civil riots, labor wars, organized banditry, filibustering expeditions, revolutions—can hardly be exaggerated. Some of these minor and virtually unknown conflicts laid waste to entire counties and lasted for years. Thus the myth of broad, free and easy frontier tolerance so cherished in the Southwest obscures the real fact of continuous and acute racial tension.[5]

These are some of the physical, social, economic, and demographic peculiarities of the Border States. Later in this chapter we will trace the impact of some of these peculiarities upon a growing minority. But there is yet another factor—of prime importance—that so dominates Mexican life in the United States that it must be considered separately and carefully. Vast numbers of Mexicans poured into the United States after 1900 in the last of the great waves of immigration to enter this country, which further conditioned the story of the Mexican American minority.

IMMIGRATION: A CLOSE
AND OPEN BORDER

From Tijuana-San Ysidro on the coast of California to Brownsville-Matamoros on the Gulf of Mexico runs the long border of more than

[5] A new generation of Chicano historians is beginning to discover these endless frontier and racial conflicts. They are often buried in regional history or in scholarly publications dealing with Western history. An interesting current rediscovery is that of Rodolfo Acuna, *Occupied America: The Chicano's Struggle Toward Liberation* (San Francisco: Canfield Press, 1972).

2,000 miles that separates Mexico and the United States. Sometimes the border is a real barrier and heavily guarded. Some areas now have electronic sensing devices adapted from the military surveillance conducted in Viet Nam. Sometimes, as in the Big Bend area of Texas, nature makes it almost impassable. More often the border is not much more than a high wire fence and dirt road running through southern San Diego County, through the lower end of California's Imperial Valley, and then across vast desert regions in southern Arizona and New Mexico to El Paso. Here the border becomes nothing much more substantial than the Rio Grande, a river that is one of the nation's longest but often shallow enough to wade across and sometimes (in dry seasons) disappearing altogether.

In this century this boundary has deeply influenced the life of Mexican Americans. The closeness and accessibility of the United States meant that a flow of immigrants constantly pressured the economic achievements of Mexicans already in this country. Then, also, the river frequently shifted channels, bringing to the affected area a rash of quarrels about property rights. Water rights in this very dry land were of critical importance and the subject of many quarrels between American and Mexican citizens and American and Mexican cities and provinces. This border is indeed a sharp contrast to that shared by the United States and Canada.

The origin of the border is itself worth some detail. Under the terms of the Treaty of Guadalupe-Hidalgo (February 2, 1848), Mexico ceded a vast territory to the United States. The line of demarcation following the Rio Grande was clear enough, but west of El Paso the treaty negotiators followed a faulty map. The ensuing arguments very nearly caused a second war. Ultimately James Gadsden was sent to Mexico City to negotiate a new acquisition. The original line of treaty would have followed the course of the Gila River across Arizona, a natural and reasonable line, but Gadsden managed to secure by purchase an additional 45,532 square miles. The new border ran south of the Gila and secured for the United States a substantial area for a proposed railroad line to California. Furthermore, as it happened (and no Mexican thinks it accidental) the Gadsden Purchase of 1853 included some of the world's richest copper mines.

But the most lasting consequence of the Gadsden Purchase was an unnatural border. Long-established commercial ties between the Mexican state of Sonora and Arizona were legally severed. A vast inland area was left without a seaport (Guayamas would have been a natural outlet). Some established cities were split in half, surviving to the present as "twin cities." Further east, where the Rio Grande marks the border the instability of the river channel generated quarrels among people who had to share the river in order to live.[6] Thus history left the two nations with a shared border that was difficult for either to defend and harder yet to share.

History of Immigration

For some reason the massive and ceaseless movements of people over this frontier have attracted little serious study. There have been only three studies of consequence, one in 1930, one in 1966, and one in 1971.[7] This neglect is hard to understand in light of two facts: first, there were huge numbers of immigrants. (During the one decade 1954–1964 more people entered the United States as immigrants from Mexico than from any other country.) Second, there have been almost continuous political and legislative wrangles about the United States-Mexican border and its control, and such quarrels are unusual in American history.

Mexican immigration differs from the much better known European immigration in many ways. It may be well to abstract some of these distinctive features before proceeding with a history of the immigration. First, it has never been regulated by formal quotas; we will discuss this point in detail shortly. Second, immigration from Mexico, though continuous, has been massive only recently—and is the only recent prolonged massive movement. Third, Mexican movement across the border has followed some very complicated patterns—some very informal. There are permanent legal and permanent illegal immigrants. Many Mexicans, some of them U.S. citizens, live in Mexico and commute to work daily across the border. Agricultural workers enter on contract or for seasonal employment. There are important flows of businessmen and tourists from both countries, and there are border area residents with business interests on both sides of the border.

Fourth (and this is related to the third point) it has been comparatively easy for Mexican immigrants to reach the United States. The large and economically attractive cities of the Border States, especially those in Texas, have been accessible by railroad, highway, and bus. It is relatively easy for both failures and successes to return home, and has been

---

[6] As Carey McWilliams states, "From El Paso to Brownsville, the Rio Grande does not separate people: it draws them together." McWilliams, *North from Mexico*, p. 61. Much of this account of the early border is based on McWilliams' work.

[7] Manuel Gamio, *Mexican Immigration to the United States* (Chicago: University of Chicago Press, 1930); Leo Grebler, *Mexican Immigration to the United States: The Record and Its Implications*, Advance Report 2 (University of California, Los Angeles: Mexican-American Study Project, 1966), and Julian Samora, *Los Mojados: The Wetback Story* (Notre Dame, Ind.: University of Notre Dame Press, 1971).

relatively easy for a prospective immigrant to make a trial journey to the United States.

Fifth, no other minority was ever deported from the United States as massively as the Mexicans. Sixth, no other minority except the Chinese has entered this country in such an atmosphere of illegality. A long, relatively unguarded border and recruiting by important economic interests insured that in some years perhaps three times as many Mexicans entered illegally as were admitted legally. No accurate estimate is possible, but the consequence was inevitable; the illegal aliens and their communities were peculiarly vulnerable to economic and social discrimination of all kinds.

Statistically it is impossible to analyze Mexican immigrants earlier than 1910. We know that an important movement took place after 1848 when thousands of Mexicans joined in the California gold rush. The chaotic condition of the border areas until 1886 prevented any government control whatever over the population movements between the two nations. Arizona, for example, was dominated by the Apache throughout most of the nineteenth century. Formal control over this human traffic began in 1886, but records were so approximate as to be nearly valueless. Not until 1907 was a definite control pattern set up. As late as 1919 the entire border was patrolled by only 151 inspectors, most of whom were actually serving at 20 regular ports of entry. Before 1954, when control was stepped up, Galarza suggests that Border State legislators succeeded in keeping Border Patrol appropriations too low to accomplish more than the most rudimentary control, thus permitting the flow of cheap labor so necessary to the southwestern economy.[8]

By 1907–1908 Mexican railroads linked interior Mexico with the border cities. This made immigration much easier, though there was not an immediate increase in the volume; most immigrants were agricultural laborers, and debt peonage, still a prevailing pattern in Mexico, kept many immobile. It was only after the sudden dissolution of peonage during the revolution after 1910 that a substantial movement to the United States began. Then, from 1910 to 1920, the immigrants apparently included a significant number of middle-class and upper-class Mexican refugees, many of whom hoped to return to Mexico.

In addition, from 1910 to 1919 American labor requirements in the Border States were increasing. The Chinese had been excluded in 1882, the Japanese in 1907, and the supply of European immigrants to the United States suddenly waned with the beginning of World War I. World War I greatly spurred both prices and demand for agricultural

[8]Ernesto Galarza, *Merchants of Labor: The Mexican Bracero Story* (San Jose, Calif.: Rosicrucian Press, 1964), p. 64.

and mine products, both specialties of the Border States. Special regulations were issued in 1917 to admit "temporary" farm workers, railroad maintenance workers, and miners. The word "temporary" had the usual meaning: in June, 1919 one report showed that two-thirds of an initial group of 30,000 Mexican workers admitted after 1917 simply remained in the United States.

This first wave of immigration in 1910–1920 was only a beginning; the next decade saw Mexican immigrants arrive in massive numbers. In 1920 there were 51,042 legal immigrants—a number large enough to raise fears in Mexico that the big neighbor in the North was pulling away far too many people. In the United States there was also some apprehension, leading to stricter administrative controls in 1929. The figures themselves tell the story, as given in Table 3–1.

In the United States there was an expanding demand for agricultural labor, while at the same time in Mexico the disruption attending the revolutionary wars prompted much of this immigration.

The influx slowed markedly after 1929. American agriculture was suffering from a prolonged decline even before the more general economic drop of the Great Depression. Further, the Mexican economy was beginning to recover from the revolutionary period. In the United States other sources of cheap farm labor became available as the migration from the Dust Bowl to the West began and as a growing number of urban workers sought refuge in farm work. By 1930, Mexican immigration dropped to only 11,915 legal entries.

The drop is only partially understandable as a response to impersonal supply-demand factors. More importantly, it reflects the impact of massive efforts to send the Mexicans "home," where, it had always been assumed, they "belonged."

U.S. Immigration Service officers stepped up the search and deportation procedures for illegal aliens. Various devices including the stoppage of welfare payments, were employed to encourage legal residents to undergo "voluntary" repatriation. Most disturbing, in many cities of the West and Midwest, Mexicans who applied for relief were referred to variously named "Mexican bureaus." The sole purpose of these agencies was to get Mexicans off the relief rolls by deporting them. The possibility that a Mexican might be an American citizen was never considered. This move was organized by local authorities with small regard for the niceties of immigration law, or, for that matter, constitutional rights. Mexican authorities cooperated, and the Mexican American (citizen or new immigrant) who wanted to stay in the United States had no recourse. Carey McWilliams witnessed one of these "repatriations" in Los Angeles:

It was discovered that, in wholesale lots, they could be shipped to Mexico City for $14.70 per capita. The sum represented less than the cost of a

TABLE 3–1

NUMBER OF MEXICAN IMMIGRANTS TO THE UNITED STATES
AND ALL OTHER IMMIGRANTS, 1910–1967

Fiscal Years	Mexican [a]	All Other	Fiscal Years	Mexican [a]	All Other
1910	17,760	1,023,810	1942	2,182	26,599
1911	18,784	859,803	1943	3,985	19,740
1912	22,001	816,171	1944	6,399	22,152
1913	10,954	1,186,938	1945	6,455	31,664
1914	13,089	1,205,391	1946	6,805	101,916
1915	10,993	315,707	1947	7,775	139,517
1916	17,198	281,628	1948	8,730	161,840
1917	16,438	278,965	1949	7,977	180,340
1918	17,602	93,016	1950	6,841	242,346
1919	28,844	112,228	1951	6,372	199,345
1920	51,042	378,959	1952	9,600	255,920
1921	29,603	775,625	1953	18,454	151,980
1922	18,246	291,310	1954	37,456	170,721
1923	62,709	460,210	1955	50,772	187,018
1924	87,648	619,248	1956	65,047	256,578
1925	32,378	261,935	1957	49,154	277,713
1926	42,638	261,850	1958	26,712	226,553
1927	66,766	268,409	1959	23,061	237,625
1928	57,765	249,490	1960	32,684	232,714
1929	38,980	240,698	1961	41,632	229,712
1930	11,915	229,785	1962	55,291	232,472
1931	2,627	94,512	1963	55,253	251,007
1932	1,674	33,902	1964	32,967	259,281
1933	1,514	21,554	1965	37,969	296,697
1934	1,470	28,000	1966	45,163	323,040
1935	1,232	33,724	1967	42,371	361,972
1936	1,308	35,021	1968	43,563	454,448
1937	1,918	48,326	1969	44,623	358,579
1938	2,014	65,881	1970	44,469	373,326
1939	2,265	80,733	1971	50,103	370,478
1940	1,914	68,842	1972	64,040	384,685
1941	2,068	49,708	1973	70,141	400,063

Source: Leo Grebler, Mexican Immigration to the United States: The Record and Its Implications, Advance Report 2 (University of California, Los Angeles: Mexican-American Study Project, 1966), p. 106. Based on Annual Reports of the U.S. Immigration and Naturalization Service and its predecessor agencies, which are the source for supplementary figures for 1965–1973.

[a] By country of birth.

week's board and lodging. And so, about February 1931, the first trainload was dispatched, and shipments at the rate of about one a month have continued ever since. [1933]. A shipment consisting of three special trains left Los Angeles on December 8. The loading commenced at about six o'clock in the morning and continued for hours. More than twenty-five such special trains had left the Southern Pacific Station before last April.

The repatriation programme is regarded locally as a piece of consummate statecraft. The average per family cost of executing it is $71.14, including food and transportation. It cost Los Angeles county $77,249.29 to repatriate one shipment of 6,024. It would have cost $424,933.70 to provide this number with such charitable assistance as they would have been *entitled* to had they remained—a saving of $347,468.41.[9] [Emphasis added.]

Again, complete figures are not available,[10] but in the four years between 1929 and 1934 more than 400,000 Mexican aliens left the United States without formal proceedings. Altogether the repatriation and sharply reduced immigration cut down the Mexican-born population in the United States from 639,000 in 1930 to a few more than 377,000 in 1940.

Only a few years later, however, the manpower emergencies of the early World War II years made the Mexicans welcome again. Immigration rose slightly but steadily, and workers were once again actively recruited, this time through the famous *bracero* (contract labor) program of 1942. For a time after the war, importations under this program stopped; but agricultural employers were able to build such a strong case for resuming the *bracero* program that in 1951 Congress enacted Public Law 78, which replaced the earlier executive agreements. The employers' arguments were familiar: the urgencies of the Korean War made them persuasive. In sum, it was argued that there were not enough domestic workers and that native Americans were unqualified or less effective for the stoop labor needed in the fields or both. Labor unions and public welfare organizations offered counterarguments without much effect.

If the *bracero* program was meant to slow down the steady flood of "wetbacks," it was a resounding failure. Again no data are available about illegal entries except some speculation that the ratio of illegals to legals might run as high as four to one. Expulsions from the U.S. continued at a rate that shortly reached 100,000 persons a year, although

---

[9] Carey McWilliams, "Getting Rid of the Mexicans," *The American Mercury* (March 1933).

[10] Immigration records on departing aliens are so confused as to be nearly useless. Departures are reported as cases, not persons. They may include nonimmigrant aliens. After World War II departures were listed only as "passengers departed," a category that simply includes international passenger traffic of all kinds. Grebler, *Mexican Immigration*, pp. 27–28. Estimates are from Abraham Hoffman, *Unwanted Mexicans in the Great Depression* (Tucson: The University of Arizona Press, 1974).

this number included many "repeaters." American farms continued to offer employment to all arrivals. (Offering employment to aliens was not illegal.) For Mexican workers the formalities of legal entry could be uncertain and expensive: often illegal entry was quicker and cheaper. Growers found it profitable to hire illegals because they could save a great deal of administrative work and substantial fees. *Braceros* and "wetbacks" often worked on the same crews. Administrative processes reached the ultimate in absurdity: illegals could be transported back across the border and then readmitted as "legally contracted" workers. It was a process aptly called "drying out" the wetbacks. American agriculture needed workers: the federal government and the Mexican government could cooperate to fill that demand.

Mexican immigration on permanent visa began to increase very rapidly in the 1950s. Both permanent and temporary immigration reached a postwar peak in 1956 when there were 65,047 permanent legal immigrants. But the real drama of the decade 1950–1960 was "Operation Wetback," which repeated the great repatriation of the Depression era, but this time with emphasis upon the illegality rather than the indigence of those sent back.

Operation Wetback was conducted by the U.S. Immigration and Naturalization Service. It was organized with military precision to begin in June of 1954. California was the first target and then Texas, but the campaign was widened to include cities as far away from the border as Spokane, Chicago, Kansas City, and St. Louis.

Operation Wetback was very successful. The apprehensions reached 875,000 in fiscal 1953 and a huge 1,035,282 in 1954. In five years the astonishing total of 3.8 million illegal Mexican immigrants were found and expelled. Only 63,515 were deported in formal proceedings; the others were simply removed under threat of deportation. Most were sent not to the border, but with the cooperation of the Mexican government to points in Mexico near their original homes.

The resulting shock waves in the Mexican American communities greatly deepened the prevailing distrust and alienation. In the process there were some important infringements of civil rights. Hundreds of thousands of American citizens were stopped and queried because they "looked Mexican." In fact, if a person who "looked Mexican" could not immediately produce documentary evidence of his legal status when questioned in the street or any other public place, he ran the risk of arrest and being sent "home" to Mexico. (This quick and rude form of repatriation is still standard Immigration and Naturalization procedure.) Yet there were many leaders, particularly in the labor unions, who saw unrestrained immigration as damaging. Mexican American spokesmen themselves were beginning to feel that a continuously supplied pool of wetback labor undermined any economic or social gains. There was also considerable resentment in the Mexican community about the *bracero* program.

Meanwhile the immigration people believed that the problem of the Mexican illegals had been solved (at least for the present) by the huge volume of these repatriations. (It seems likely, however, that many of the expellees simply reentered with clean papers, because the totals of legal immigration grew considerably in the following years.) One consequence of Operation Wetback was more pressure for the importation of *braceros* because there were not enough aliens for labor on the ranches of the Southwest. Another and more damaging consequence was a stifling of those leaders in the Chicano communities who were beginning to realize the necessity for some control of illegal aliens. Operation Wetback made it impossible for them to agree publicly with the Immigration and Naturalization service and the labor unions.

By 1960, sentiment against both Mexican immigrants and Mexican contract laborers had hardened considerably. Congress listened more attentively to labor interests. It is also very probable that the long decline of agricultural power in the Border States meant that agriculture no longer dominated legislative opinion. Whatever the reason for the change in attitude, any reasonable future projection of the 1960 to 1963 immigration totals was frightening to Border State residents. Legally there had never been any quotas. There was, however, a convenient administrative mechanism available in the Act of 1952. Accordingly on July 1, 1963, the U.S. Department of Labor announced simply that any job offer to a potential Mexican immigrant would have to be certified by the department. In turn, the department required verification from state employment agencies. No Mexican could take a job that would adversely affect domestic wages and working conditions or one that had domestic applicants.

The same slow reversal of public opinion had yet other important consequences. First, the *bracero* program was halted (with some minor exceptions) at the end of 1964. The next year Congress imposed a ceiling of 120,000 immigrants a year from all Western Hemisphere countries, to become effective in 1968. This created a new and unprecedented atmosphere of control: the "close and friendly" border had disappeared, perhaps forever.

WHO WERE
THE MEXICAN IMMIGRANTS?

Immigration statistics offer only a crude profile of the immigrants, but it is possible to make some important comparisons. We know that the Mexican immigrants tended to have been even younger, less skilled, and less well-educated than immigrants from other countries. They have been predominantly male, except in recent years when the legal immigrant quota has shifted to wives and children.

In earlier years the American economy could easily use such immigrants; those coming from Europe included a large proportion in occupations requiring little training. Unskilled Italians, Poles, Scandinavians, and Irish were absorbed by construction and other industries needing a great deal of labor. However, such opportunities have rapidly declined, even in the relatively underdeveloped Border States.

Over the years there have also been important changes in the announced destinations of the new Mexican arrivals, some of great significance. Typically the immigrant of earlier years was bound for a company town, an agricultural work camp, or perhaps an urban enclave somewhere in the Border States: from 1910 to 1929 Texas was the most popular destination. Slowly California became more attractive, and figures from 1960 to 1964 show an impressive 55.7 percent going to California and only 25.1 percent to Texas. Arizona took 5.7 percent and New Mexico 2.5 percent. Areas outside the Border States were not important. During this period only 10.6 percent intended to go outside this very limited area. Recent trends show that California is still taking a very high proportion and large midwestern cities, notably Chicago, are of dramatic new importance. These shifts in distribution of the immigrants (as well as the shifting proportions of the foreign-born within each state) greatly affect life opportunities in all Chicano communities.

Whatever their destination, it seems that the rural population of inland Mexico has been the main source—either directly, or by way of an intervening move to one of Mexico's larger cities. The most important single geographic source is probably the great Mesa Central, a large plateau area in central Mexico far from the U.S. border which contains, as it happens, a great many of Mexico's most acute social problems. Most Mexicans who wanted to leave Mexico tended to be impoverished and unskilled. There have always been many such persons in Mexico, and Mexican economic growth has seemed ironically to mean that her lower-class groups are getting an even smaller share of the total national income of Mexico. The real question about Mexican immigration is not why so many Mexicans came to the United States, but why so few?

Leo Grebler suggests that much of the ebb and flow of Mexican immigration can be explained by four factors. First, the urge to immigrate simply lay dormant until the Mexican revolution released masses of agricultural peons. Second, alternative methods of immigration were nearly always available. An increase or decrease in the number of recruited contract workers often meant a corresponding increase or decrease in permanent immigration. Third, changes in the volume of Mexican immigration tend to be related to business cycles in the United States. Fourth, administrative controls affected the movements. The real force at all times, Grebler concludes, was a "persistent disparity in per-capita real income, together with a highly and perhaps even increasingly uneven distribution of income in Mexico itself."[11]

LAWS, COURTS, AND IMMIGRANTS

Before 1875 there were no federal statutes in the United States regulating immigration.[12] Two concepts determined this policy of presenting an "open door" to all the world. It was felt that America was to be an asylum and a place of opportunity for Europe's "downtrodden masses." It was also widely believed that any mixture of nationalities that would enter this country could be "melted" into American life. Both these ideals—and a practical need for unskilled labor in American industry and agriculture—had to be faced down in Congress before there could be any restrictions on immigration.

However, Congress could and did control the quality of the immigrants. Qualitative restrictions appeared as early as 1875, and the list of aliens excludable for physical or moral reasons grew with each revision of the laws governing immigration. There were specific acts against Chinese immigrants in 1882 and against alien contract labor in both 1885 and 1891, although neither much affected Mexican immigration. These dilutions in practice of the traditional American welcome were based on a feeling that the newer immigrants were "less American" than the older. Americans began to feel more receptive to racist ideology. Large-scale importations of unskilled labor were less needed in the late nineteenth century in every part of the nation except in the Border States. Further, the nation suffered a series of acute agricultural and financial depressions that created much domestic unemployment. In Congress the debates about immigration reflected a new and tough nationalism quite typical of the early twentieth century. And although Mexican immigration did not yet figure importantly in the debates, the new feeling did lead directly to the Quota Law of 1921 and thus to the first overall control of the *number* of immigrants attempted in this country. The Quota Law was revised in 1924 and became the basis of all future immigration policy.

Not until later did Mexican immigration become a subject for

[11] Grebler, *Mexican Immigration*, p. 93.
[12] This study of federal laws and Mexican immigration is based on a section by Ronald Wyse in Grebler, *Mexican Immigration*.

national debate. The qualitative restrictions of 1917 were a reaction to the large numbers of immigrants coming not from Mexico but from southern and eastern Europe. Mexicans were exempt from the quantitative controls imposed in 1921 and 1924, as were all Western Hemisphere countries. In Congress the exemption was justified on the basis of "pan-Americanism" as a principle and traditional policy. There were, as yet, comparatively few immigrants from either Mexico or Canada and it was easy for Congress to be a "good neighbor." Nonetheless the idea of both qualitative and quantitative controls over immigration had been established by 1924. The actual mechanism of exclusion was available for use when needed.

By 1926 a great increase in Mexican immigration encouraged the Congressional restrictionists to make a strong drive to "close the back door." The racial argument against Mexicans appeared again. As Congressman John Box of Texas put it, Mexicans were "illiterate, unclean, peonized masses" and racially speaking, he felt they were a "mixture of Mediterranean-blooded Spanish peasants with low grade Indians who did not fight to extinction but submitted and multiplied as serfs."[13] But the restrictionists overreached themselves. If they excluded only Mexicans they would anger powerful economic interests. If they excluded all Western Hemisphere nationals, they would have a difficult time applying the policy to Canadians. Moreover, there was always the danger that the Republic of Mexico might be offended. But, in fact, no new legislation was needed. Merely enforcing the qualitative provisions would achieve the desired effect. Accordingly, in 1929, consular officers in Mexico began to turn down applicants for legal admission on the grounds they were likely to become "a public charge" in the United States. Thus Congress could be persuaded that no unseemly anti-Mexican legislation was needed.

The Depression era and the rise of facism and communism in Europe brought a new concern with national security. By 1950 a substantial overgrowth of modifications and exceptions meant that the basic immigration law needed rewriting. The result was the famous McCarran-Walter Immigration and Nationality Act of 1952. Fundamentally, it recodified and retained the national origins quota system. Subsequent legislation as late as 1965 would do nothing more than modify certain particularly harsh provisions of the McCarran-Walter Act.

All the basic laws concerning immigration left loopholes to allow importation of Mexican workers even when the main purpose of the laws seemed to be to restrict such importation. The Immigration Act of 1917 and the McCarran-Walter Act both contain such exceptions and pro-

13 Quoted in Grebler, *Mexican Immigration*, p. D-10.

vide for a fully developed administrative apparatus to control the flow of workers. Whatever the intent of Congress, the loopholes could always be opened or closed administratively.

One excellent example of such a loophole is the continuous admission of Mexican workers as "commuter" workers. Under the Quota Law of 1924, a Mexican "immigrant" who qualified for immigration could be issued a card which permitted him to enter the United States every day to work in Border State cities and then return home to Mexico at night.

Mexican contract labor has entered continuously under a series of complicated special laws and agreements in addition to loophole provisions of both the Quota Law of 1924 and the McCarran-Walter Act. Sometimes the importations were made under joint control of the United States and Mexico and sometimes not. When Congress passed Public Law 78 in July of 1951 allowing the *braceros*, strong governmental controls became effective for the first time. Notable among the controls were two laws that made the illegal smuggling of aliens a felony and gave federal officials the right to patrol private lands within 25 miles of the United States-Mexico border.

A considerable body of administrative law affects Mexican immigrants although it is much too complicated to sketch here.[14] Most of this regulation was created by the Immigration and Naturalization Service (of the U.S. Department of Justice) and by a series of judicial decisions on the nature of American citizenship. The growth and administration of this law is a story in itself and sometimes not very pretty. The Service has not always observed either its own regulations or the ordinary civil rights of the citizens and aliens affected. (A U.S. Supreme Court decision in 1886 established that the "person" in the Fifth Amendment guarantee of due process of law includes not just citizens and nationals of the United States but also resident aliens.) Nor does the Mexican American population, alien and non-alien, regard *la migra* (a nickname for the Immigration Service officers) with any feeling except varying degrees of resentment. Service regulations have often been invoked in punitive and arbitrary fashion by employers and local authorities throughout the Border States. In theory, of course, there was always recourse to the courts, but such alternatives were for the wealthy, not for poor and ill-informed Mexican immigrants.

In recent years the Mexican American population has been profoundly affected by a series of judicial decisions regarding the "dual national." In fact, much of the current legal doctrine on loss of nationality stems from decisions affecting Mexican immigrants. These decisions

14 For a short but excellent summary, see Ronald Wyse in Grebler, *Mexican Immigration*, p. D-19.

were a direct result of the heavy illegal immigration and the equally massive repatriations of Mexicans. Legally speaking, children born to Mexican contract laborers (or even to illegal aliens) are American citizens who hold "dual nationality." Thus many U.S. citizens were illegally repatriated to Mexico. Many then endangered their U.S. citizenship by voting in a Mexican election or by serving in the Mexican army. Without going into the details, the general effect of the judicial decisions is that a "dual national" Mexican, although residing in Mexico, has no special handicaps in U.S. citizenship. If he wishes to renounce his allegiance to the United States, he must do so formally and at a mature age.

Ultimately the right to vote and, to some degree, acceptance by the larger American society depends upon citizenship, which is normally acquired through naturalization. Mexicans have been extraordinarily slow to become naturalized. Between 1959 and 1966 only 2.4 percent to 5 percent of the eligible Mexicans became citizens each year. Other immigrants entering at the same time with the same length of residence naturalized at a rate of between 23 percent and 33 percent.[15]

None of the explanations advanced for this low rate of naturalization is conclusive. A low rate is consistent with the social isolation of Mexican Americans. In earlier years the Mexican consuls made a deliberate effort to promote loyalty to the homeland. Mexicans have mistrusted U.S. government authority, and many Mexicans did not intend to remain permanently in the United States. Finally, the generally low economic and educational level of the immigrants has made naturalization more difficult than for other immigrant groups. Illiteracy rates are very much higher in Mexico than in any European country.

ILLEGAL ALIENS: THE NEW INSECURITY

In the previous chapters it was assumed that American immigration laws are enforced, that the Mexican immigrants entered legally in the numbers recorded, and that the Immigration and Naturalization Service is able to regulate entries in its time-honored fashion. While there always has been illegal entry, during the years 1968 to 1974 the long border leaked such a flood of illegal Mexican aliens that the character of Mexican immigration is changing greatly. We cannot now assume that all, or even the largest fraction, of immigrants are legal. Nor can we assume that the Border Patrol is able to do much more than restrain illegal immigration in symbolic fashion. Nor can the existing demo-

15 See Leo Grebler, "The Naturalization of Mexican Immigrants in the United States," *The International Migration Review* 1 (Fall 1966): 17–32.

graphic data about Mexican Americans be accepted without remembering the huge and expanding subclass or "underground" fraction of Chicanos that must now live in the United States quite beyond the reach of the Census. Julian Samora notes that they live a sort of "half-life" as "invisible people" who are almost unknown to sociologists.[16] Their adjustment to urban life will be far different from that of the legal immigrant who will have some limited ranges of community and agency resources.

The dimensions of this new surge of successful illegal immigration can only be guessed. In 1973 illegals entered at the rate of no less than 600,000 persons a year. The true figure might be as high as 1,000,000 persons a year and the rate is increasing rapidly. These estimates are based entirely on the numbers of illegals caught and deported by the Border Patrol, but no responsible officers of the Immigration and Naturalization Service claim that more than half of the illegals are apprehended. (In 1973, 480,588 illegal Mexican aliens were apprehended and repatriated. In 1972 the comparable figure was 355,099; in 1971 it was 290,152. About a third of the apprehensions are "repeaters"—that is, illegal aliens previously apprehended at least once.) As a consequence the *lowest* estimate of the number of illegal Mexican nationals now living in the nation's Chicano communities is one million persons.[17]

If anything, the border is harder to cross illegally now than before. New fences, increases in the number of Border Patrol officers, aircraft, electronic sensors, and sophisticated communications and deportation techniques have greatly increased the efficiency of the Patrol. The reason for the sudden increase is simple—many more Mexican nationals want to cross the border. For nearly all of the *mojados*, walking across the border or overstaying a legal permit is a simple and understandable reaction to hunger. Alejandro Portes suggests that since 1968 the rapid economic growth of Mexico has displaced vast numbers of rural workers who migrate to urban centers such as Mexico City and Monterrey or to the cities along the Mexican side of the border. Portes believes the wetback flow relieves many tensions in Mexico and assists the balance of payments.[18] Mexico's unwillingness to stop this form of immigration is noticeable. In the United States new anti-alien legislation is opposed by the State Department in the interests of amicable relations. In general,

[16] Samora, *Los Mojados*, p. 59.

[17] This material is based on statistics from the U.S. Immigration and Naturalization Service and from testimony and summaries in *Review of Hearings Before the House Committee on the Judiciary, Subcommittee No. 1, Immigration and Nationality* (Washington, D.C.: February 1973). All figures are based on the federal fiscal year, July 1 to June 30.

[18] Alejandro Portes, "Return of the Wetback," *Society* 2, no. 3 (March/April 1974): 40–46.

the Mexican position is that illegal immigration is an American problem.

For the first time a large-scale traffic in organized smuggling has appeared. It is considered a dangerous new development by the Border Patrol. *Coyotes* and *polleros* ship illegals in large numbers and greater distances than before for prices now at about $300 for Los Angeles and $1,000 for New York City. They are efficient. A few have inside connections with the Border Patrol itself. They do not hesitate to endanger the lives of their "chickens" or *pollos*. The penalties for smuggling are not very great. The use of falsified documents is increasing also.

Ultimately the successful illegals will disappear into the larger society, but until this time the impact on the Mexican American communities is likely to be profound and a new source of insecurity. It may also tend to increase discrimination. Some hints of other possible effects are given in other chapters. At this time not many persons in the Anglo community are aware of this movement, and the most important effect may be the impending debate on new federal legislation. Opinion differs on just how seriously a large new supply of unskilled labor will affect the U.S. labor market. Official witnesses at the 1972 hearings felt this supply would greatly increase the competition for certain kinds of jobs now held by American citizens, primarily Blacks and Chicano citizens. It can also be argued, however, that these jobs are badly paid and not desirable; in effect, that nobody else will do them. There is also some evidence that illegals receive a large enough share of the limited social services in certain areas to draw some official attention. True or not, these arguments are very reminiscent of the justification for Operation Wetback in 1954—and this reminder alone is beginning to create some anxieties.

Labor leaders are understandably upset over the influx of illegals. A number of Chicano community-based organizations are working in some cities to support federal legislation which will restrict the employment of aliens. Others are equally concerned with the racist implications of such legislation. The willingness of many employers to exploit the *mojados* adds a touch of urgency. Meanwhile the nation's urban and rural *barrios* offer homes and a sheltering environment for people who are, after all, countrymen and relatives.

THE NEW BORDER

A number of powerful interests worked together to tighten the border gradually. Probably the slow erosion of political power suffered by the railroads, the great ranches, and the mining interests of the Border States is the single most critical factor. Also important in the debate were northeastern businessmen who saw no reason for supplying cheap labor to their southwestern competitors, along with state and local welfare agencies, and organized labor. These forces dominated Congressional debate on the Immigration and Nationality Act of 1965. It is very likely that these same forces will continue to oppose any relaxation of its application.

This bill was designed by a pro-labor administration to eliminate the national origins quotas embodied in the McCarran-Walter Act. The original form of the new bill would have left Western Hemisphere provisions almost unchanged. But in the House and Senate hearings, the Western Hemisphere unexpectedly became the main concern. The bill was amended to allow no more than 120,000 persons per year from the New World countries. To soften its impact, the ceiling would not take effect until 1968 and not until a final deliberation from a special commission on Western Hemisphere immigration.

According to this law, immediate relatives of earlier immigrants are in a preferred category without reference to either quota or job skills. This provision has meant changes in the characteristics of legal immigrants. Only 32,967 Mexicans entered in 1964. The total rose to 37,969 in 1965 and 45,163 in 1966, and the proportion of housewives and children reached 78.1 percent for 1965–1966. This is an important increase over earlier averages in which the proportion of housewives and children ran as low as 50.1 percent (1955–1959). Furthermore, the proportion of eligible relatives is still increasing.

These increases probably only reflect the increasing numbers of illegal immigrants who are able to establish themselves as citizens by marriage or by having children. The children become U.S. citizens by birth and, of course, both parents enter a preferred category. In this manner the figures on legal immigration become more and more meaningless, reflecting only the enormous pressures for entry.

Administrative rulings are gradually tightening the labor certification procedures. But none of these changes nor even the federal legislation will be as meaningful as the social pressures on the Mexican American minority. Some of these pressures can be inferred from the present condition of the Chicanos; others will be subtle and harder to anticipate. It may well trigger fresh discrimination from the Anglo majority or from Blacks and other groups who feel themselves threatened by a pool of cheap and willing unskilled labor. It may greatly strengthen the cultural distinctiveness of the Mexican American community. It has surely sharpened and made even more poignant the divided loyalties of many Chicano community leaders. Meanwhile the current internal migration from Texas to California and from Texas into the industrial cities of the Midwest will continue to supply urban Mexican American communities with rural laborers. (In nearly every respect the new arrivals from such areas are as impoverished and as "green" to city life as are the immigrants, legal or illegal, from Mexico.) This reservoir of new arrivals may affect Mexican American social stratification, both internally and in the larger society, as profoundly as it has affected everything else Mexican in the United States.

The pressure to stop the new flow from Mexico will surely grow stronger in the near future. The suggested legislation, both federal and state, has so far been restrictionist and often racist, but carries a certain air of desperation. A "Mexican problem" and a long border almost unnoticed in American history has become an "American problem."

Mexican Americans have certain special and distinctive characteristics as a population. These characteristics are the realities behind Chicano social life and values. To understand them, we must answer questions like the following: How many Mexican Americans live in the United States? Where do they live? How many were really born in Mexico? What is their position in the labor markets of the Southwest? Compared to other subpopulations, what is the nature of their family structure? What does "poverty" mean in the Chicano context?

PORTRAIT OF A POPULATION

Profile of the Mexican American

It is characteristic of the Mexican American population that there has always been a certain amount of ambiguity about the basic facts—even how many Chicanos live in the United States. The U.S. Census, our primary source of information about the American population, has counted the Mexican Americans by different criteria in almost every one of the decennial censuses since they first were officially noticed as a portion of the population—that is, since 1930. Often these definitions have not been comparable with those used in prior years. In 1970 anyone but an expert could be confused by the three separate definitions used for the Mexican Americans.[1] Thus according to Census data there are probably between 6 million and 7 million Chicanos living in the United States in 1973.[2] However, because of the ambiguity of the criteria used by the Census, all estimates based on Census data have been brought into question, especially by community groups concerned with the allocation of federal funds based on Census figures.[3]

[1] One of these, "Persons of Spanish surname" for the southwestern states, is identical with that of the 1960 and 1950 censuses. A second, also used for the southwestern states is "Persons of Spanish Language or Surname." A third, "Persons of Spanish Origin," is a self-identification question that was used for a very small sample for the total United States.

[2] U.S. Department of Commerce, Bureau of Census, "Persons of Spanish Origin in the United States: March 1973," *Current Population Reports*, Series P-20, no. 259, January 1974.

[3] Persons of Spanish surname in 1970 were counted as 4,546,000 (PC(2)-1D) "Persons of Spanish Surname." Persons of Spanish language and surname for the same

But even if there were a million more Mexican Americans (a real possibility), this is not many people in a nation of more than 200 million. But Chicanos are concentrated into an area of only five states, a fact that makes them the most significant minority in the Southwest and thus of great importance. In 1970 in the five southwestern states they were about 15 percent of the roughly 36 million inhabitants. By contrast, the Puerto Rican minority in the East receives much more attention and yet is much smaller, including only about 1.5 million in 1973. Even Puerto Rico shelters only about half as many people as there are Chicanos in the United States. Mexicans and their descendants now form the largest concentration of people of Latin American descent outside Latin America. Further, there is every chance that this minority will continue to grow rapidly.

In 1970, approximately 90 percent of the Mexican Americans in the United States lived in the Southwest (PC(2)-1C, Table 1). Moreover, an overwhelming proportion of them lived in just two states—California and Texas. Thus 84 percent of the Southwestern Chicano population lived in just those two states and each state had more than a million and a half (California had close to two and one-quarter million). The three remaining states of Arizona, Colorado, and New Mexico held only 16 percent although in all three states Chicanos were the important minority by a wide margin, considerably outnumbering Blacks and other non-whites (Indians and Orientals). The Los Angeles metropolitan area alone had 980,000 Mexican Americans, a concentration exceeding the total number living in the combined states of Arizona, Colorado, and New Mexico. Changes since 1960 have increased the proportion living in California. In 1960 roughly equal numbers of Mexican Americans lived in Texas and California. By 1970 almost 50 percent of the total Southwestern Chicano population lived in California, as compared to 36 percent in Texas. As a consequence the social and economic milieux of just two states, California and Texas, is of critical importance.

Even by the most conservative of the Census figures, Chicanos are the fastest growing segment of the Southwestern population. Between 1950 and 1970 the Spanish-surnames increased 99 percent—or nearly

---

area yield a figure of 5,988,000 (PC(2)-1D). Persons who identify themselves as of Mexican origin in the entire United States equal 4,532,000 (PC(2)-1C). It is evident that the first figure is a subset of the second but that the "Persons of Mexican Origin" is based on a far larger sample base, that is, the total U.S. population and includes many persons who are not counted in either of the two preceding estimates, just as it excludes many persons who are counted in both of them. In 1974, the U.S. Civil Rights Commission published a report, *Counting the Forgotten*, emphasizing these problems.

doubled. By contrast, the Anglos increased only 67 percent and the Blacks 61 percent. In the single decade between 1960 and 1970, Chicanos increased 32 percent, the Anglos gaining 25 percent and the Blacks only 7 percent.[4]

Not all Mexicans live in the Southwest, although their failure to move deeply into the northwestern and midwestern states is largely unexplained. Small communities of Mexican Americans are found in all large western and midwestern urban areas, with notable and increasingly large enclaves appearing in Illinois, Michigan, Indiana, Kansas, and Ohio. However, as indicated above, no more than 10 percent of the total Mexican American population lives outside the Southwest (PC(2)-1C, Table 1).

Not only do most Chicanos live in California or Texas, but even inside these states, they are concentrated in particular areas. Los Angeles and smaller nearby cities in southern California hold most of the California population. South Texas, particularly the lower Rio Grande valley and some of the larger border cities, houses most of the Texas Chicano population. Laredo was 80 percent Chicano in 1970, and Tyler, in east Texas, only 3 percent. These disparities are historical and social "accidents" of considerable consequence.

Still other historical and social accidents have forced many Mexican Americans into an unusual community pattern in their areas of greatest concentration. Although the degree of actual separation from the dominant Anglo and the subordinate Black populations varies considerably from city to city, Mexican Americans generally live together in distinctively "Mexican" neighborhoods. (These are often called *barrios.* The term is roughly equivalent to "neighborhood," although sometimes the word "ghetto" carries a more exact connotation.) It is interesting to compare origins of the Chicano *barrio* with the more common patterns by which ethnic enclaves were established in the U.S. Most of these enclaves were produced when a subpopulation appeared in a city quite suddenly. Classically (as with the Irish in Boston and the Blacks in Chicago) the newcomers settled in cheap housing in the older central areas of a big city. There are such Mexican enclaves in the Border States, but most pockets had quite different origins from those of the Little Italys and the Chinatowns of classic sociology, simply because Mexicans were the original settlers of so many towns.

One typical town plan in the Border States was the settlement around a traditionally Mexican *plaza* (central area). When the railroads and highways brought growth of the Anglo population, such growth

4 Sources: 1950 U.S. Census of Population PE No 3C, Table 1; 1960 U.S. Census of population, vol. 1, part 1, Table 158, parts 4, 6, 7, 33, and 45, Table 15, and PC (2)-1B Table 1; 1970 U.S. Census of Population PC (1) -C1.

tended to center around the new terminals or nodes of transportation. The Mexican plaza area was bypassed and tended to deteriorate. In time, as in Albuquerque, Los Angeles, and dozens of other cities, the plaza area remained as the "Mexican Downtown" or as a carefully reconstructed and often glamorized tourist center.

Still other Mexican enclaves are the residue of early labor camps. In southern California such remnants of times past as Santa Fe Springs and Pacoima in Los Angeles County and the Casa Blanca area of Riverside are really new growth on the skeletons of old labor camps bypassed and isolated inside growing, spreading cities. Whole families of Mexicans emigrated or were imported into these camps to serve such functions as ranching, railway maintenance, citrus harvesting and packing, and brick-making. The ethnic population may remain but it ceases to be employed at its old occupation. In yet other areas the enclaves remain on the fringes of the metropolitan area and continue to serve as agricultural labor markets. The Mexican American population may then work both inside the city and outside in the fields as the season demands, as in Fresno, California. Many such settlements have disappeared; some are in the process of urban renewal; some have been overwhelmed and displaced by a rapid rise in land values.

There are also some parts of the Border States in which Mexican Americans are not found in ghettos or enclaves but rather dominate the life of the community. This pattern appears frequently in the small towns of northern New Mexico and southern Texas and also in large Texas border and near-border cities like Laredo. No other American minority shows such an extraordinary range, from highly segregated to almost completely nonsegregated living patterns.

Although comparatively few Mexican Americans live in rural areas, the stereotype that the Mexicans are primarily a rural people still prevails. Actually, Mexican Americans have been moving into cities at a very rapid rate since World War II. By 1970 any portrait of the American citizen of Mexican descent as an agricultural laborer or rural resident had become a serious distortion. They did not even hold half of the farm labor jobs in any state in the Southwest except New Mexico. This segment of the labor market has been shrinking rapidly since World War II and with it, has gone much of the incentive for a minority population to remain in rural areas where there is comparatively little farm ownership.

By 1970 only 15 percent of the Mexican population lived in rural or rural nonfarm areas (PC(2)-1D, Table 2). Of those who do work in agriculture, most of them tend to be foreign-born Mexicans. Only in the "Old Colonies" of Colorado and New Mexico is this proportion of rural residents significantly higher, reaching 35 percent of the Mexican American population of New Mexico. Urbanization is most apparent in California with 90 percent of the Mexican population living in cities.

The importance of this rapid urbanization cannot be overstated. As recently as 1950, a third of the total Chicano population was rural—and more than half of those were living in New Mexico and Colorado. The rapid pace of urbanization reduced many agricultural towns in those two states to ghost towns. Large numbers of younger people moved to Albuquerque, to Denver, or even to other states, notably California. In fact, the population shift to California may well be part of the urbanization process with a net loss of rural population from the other states to California.

The nativity patterns of Mexican Americans have also been changing, but not as dramatically as their settlement patterns. In the nineteenth century, most Chicanos were U.S. citizens; they became so by treaty in 1848. Then the great waves of immigration in the early part of the twentieth century tipped the scales toward the foreign-born. (See Chapter Three.) Since then the proportion of native-born has been increasing slowly. In 1970 about 85 percent of Mexican Americans counted by the Census were born in the United States. Immigration patterns during the 1960s have been heavy and immigration legislation is still controversial. Thus the proportion of Mexican-born persons has not declined as sharply between 1960 and 1970 as one might anticipate simply from looking at the tight immigration restrictions.

There are some important differences between the foreign-born and native-born Mexican Americans and between the native-born Mexican Americans who are of foreign parentage and those who are "old Americans." For a rough notion of the relative importance in the population of each of these classes, we may note that in 1970 the foreign-born formed 16 percent of the Spanish surname population of the Southwest. The native-born of foreign parentage formed 29 percent and the native-born of native parentage formed 55 percent of the total population. Proportions differ greatly from area to area. The native-born of native parentage were heavily concentrated in Colorado and New Mexico, forming 86 and 87 percent of those populations, respectively. It is grossly misleading to call them "third generation" since they often represent descendants of colonial stock that oftens goes back to the sixteenth century. (We discuss this interaction between nativity and locality in Chapter Seven.) In general, the differences between nativity classes or "generations" follow the patterns one might anticipate from American immigrant populations: third or later generation Mexican Americans generally tend to be better educated and to make more money than foreign-born, but tend not to receive higher incomes than do the second generation (native-born of foreign parentage).[5]

Generally the native-born tend to have a lower proportion of families which have been disrupted by divorce or separation. The native-born are also far more likely to work in white collar occupations than are the foreign-born.[6]

In all the Census data made available since the end of World War II, the foreign-born consistently appear considerably worse off. They are consistently well below the educational level of the native-born; consistently far more overrepresented in farm labor and other unskilled jobs; and consistently appear to show signs of some stress in adaptation to this society. Of course, many of these figures must be put into context. For example, a high proportion of the elderly people of Mexican descent are foreign-born and one is thus seeing the continuation of an old pattern of disadvantage. Agencies working with newly arrived immigrants from Mexico corroborate the statistical indicators of the struggle of newer Mexican immigrants to find a respectable place in the new society. Much of this struggle is the consequence of certain lags in the process of adjustment of such institutions as the schools and employing agencies to the persistent presence of the foreign-born. It is with these lags that a combination of informed legislation, both federal and state, and adequate linkage between the activities of the Immigration and Naturalization Service on the one hand and community based agencies responsive to the needs of the immigrants on the other could make an enormous difference.

The median age of Mexican Americans is low: 20.2 years. The median age of the native-born of native parentage is even lower—only 15.8 years. This age structure is the result of a very high birth rate. Using as a measure the number of children ever born per 1,000 women ever married, the great difference between Mexican and Anglo fertility begins in the 15- to 19-year-old group. The fertility difference increases with every age group thereafter. This difference is of long historical standing, going back as far as we have records, that is, as far back as 1850. By 1969 the Mexican American women were 40 percent more fertile than were Anglo

[5]Thus 13 percent of the foreign-born were high school graduates, 30 percent of the native-born of foreign parentage were high school graduates, and 37 percent of the native-born of native parentage were high school graduates (PC(2)-1D, Table 11). In income, the median income of foreign-born family heads was $6,127, median income of family heads of native-born of foreign parentage was $7,604, and the median income of native-born family heads of native parents was $6,795 (PC(2)-1D, Table 12).

[6] Twenty-five percent of the men who were native-born of native parents worked in white-collar occupations; 22 percent of the native-born of foreign parentage and 12 percent of the foreign-born of foreign parents worked in such occupations (PC(2)-1D, Table 11) .

American women.[7] Although the fertility of Mexican American women as compared to Anglo women is declining somewhat, the difference between the two populations is still very great.

As one might expect from the high fertility rates, Mexican American families are extremely large. They are large enough, in fact, to make Mexican American participation in the ordinary material rewards of American life much more marginal than that of most other populations. No other category of people in the United States matches the typical Mexican American family size of 4.5 persons. The average American family size in 1970 was 3.6 persons. The size of Black and Puerto Rican families was 4.1 persons, and even American Indians only barely approximate the size of the Mexican American family.[8] These and other age disparities between urban Anglo Americans and urban Chicanos show clearly in the age pyramids in Figure 4-1. (This chart is based on 1960 data, but the change in age structure has been negligible since then.) In 1970 the median age of the Mexican American population was nine years lower than that of the U.S. population as a whole and two and one-half lower than that of nonwhites in the United States.[9] Forty-six percent of the Mexican American population were children of less than 18 years of age. By contrast, only 33 percent of the U.S. white population was less than 18 years of age.

Of course these figures have some important implications. For example, a far higher proportion of the Southwest's schoolage children are Chicano than the proportion of adults who are Chicano. The persistence of the large family pattern among Mexican Americans means a continuing challenge to schools and to youth-serving agencies. The age figures also imply a high rate of future population growth, unless the large number of Chicano children depart substantially from the family patterns of their parents. There are indications of a receptivity to birth control: family planning clinics do not beg for clients even though their information booths at "health fairs" may be placed next to a conservative Catholic "Right to Life" display. Apart from religion, however, there is the obvious and pragmatic problem of caring for large families.

The "dependency ratio" is a way of stating the fraction of the population that is of working age as compared to the fraction that is not

[7] This figure is adjusted for age differences between the two populations. Benjamin S. Bradshaw and Frank D. Bean, "Trends in the Fertility of Mexican Americans: 1950–1970," *Social Science Quarterly* 53 (March 1973): 688–696.

[8] Mexican American data from PC (2)-1D, Table 11; Puerto Rican data from PC(2)-1E, Table 8; Indian data from PC(2)-1F, Table 8; and Black data from PC(2)-1B, Table 8. U.S. total data from U.S. Bureau of the Census, *Statistical Abstracts of the United States*, 1972, p. 39.

[9] *Statistical Abstracts*, p. 24.

FIGURE 4–1

AGE PYRAMIDS FOR URBAN ANGLO AND SPANISH-SURNAME
POPULATION IN THE SOUTHWEST, 1960

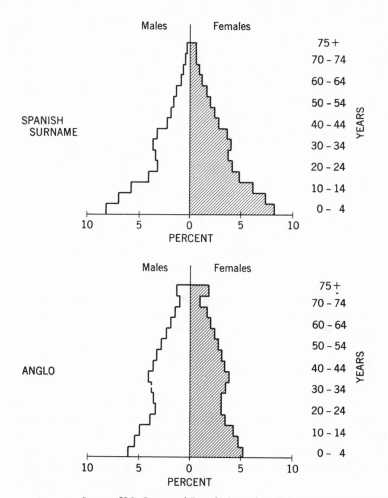

Source: U.S. Census of Population, 1960, Vol. 1, Parts 4, 6, 7, 33, 45, Table
96: PC(2)1B, Table 2. Compiled by Mexican-American Study Project (Los
Angeles: University of California 1966).

likely to work—that is, dependent. It is a statistical measure that expresses
the actual economic burden on the working population. For Mexican
Americans this dependency ratio is higher than for either Anglos or nonwhites. In the Southwest as a whole there were 101 dependents in 1970
for every 100 Mexican Americans between the ages of 18 and 64. For the

U.S. Anglo population as a whole, there were only 77 dependents for every 100 individuals in the same age range and 93 dependents for every 100 nonwhites. This high dependency ratio has declined somewhat between 1960 and 1970 as Mexican American fertility has declined slightly. In short, the high Mexican dependency ratio is due almost entirely to the large number of dependent young people. Less than 5 percent of the Chicano population was over 65 in 1970 as compared to over 10 percent of the Anglo population in the U.S. Dependency ratios run the highest in rural nonfarm areas where the child population is the highest.

But, of course, dependency ratios do not express the whole story of the burden on the wage earner. Mexican American families also suffer disproportionately from family disruption—far more than might be expected from the traditional stereotype of the strong Mexican family. "Broken families"—that is, families headed by persons other than husband and wife—reached 18 percent in 1970, a figure much larger than for Anglos.[10]

America's Chicano minority is also distinctive in its sex ratio. Generally the census reports slightly more males than females, in contrast to the ratio in most other population groups in the United States. In rural areas there is an even higher disproportion of men to women. It is probable that most of this difference is the result of the presence of farm laborers who are predominantly male. The sex ratio favoring men is most notable in the working ages. By old age, women predominate as they do in other segments of the United States population.

TO EARN A LIVING

These patterns, generally quite different from those of the dominant Anglo American population, profoundly affect the share of income available to each Mexican American individual. Except for the relatively small Indian group, no population in the Southwest is so severely pinched economically. The Chicano head of a family must make his lower income stretch to cover a larger household. The chances of his earning a livable wage are relatively low and have been increasing very slowly. His chances also vary from state to state and even from city to city throughout the Southwest.

For example, the median income of Spanish-surname males over 16 was $4,839 in 1969. In Texas, Spanish-surname males earned 60 percent of the median earned by an Anglo male in the same area while in California and Arizona they earned 75 percent of the median earned by

10 PC(2)-1D, Table 11.

Anglo males. Further, when older males in both groups are compared, relative Mexican income declines steadily. Few Chicanos have had life-time job mobility, and foreign-born immigrants form a larger proportion of older age groups than they do of younger groups. Absolute median income differences between the states are great, ranging from $3,800 in Texas to $5,900 in California. The median income of Texas nonwhites (mostly Blacks) is almost exactly the same as that of Spanish-surname males in Texas. In Arizona, by contrast, the Black median income is substantially below that of Chicanos.[11]

In summary: about 24 percent of all Spanish surname families counted by the Census fell below the "poverty line" as defined by the federal government in 1970. (The average poverty threshold for a non-farm family of four was $3,743 in 1969.) This represents a statistical improvement over 1960 Census figures when about 35 percent of the Spanish-surname families fell below the poverty line as then defined. Once again, the proportion of Spanish-heritage families living in poverty ranged from state to state with the highest proportion of poor families living in Texas.

The tiny share of income cannot be ascribed entirely to the "qualifications" of Mexican Americans, although there are relationships with age and education, as there are for other segments of the population. The correlation between education and income is not as great as it is for the majority population. These disparities between qualification and income attainment have been narrowing somewhat over the past decade.

These are definitely hopeful signs for this minority. The decline in the proportion of families that live in poverty and the somewhat narrowed gap in income are also hopeful signs. However the gains in part reflect a shift in the population by migration from Texas to California where incomes and other opportunities tend to be greater. The gains also reflect a changing pattern of industry in the Southwest.

Income directly reflects the occupational pattern of the Mexican American in the Southwest. Their disadvantage is illustrated clearly in Table 4-1. Less than a quarter of the Spanish-surname males held white-collar jobs as compared to more than half of the Anglo American males

---

[11] These income figures represent a relative increase as compared to data for 1959 when Mexican American males earned only 57 percent of the Anglo male median. In these figures we have used data for Spanish surname males from PC (2) -1D, Table 9, comparing them with data for "whites" and "Negroes" from the PC(1)-D series. It is notable that the Census definition of the population produces very different income figures. We have chosen to remain with the figure that is comparable to 1959—that is, Spanish surname only. When the more widely used and available Spanish-language, Spanish-surname definition is applied, Mexican Americans male income goes up notably and the gap between the Anglo and the Spanish heritage population declines markedly.

TABLE 4–1

OCCUPATIONAL DISTRIBUTION OF MALES AGED 16 AND OVER
BY ETHNIC GROUP, 1960 AND 1970

Occupational Category	Anglo [a]		Spanish Surname [b]		Nonwhite [c]	
	1960	1970	1960	1970	1960	1970
White Collar	46.8	53.3	19.1	21.6	18.1	21.0
Professionals	15.1	17.2	4.6	6.4	6.1	6.8
Managers and proprietor	14.7	12.3	4.9	5.2	3.6	3.3
Clerical workers	7.8	15.9	5.5	6.6	6.1	8.5
Sales workers	9.2	7.9	4.1	3.4	2.3	2.4
Blue Collar	53.2	46.7	80.9	78.4	81.9	79.0
Skilled craftsman	21.5	18.5	18.2	20.8	10.8	15.9
Semi-skilled operatives	15.8	13.4	25.4	25.4	20.0	26.2
Private household workers	0.1	0.1	0.1	0.1	0.9	0.3
Service workers	5.4	6.8	8.4	10.5	18.6	17.6
Laborers	4.4	4.7	15.8	12.6	18.3	16.3
Farm laborers	0.6	1.4	7.3	8.1	2.1	2.4
Farmers and farm managers	0.7	1.8	0.6	0.9	1.9	0.4
Occupations not reported	4.7	—	5.1	—	9.3	—

Sources: 1960 U.S. Census of Population, OH 1, Parts 9, 6, 7, 33, 45, Table
58; PC(2)-1B, Table 6. 1970 U.S. Census of Population, PC(1)-D4, 6, 7, 33,
45, Table 172, PC(2)-1D, Table 10.

[a] 1960 "Anglo" = White − (Spanish surname + nonwhite).
1970 "Anglo" = White − (Spanish language/surname + Negro).

[b] 1970 Spanish surname employed males 16 and over; all other figures are
for males 16 and over in the experienced labor force.

[c] 1970 "Nonwhite" = "Negro."

in the region. Occupationally, Blacks and Chicanos in the Southwest
show very much the same profile, one that is weighted heavily toward
blue-collar jobs. There are more Black service workers and laborers and
fewer craftsmen than there are Chicano, although in the blue-collar occupations Blacks have been improving their position during the decade of
the 1960s much more rapidly than Mexican Americans. For example, the
Black segment has been increasing proportions in the skilled and in
the semi-skilled occupations.

The most striking fact about the occupational profile of Mexican
Amercians is the very slow and slight change between 1960 and 1970. In
fact, the change has been smaller than it has been for Anglos. Seven
percent more Anglo Americans were in white-collar jobs in 1970 than in
1960 as compared to only 2.5 percent more Chicanos. Thus it is clear that

the Mexican Americans have failed to keep pace with the general occupational shift toward white-collar and somewhat better-paying positions.

The implication of all these rather depressing figures can be summed up by saying that a high proportion of Mexican Americans are—and will probably remain—in what some economists call the "secondary labor market." Essentially this means that they have neither job skills nor, more importantly, do they enter the kind of world that could lift them out of the endless cycle of dead-end jobs. Paul Bullock recently studied Chicano and Black youth in Los Angeles and concluded that such workers often are involved in "subeconomy" or street economy activities (gambling, betting, drugs, and the like) as well as the legitimate labor market. His figures show that one third of the young Chicano men under 24 in Los Angeles either are unemployed or "discouraged," and in fact, have given up the search for a job. Bullock argues that although the street economy has existed throughout American history, the present minorities (Black, Chicano, Puerto Rican) do not show signs of movement into the primary labor market—that is, of full participation in the higher wage jobs that offer security and a career, whether blue-collar or white-collar. He concludes that their special handicaps of poor education, arrest records, and discrimination are unique and thus cannot be compared with other ethnic groups in American urban history. Perhaps most poignant is Bullock's finding that young Chicanos themselves recognize their own handicaps—and at a very early age.[12]

Several other careful studies of Mexican American occupational patterns offer similar and rather depressing facts. Walter Fogel did a study in 1966 based largely on 1960 Census material.[13] Fred Schmidt analyzed employment patterns in twenty southwestern counties in detail using data supplied by the Equal Employment Opportunity Commission.[14] Schmidt is careful to note that only larger employers are required to supply EEOC reports, but his conclusions (even from these larger firms) are very much the same as those of Fogel: Chicanos hold the poorer jobs inside broad occupational classifications. Mexicans get lower pay than Anglos for similar kinds of work.

Recently, several labor market theorists have conceptualized these patterns as characteristic of an increasingly well-institutionalized "sec-

---

[12]Paul Bullock, *Aspiration vs. Opportunity: "Careers" in the Inner City* (Ann Arbor, Mich.: Institute of Labor and Industrial Relations, 1973).

[13] Walter Fogel, *Mexican Americans in Southwest Labor Markets*, Advance Report 5 (University of California, Los Angeles: Mexican-American Study Project, 1966).

[14]Fred H. Schmidt, *Spanish Surnamed American Employment in the Southwest*, a study prepared for the Colorado Civil Rights Commission under the auspices of the Equal Employment Opportunity Commission (Washington, D.C.: Government Printing Office, 1970).

ondary labor market."[15] According to this theory, the work force in the United States is increasingly bifurcated. There is a significant cluster of workers involved in "primary" or "core" industries, in which there is a stable market for employment, established fringe benefits, and opportunities for promotion. These wages and conditions are guarded by unions or other institutionalized agreements. Minorities and women, by contrast, are concentrated in "peripheral" industries forming a "secondary labor market" that is characterized by instability and unpredictability. Although no strong effort has been made to apply this idea to the situation of the Mexican American working force, it does seem to fit the available data. Thus it may be that the employment and occupational patterns of Chicanos are institutionalized to serve the needs of this secondary labor market; further, that this secondary labor market was created and is maintained by established elements of American society and is actually being extended and perpetuated by current agency efforts to train minority workers.

TO GAIN AN EDUCATION

Mexican educational accomplishment offers only little hope for those who suggest that southwestern schools will soon be able to end the Mexican American labor market handicap. Some of these results are the natural consequence of generations of *de jure* and *de facto* segregation. Others reflect inept if not downright bad teaching. (See Chapter Five.) American schools must be judged by their results, not their intentions. By any standard other than those of schools in underdeveloped countries, the output for Mexican Americans is exceptionally poor.

Throughout the Southwest the Mexican American adult population was too badly educated to participate effectively in modern economic life. On the average in 1970 the adults over 25 years of age had attained less than 9 years of schooling as compared with more than 12 for Anglos. Black educational attainment is substantially higher than that for Mexican Americans. When we compare states we find that the schooling is highest in California with 9.7 years. It is lowest in Texas with 6.7 years— or only slightly better than literacy. In all states Blacks are better educated than Mexican Americans. (Nonwhite medians are pulled down in New Mexico and Arizona by the large proportion of Indians with extremely low levels of schooling.) In 1960 the incidence of functional illiteracy (0 to 4 years of elementary school) is seven times that of the Anglo popu-

---

[15] David M. Gordon, *Theories of Poverty and Underemployment* (Lexington, Mass.: D.C. Heath & Company, 1972).

lation and nearly twice that of the nonwhites as a whole.[16] It should be noted that even the variation between the "good" state of California and the "bad" state of Texas is not very significant in terms of capacity to function in the late twentieth century. Less than a tenth grade education does not equip people for much in the way of economic success.

There has been a definite improvement over time, especially in urban areas. The median school years completed rose from 5.4 years in 1950 to 8.6 years in 1970. In effect, this means that the gap between the Anglo population and the Mexican American population has been reduced. The gap is even smaller when only the youngest adults are considered. In the case of persons aged 20 to 24, for example, the Mexican American men and women of this very narrow age cohort had attained a median of approximately 12.1 years of school.[17] In effect this cohort is close to a schooling level that is attained by Anglos of all ages in this region.

As indicated in Table 4–2, we are actually dealing with a population that in city after city averages less than a high school education. In the same communities, on the average, the total population has more than a high school education—holding, in fact, several months of college. The last two columns of Table 4–2 show that there is relatively little variation from city to city throughout the Southwest in the school achievement of the total population. There is a low of 11.5 years in San Antonio and Corpus Christi and a high of 12.6 years in San Jose and Santa Barbara.

But when we look at the school years attained by Mexican Americans we see not only that there is not only a substantially lower level on the whole, but that there is much wider variation. We find figures as low as 5.3 years of school in Lubbock in south Texas and a high of 11.3 years of school in the San Francisco-Oakland area.[18] These city variations in educational attainment clearly show the diversity of opportunity for Mexican Americans throughout the Southwest. One sees not only the state variations in the opportunities provided for Chicanos but also varia-

[16] Leo Grebler, *The Schooling Gap: Signs of Progress*, Advance Report 7 (University of California, Los Angeles: Mexican-American Study Project, 1967), p. 13.

[17] These data are from PC(2) -1D, Table 7 and 8, U.S. Census 1970.

[18] It should be emphasized that these data on Mexican American school attainment are derived from the Census definition of "Persons of Spanish Surname" (PC (2)-1D). They are therefore strictly comparable with the data reported in Table 4–2 for 1950 and 1960. When one uses the Census data by states (for example, the PC (1)-C and D series) we find a somewhat higher level of educational attainment. The reason for this is a matter of speculation. This source employs the most widely used Census definition of "Mexican American," i.e., Spanish-speaking and/or Spanish surname. It produces data that show better attainment in nearly all areas, notably income, occupational level, and education than does a definition that is comparable with the 1950 and 1960 data—that is, by "Spanish surname."

TABLE 4-2

MEDIAN SCHOOL YEARS ATTAINED BY VARIOUS SUBPOPULATIONS
IN 25 SOUTHWESTERN METROPOLITAN AREAS 1950, 1960, AND 1970

Standard Metropolitan Statistical Area	1950		1960				1970	
	Total Pop.	Spanish Surname	Total Pop.	Anglo	Spanish Surname	Non-White	Total Pop.	Spanish Surname
Albuquerque	11.7	7.7	12.2	12.5	8.7	10.9	12.5	10.5
Austin	10.9	3.5	11.7	12.3	4.4	8.6	12.4	7.9
Bakersfield	9.9	6.5	10.8	11.4	7.3	8.5	12.1	8.1
Brownsville Harlingen San Benito	6.3	2.7	7.9	12.3	3.9	9.5	8.4	5.4
Corpus Christi	9.4	3.2	10.1	12.2	4.5	8.0	11.5	6.7
Dallas	11.0	4.4	11.8	12.1	6.4	8.6	12.2	8.1
Denver	12.0	8.0	12.2	12.3	8.8	11.4	12.5	10.3
El Paso	9.2	5.2	11.1	12.4	6.6	11.7	12.5	8.0
Fort Worth	10.7	5.4	11.4	11.9	7.7	8.7	12.1	8.5
Fresno	9.8	5.6	10.4	10.7	6.1	8.8	12.1	8.0
Houston	10.4	5.2	11.4	12.1	6.4	8.8	12.1	8.0
Laredo	5.4	5.2	6.7	N.A.	5.4	N.A.	7.1	6.6
Los Angeles Long Beach	12.0	8.2	12.1	12.3	8.9	11.1	12.4	9.8
Lubbock	11.0	1.7	11.6	12.1	3.1	8.3	12.2	5.3ª
Phoenix	10.6	5.3	11.6	12.1	6.1	8.5	12.3	8.4
Pueblo	9.1	6.3	10.2	11.0	8.1	9.2	12.1	9.2
Sacramento	11.3	7.9	12.2	12.3	9.1	10.9	12.4	10.2
San Antonio	9.1	4.5	10.0	12.1	5.7	9.4	11.5	7.4
San Bernadino Riverside Ontario	10.9	6.7	11.8	12.1	8.0	9.8	12.2	9.2
San Diego	12.0	8.1	12.1	12.2	8.9	10.7	12.4	10.2
San Francisco Oakland	12.0	8.9	12.1	12.3	9.7	10.2	12.5	11.3
San Jose	11.4	8.0	12.2	12.4	8.3	12.0	12.6	9.8
Santa Barbara	11.8	7.0	12.2	12.4	8.3	9.9	12.6	10.1
Stockton	9.1	7.2	10.0	10.7	7.5	8.2	11.9	8.7
Tucson	11.2	6.5	12.1	12.3	8.0	7.8	12.4	9.1

Sources: 1950 U.S. Census PE No. 3c Tables 8, 9, Vol. 2, Pts. 3, 5, 6, 31, 43, Table 42; City and County Data Book, Table 2, Item 28 and Table 3, Item 28. 1960 U.S. Census, PC (2)-1B, Table 13; Vol. 1, Pts. 4, 6, 7, 33, 45, Tables 73, 77, 103. Census Track, Table P-1, P-4, P-5. 1970 U.S. Census, PC(2), 1D, Table 14; PC(1)D-33, D45, D6, Table 148; PC(1)C4, Table 83.
ª For the City of Lubbock.

tions *within* the states. For example, the agricultural areas of California (such as Stockton, Fresno, and Bakersfield in the San Joaquin Valley) do relatively little better than do communities in Texas. The size of the urban area does not always guarantee educational opportunity. Houston, as an example, managed only eight years of education for Mexican Americans. A comparison of the 1950 attainment with the 1970 attainment also gives some indication of comparative educational opportunity. We note, for example, in some central San Joaquin Valley cities in California (San Jose and Stockton) relatively little gain in twenty years. This is also true in the Los Angeles-Long Beach area. Here we note an advance of only one year and six months in school attainment between 1950 and 1970. By contrast, some other areas in the Southwest show an advance as great as 4 years or more. Obviously, these comparative advances depend upon the amount of effort put into the school system but they are also heavily conditioned by patterns of movement throughout the region. Thus it is likely that the very small advance shown in the Los Angeles area is largely determined by the heavy in-migration from the state of Texas so characteristic of the decade of the 1960s, as well as substantial immigration from Mexico. We are suggesting that those areas in which the greatest effort is expended may not necessarily show the greatest advance in schooling given the shift in patterns of Mexican American population. It is probable (according to Grebler)[19] that this gap might have been even greater except that it is the better-educated Mexican Americans who chose to migrate from Texas to southern California and other urban areas with better school systems. More careful study of the available statistics points to some disquieting departures from the Southwest educational norms at very young ages. Typically, the schooling of Spanish-surname children begins later than for either Anglo or Black children, as is shown in the lag of enrollment among 5 and 6-year-old youngsters. Figure 4–2 (from an extensive study by the U.S. Civil Rights Commission) shows the "school holding power" for various ethnic groups in five southwestern states. The graph shows dramatic differences in the ability of schools to hold youngsters of Mexican ancestry as compared to Blacks and especially to Anglos in high school and college. There are also differences according to age and to nativity. Thus the older Mexican American youngsters and those who are foreign-born are less likely to obtain schooling above the norm. Figure 4–3 also gives clues to the sources of this failure in education. In essence they show that as early as the 4th grade Mexican American young people begin to be seriously behind "average" grade level in reading. By the 8th grade an astonishing 64 percent of the Mexican Americans are below grade level. This, of course, is the period during which drop-outs begin to appear in large numbers. By the 12th grade when most drop-outs have already left school, about two thirds of the remaining Mexican American students are reading below grade level. These data are based on the U.S. Civil Rights Commission study of schools throughout the Southwest.

[19] Grebler, *The Schooling Gap*, p. 19.

FIGURE 4-2

SCHOOL HOLDING POWER: RATES FOR EACH ETHNIC GROUP
IN FIVE SOUTHWESTERN STATES

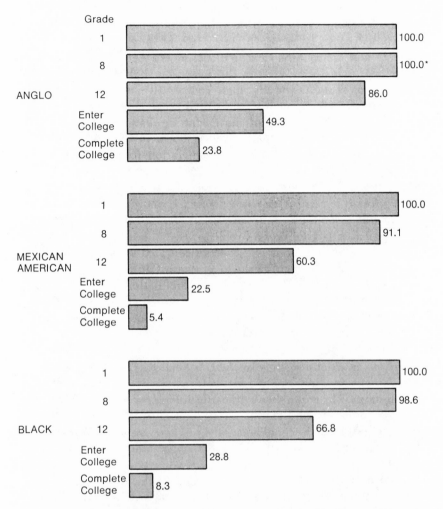

Holding power rates are approximate estimates based on questionnaire data modified from U.S. Bureau of the Census and HEW. Consequently, rates are not to be interpreted as representing exact percentage of students retained. In this instance, a rate of 100 percent holding power for Anglos at grade 8 does not mean that no Anglo student whatsoever has left school between grades 1 and 8, but rather that nearly all students remain through that grade.

Source: U.S. Commission on Civil Rights, *Ethnic Isolation of Mexican Americans in the Public Schools of the Southwest*, Mexican American Education Study, Report 1 (Washington, D.C.: U.S. Government Printing Office, 1971).

FIGURE 4–3

ESTIMATED READING LEVELS IN THE SOUTHWEST

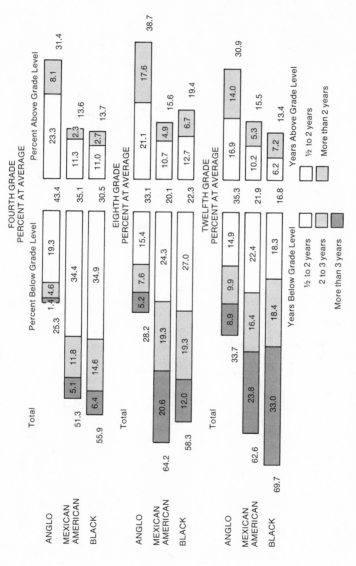

Source: U.S. Commission on Civil Rights, *Ethnic Isolation of Mexican Americans in the Public Schools of the Southwest,* Mexican American Education Study, Report 1 (Washington, D.C.: U.S. Government Printing Office, 1971).

Reading attainment also shows very wide variation between cities and within the same city. Reading attainment is important because it is a major cause of dropping out of school. When students are compared inside Los Angeles there is a rough correlation between the number of students who are significantly below grade level and the percentage of Mexican American students. Achievement scores in other subject-matter areas show a similar correlation.[20] It is also clear in a general way throughout the Southwest that school systems that badly educate one minority are almost certain to badly educate another. Thus a community in which Mexican American youngsters do poorly in school is also a community in which Blacks or (in New Mexico and Arizona) Indians are also badly educated.

The Civil Rights Commission report on segregation also notes that the larger school districts of the Southwest are very important in the education of Mexican Americans. By way of illustration, the Los Angeles Unified School District contains slightly more than 20 percent of all Mexican American pupils in California.[21]

By and large, state educational attainment tends to be inversely correlated with the segregation of Mexican American students. For example, the Civil Rights Commission study showed that in Texas two thirds of the Mexican American students were attending schools that were more than half Mexican American. In California only about one fourth of the Mexican American students were attending predominantly Mexican American schools.[22] It also should be noted that Mexican American teachers are few and far between. More precisely, there was one Anglo teacher for every 20 Anglo students; one Black teacher for every 39 Black students and one Mexican American teacher for every 120 Mexican American students in southwestern school systems in 1968.[23] Where the Chicano teachers work is also significant. In California Mexican American teachers tend to be assigned to non-Mexican American schools while in Texas almost all Mexican American teachers work in predominantly Mexican American schools. This is simply a way of underlining the racist nature of segregation in the Texas school system. Variations from state to state and from system to system can be at least partially

20 Data on achievement and IQ scores are regularly made public by the Research and Evaluation Branch of the Los Angeles Unified School District. Data are published on a school by school basis, while the ethnic composition of each school is published separately.

21 U.S. Commission on Civil Rights, *Ethnic Isolation of Mexican Americans in Public Schools of the Southwest,* Mexican American Education Study, Report no. 1, April 1971, p. 20.

22 *Ethnic Isolation,* p. 26.

23 *Ethnic Isolation,* p. 42.

explained in terms of the historical position of the Mexican Americans in combination with the general effort made to educate all their children. Only recently has there been expenditure of federal funds in an effort to educate Mexican American children through, for example, the development of bilingual programs. (See Chapter Five.) The overall 1964 expenditure in California of $565 per pupil in average daily attendance in public elementary and secondary schools is much greater than the comparable expenditure in Texas of $396. (A decision by the U.S. Supreme Court in 1973 stated that similar intrastate differentials in expenditure were constitutional.) Nonetheless such disparities based on the taxing power of governmental units are clearly related to the educational problems of Mexican Americans. Another report from the Civil Rights Commission points out the clear disparity in district funding within Texas. Basically, the higher the proportion of Mexican American students in a school district, the less money spent on education in that district. This means that teaching personnel in predominantly Mexican American districts earn, on the average, $400 per year less than in predominantly Anglo districts.[24] The survey conducted by the Commission showed that in districts in Texas that had between 10 and 20 percent Mexican American enrollment, the expenditure was .$464 per pupil. Districts with 80 to 100 percent Mexican American enrollment expended $296 per pupil.[25] (In the *Rodriguez vs. San Antonio Independent School District* case brought to the Supreme Court the argument was advanced that this disparity in district expenditure violated certain "equal protection" guarantees in the U.S. Constitution.) In fact, until such gross disparities between states and within districts in a single state are corrected, many of the more esoteric arguments about the nature of the conditions under which learning is optimized are simply academic.

THE CONSEQUENCES OF POVERTY

This profile of the Mexican American is based on the raw materials supplied by the U.S. Census and other sources. All the available materials indicate the prevailing poverty of this second largest American minority. Regrettably, they also show that poverty will dominate the lives of most Chicanos for the next decade or so. The unknowns and unmeasured factors are not hopeful. This is partly because it is very nearly impossible to appraise the impact of the Mexican nationals entering in very large

[24]U.S. Commission on Civil Rights, *Mexican American Education in Texas: A Function of Wealth*, Mexican American Education Study, Report no. 4, August 1972, p. 16.

[25] *Mexican American Education in Texas*, p. 26.

numbers in the mid-1970s. (See Chapter Three.) Partly it is because the Chicano poor are affected differentially by nationwide trends in the economy: thus the energy shortage meant that many Chicanos in Los Angeles could not afford the higher price of gasoline to travel long distances to work—and many poor Mexican Americans in San Antonio were hurt by a "sudden" shortage in natural gas and an enormous increase in price. The inflation of food prices meant a greater demand for staple cheap foods as middle-income families "buy down." An ironic consequence was that in 1974 the price of a Mexican staple, beans (*frijoles*), had risen to very nearly the price of cheap hamburger. Neither was within easy reach of the large and poor family.

This prevailing poverty greatly affects the quality of life available to Chicanos. It also creates certain difficulties which one must describe, because there is no better phrase, as "community problems."

Bad housing is one difficulty. In 1960 more than one third of the Mexicans living in this country inhabited overcrowded housing compared to less than 8 percent of the Anglo families and 22 percent of the non-whites.[26] Also, the quality of this housing is poor. The incidence of dilapidation in 1960 was seven times as great among housing units occupied by Chicanos as among homes occupied by Anglos. Unfortunately, the Census procedures in 1970 did not permit an evaluation of the quality of housing as did the 1960 Census. "Dilapidation" is a technical but important standard, nearly always reflecting substandard housing.

Overcrowded homes are yet another standard of housing and in 1960 in urban areas of the Southwest more than one third (34.6 percent) of the Chicano families lived in overcrowded housing. ("Overcrowding" is defined as more than 1.01 persons per room.) Comparative figures are not available in 1970 for Spanish-surname families in the entire Southwest, but Census figures do show that Mexican Americans were overcrowded to a noticeable extent. On the basis of a percentage of the available housing for Mexican Americans, in the Brownsville-Harlingen-San Benito area of Texas, 44 percent of the Chicano homes were overcrowded. In Albuquerque, N.M., 24 percent were overcrowded; in Houston, Texas, 32 percent; Denver, 19 percent; Los Angeles 28 percent; and Phoenix, 26 percent; Comparable figures on overcrowding for the total population in these cities show 39 percent, 10 percent, 10 percent, 5 percent, 8 percent, and 10 percent, respectively.[27]

Beyond these bald statistics, the Mexican American *barrios* are

26 Much of this section is based on Mittelbach and Marshall, *The Burden of Poverty*.

27 When we realize that the "total" *includes* Chicanos and that 65 percent of the Brownsville population is Chicano, we realize that the disparities are even greater than shown by the figures. Spanish surname figures are from PC (2)-1D. Total figures are from the PC (1) series.

often of a quality that reflects both the poverty of the inhabitants and the peculiar lack of institutional response to their problems. Thus when a visitor enters Mexican American *barrios* in many urban areas, ordinary urban facilities tend to disappear. Streets are unpaved; curbs and side-walks and street lights disappear, traffic hazards go unremedied, and the general air of decay and neglect is unmistakable. (In many cities in the Southwest, "improvements" considered normal and essential in other neighborhoods are financed by per capita assessments of local property owners. These special assessments are often impossible to obtain in poor neighborhoods.) Abandoned automobiles, uncollected refuse, and the hulks of burned out buildings are monuments to the inadequacy of public services in such areas. It is typical of many Mexican American neighborhoods in the Southwest that they are carelessly zoned. Cheap shops, small factories, tumble-down houses, and tiny urban farms sprawl together in unregulated confusion. Often, as in the near downtown areas of Los Angeles, Mexican American *barrios* have been destroyed by the march of civic progress. A railroad station, a baseball stadium, and a cluster of government buildings each cost the existence of a separate Los Angeles neighborhood. Mexican neighborhoods have been destroyed by the march of freeways across many southwestern cities. This easy eradication of Mexican American communities reflects both their political impotence and the fact that these neighborhoods never enjoyed the great rise in land values so characteristic of the urban Southwest.

Inevitably illness and early death are the companions of the over-crowded and undernourished poor. These conclusions are roughly re-flected in the available statistics for Mexican Americans. But the statistics of death (mortality) and illness (morbidity) have some problems in meas-urement, not the least of which is the fact that diseases which limit activity and destroy earning power may not even cause death and thus escape certain types of data-gathering. Mortality is reflected directly to health care and to the social and economic characteristics of the population group and proper analysis is thus very difficult.

Some of the rough data available, as for Mexican Americans in Houston, Texas, for 1950 and 1960 and for San Antonio in 1950 plus the standardized mortality ratios in 1950 and 1960 show that Chicanos are considerably more likely to die at an early age than Anglos in the same area. Blacks also die earlier than do Anglos and at about the same rate as Chicanos. Standardized mortality ratios indicate that in 1950 Chicano males had an observed mortality rate 1.66 times greater than Anglo males. In 1950 Chicano females suffered a death rate 2.43 times greater than Anglo women and a shorter life span. This difference fell rather sharply by 1960, although neither the significance of this drop nor the difference between ethnic groups is understood. The Black death rate for both men and women also fell sharply during the same period.[28]

There is virtually no useful data across the Southwest on the state of health of the Chicano population generally, in contrast to other groups, adjusted for age. This is rather surprising considering the rapid growth in health care services, a new outreach effect in health care institutions that may substantially affect all Mexican communities in the Southwest. Much of this change has been accelerated by community-based groups which are acutely aware of the need for health care. In a way, except for the strategic use of resources, the gathering of statistics about *need* is almost irrelevant. The need is very nearly limitless; some recent survey work shows basically that the demands of a disadvantaged area tend to surface in exact measure with the availability of health care resources. The new federal Medicare program and the state program in California (Medi-Cal) have greatly benefited Chicano communities simply because they were designed to benefit poor people and were actually reaching poor people. On a practical note, much of the health work done by community-based groups is that of increasing community access to existing facilities as was done in Los Angeles with a series of Health Fairs.

Poor people suffer excessively from mental illness—and the large amount of federal money being spent on programs in this area in the Mexican *barrios* of the Southwest has demonstrated this fact. More happily, there is an increasing ability to differentiate between the "culturally mentally retarded," a condition which may be created by certain types of school systems (see Chapter Five) and the biologically determined mental retardation which affects all populations for biological reasons whether they be Anglo, Black, or Chicano. In some instances malnutrition may be a factor. All these causes and results are complex and beyond the scope of the book. Mexican American community leaders are perfectly familiar with the consequences of poverty. In a very real way it is not only agonizing but insulting to search out the threads of deprivation when the root is nothing more exotic than poverty.

Poverty is also clearly associated with crime for the continuously urbanizing Mexican American populations of southwestern cities. This is true both for youthful and for adult offenses. Chicanos share disproportionately in two types of arrests and convictions—in youth crime, particularly in activities related to the traditional Mexican urban gangs, and in narcotics. An exceptionally high proportion of the Mexican American individuals incarcerated in California state institutions are persons in-

---

[28]This discussion is based on a valuable paper by Robert E. Roberts, "Mortality and Morbidity in the Mexican American Population," given to the Mexican American Population Conference, Austin, Texas, May 17–19, 1973. A useful bibliography is attached.

volved with narcotics, either directly or indirectly, and who have a history of juvenile offenses. There appears to be a direct historical link between these patterns and between the processes of urbanization of the Mexican American from the earliest history of the Southwest, although juvenile gangs only came to public attention at the time of the so-called "Zoot Suit riots." (See Chapter Two.) Gangs appear to be a long-standing form of social organization in southwestern metropolitan areas. Often they have a clearly age-graded structure that includes by association fairly large numbers of older people as well as young persons. These gangs are territorially *barrio* based. They are intimately related to neighborhood social structure and to the patterns of Chicano settlement in urban areas. They are quite different in social structure and in crime patterns from gangs in other metropolitan areas in other parts of the United States. They are also very different from gangs of other ethnic groups with different patterns of urban settlement. There is very little in the existing literature on criminology or juvenile delinquency that aids very much in understanding these patterns.[29] Thus, for example, it has been extremely difficult for public agencies to deal effectively with the high rate of narcotics addiction in Mexican neighborhoods. Psychiatric techniques are often misapplied toward an understanding of complex traditional social relationships. Some noteworthy examples of this misapplication took place in the federal narcotics hospital in Fort Worth, Texas, in the California Rehabilitation Center, and in drug programs in California state hospitals. In recent years strong community-based Chicano addict service centers have developed in every large city. These self-help groups reflect both the new federal money available for narcotics work and the increasingly recognized inadequacies of most clinically based hospital programs. "Street drug programs" also reflect the increasing strength of Chicano prison-inmate self-help groups. In some parts of the Southwest they have begun to share not only in drug programs but in overall community development, as with *Aliviane* in El Paso.

Although the bald statistics of personal and social problems add up to a depressing and somewhat overwhelming picture, the trends of the data show signs of a change and something of an improvement in social indicators. In addition, the growing organization of Mexican American communities reflected in such self-help groups as those dealing with narcotics addiction gives some hope. There is a faint promise here that the distinctive conditions of Mexican American urban settlement can, from itself, produce a distinctive set of self-generated solutions for their all-too-familiar problems.

[29]See Chicano Pinto Research Project, *The L.A. Pinto* (Los Angeles: University of Southern California, School of Planning and Urban Studies, 1975) for an analysis of these interactions from the "pinto" (ex-convict) perspective.

The first confrontation of Mexican Americans with American society involved a relationship between two separate societies, each with its own institutions. But Mexican institutions did not long survive the arrival of Anglo American settlers. Thus Mexicans coming to the Southwest in the twentieth century passed into Anglo society as a minority confronting Anglo institutions. The "little Mexican church" of the 1930s and the "little Mexican school" were never, in fact, Mexican. They were an integral part of the American Catholic church (probably with a Spanish, Irish, or French priest) and of a segregated American school system.

Between 1848 and the first large wave of immigration in the 1920s, the old-country institutions of the Mexicans were largely obliterated. It was not possible to transplant institutions that could ameliorate life in the *barrios*. Here again the marginality of the Mexicans in American life was demonstrated by the marginality of their institutions. Few priests came from Mexico with their people. Only in a very few isolated places were there any Mexican-administered Spanish-language schools. Perhaps even more important, the Mexicans did not come into a region where the government was committed to welfare state measures in even a small degree.[1]

American Institutions in the Mexican Experience

This chapter will discuss the work of the institutions most concerned with Mexican Americans. The first and most important of these is the public school system.

THE SCHOOLS AND THE CHILDREN

There is no doubt whatever about the massive failure of southwestern schools to educate Mexican American children. The magnitude of this failure is detailed in Chapter Four in the bare statistics of dropouts, low achievement, and low grade attainment of Mexican Americans

---

[1] This distinguishes Mexican immigration from the contemporary movements of Puerto Ricans from Puerto Rico and of American Blacks from the South. The mass movements of these groups are often compared to Mexican immigration. Oscar Handlin, *The Newcomers* (Garden City, N.Y.: Doubleday & Company, 1962).

throughout all the Border States.[2] The schools themselves perceived this reality only since the 1930s. Before that time there could have been no recognition of success or failure because there was no problem defined as such—and hence no special effort to educate Mexicans. Nearly all educators saw the Mexican as an outsider to our society, not to be expected to participate in American life. As Carter states,

> Frequently attitudes were tinged with racial prejudice; the literature emphasized the differences between the two cultures rather than their similarities. The typically low intelligence test scores were used as "evidence" of innate inferiority. This in turn was used to justify the commonplace segregation in the schools. Although some concern was expressed for the state of the Mexican-American's health, most of the literature reveals little interest in his economic or educational plight.[3]

Once the problem was recognized and defined as a "problem," then there were attempts to cope with it by explanation. In the process many shallow and overgeneralized stereotypes regarding Mexican children and Mexican culture attained institutional validation as "reasons" for the disproportionate failure rates. It is plain that many Mexican children are bilingual. Educators often saw *the* explanation of Mexican school problems in this bilingualism, assuming that it is detrimental to intellect and thus to the child's "teachability." A second generalization was that Mexican American culture produces "lack of motivation." Cultural traits conceptualized on this shallow level were used to explain the behavior of Mexican Americans in places as diverse as Laredo, Los Angeles, and the villages of northern New Mexico. It was applied to new immigrants from the vast landless peasantry of Mexico as well as to second generation residents of the large cities of the American West. A study of a Los Angeles high school in 1938 from the University of Southern California produced this very typical conclusion, a minor masterpiece of Lysenkian genetics, as quoted by Thomas Carter:

> The Mexicans, as a group, lack ambition. The peon of Mexico has spent so many generations in a condition of servitude that a lazy acceptance of his lot has become a racial characteristic.[4]

This evaluation of the effect of language and culture has become

[2] See also the detailed data in the U.S. Commission on Civil Rights, *The Unfinished Education: Outcomes for Minorities in the Five Southwestern States*, Mexican American Education Study Report no. 2, (October 1971).

[3] Thomas P. Carter, *Mexican Americans in School: A History of Educational Neglect* (New York: College Entrance Examination Board, 1970).

[4] Lillian Graeber, "A Study of Attendance at Thomas Jefferson High School, Los Angeles, California" (Master's thesis, University of Southern California, 1938).

somewhat more sophisticated in recent years, although it is still widely held that Mexican American children are the products of a folk culture dominated by traditional values that make it difficult for them to learn in American schools. Many educators believe that most Mexican American children are essentially "alingual" (or "bicultural illiterates"), not truly speaking either Spanish or English. The culture is also blamed for the self-derogation that is held to be characteristic of a larger than normal percentage of Mexican children, especially adolescents. Mexicans have been further supposed to be characterized by an apathetic, noncompetitive attitude.

The "diagnosis" reported above is, of course, the picture of an excluded child. Nonetheless these evaluations by educational institutions have given some directions toward changing and improving the schools. Other directions have been given by the increasingly well-organized and articulate Mexican American and other educators in the Southwest and elsewhere. But to return to these diagnoses and the possible therapies—the most obvious measure of action, of course, would be that of the comparative speed with which the reasonably neutral question of language is attacked. Thus in the Elementary and Secondary Education Act of 1965, one major section (Title VII) is set aside for bilingual, bicultural education. But after three years of operation, a report for 1972–1973 notes that a total of approximately 120 programs were funded to serve Mexican American children. These programs reached less than 2 percent of the Chicano children in the Southwest—even when supplemented by certain state-funded programs.[5] These programs are overwhelmingly concerned with technical aspects.[6] The usual catch phrase for such concern is "learning to become functionally bilingual in both English and Spanish." "Bicultural" education as outlined in the federal bill has yet to be implemented in any but a few places. A recent state law in California (the Ryan Act) called for the creation of bicultural teacher training. These tiny effects only dimly reflect the strenuous attempts by Mexican American educators both in the past and recently to create a viable educational institution in the Southwest. An exceptionally valuable series of studies undertaken by the U.S. Commission on Civil Rights reflects in detail the

---

[5] U.S. Commission on Civil Rights, *Toward Quality Education for Mexican Americans*, Mexican American Education Study Report no. 4, February 1974 and *Guide to Title VII Bilingual Bicultural Projects in the United States* (Austin, Texas: Dissemination Center for Bicultural Education, 1972–1973).

[6] The varieties of goals of bilingual educational programs are illustrated in Rolf Kjolseth, "Assimilation or Pluralism," in *Bilingualism in the Southwest*, ed. Paul R. Turner (Tucson: University of Arizona Press, 1973). Kjolseth equates technical programs with an assimilationist goal emphasizing a one-way power structure—with the English dominant.

failure of the schools of the Southwest and many of the hopes for change. These hopes and plans, as summarized by the Commission, include most of the current educational philosophies that are being developed in the region. The reports are also very closely tied to documentary evidence of discriminatory practices. Thus the first report ("Ethnic Isolation of Mexican Americans in the Public Schools of the Southwest") deals with the painful issue of segregation of Mexican Americans. Although it is difficult for most Americans to imagine racial segregation outside the Black-white context, "Mexican schools were a pervasive feature of the Southwest for many decades, clearly segregated by intent as well as by the accidents of location."

The rationale for segregation followed the idea of the "unassimilable" Mexicans and carried a strong air of patronization. Separate schools were built and maintained, in theory, simply because of residential segregation or to benefit the Mexican child. The Mexican child had a "language handicap" and needed to be "Americanized" before mixing with Anglo children. As Thomas Carter notes, Anglo educators felt Mexican American children could better overcome their deficiencies by separation from Anglos and would not suffer from excessive competition.

This patronizing approach was used to justify many inequalities and rigid segregation. "Mexican schools" generally were inferior in physical plant and in teachers and generally there were larger classes. Black children were sometimes assigned to these schools, implying a low social status. There was a notable lack of effort in enforcing the weak school attendance laws. At secondary level schools, students were often discouraged from attending school at all. These and other restrictive practices were not illegal until a series of court cases in 1946 and 1948 proved the intent and practice of segregation.

Segregation is now illegal, but separation is an institutional pattern. Ironically, when some recent court orders in east Texas forced desegregation, the school boards merely mixed their Black children and Mexican children, leaving the Anglo children in quite separate schools. (Legally speaking, Chicano children are "white" and this satisfied the letter of the law.) *De facto* segregation based upon patterns of residential segregation is widespread in the Southwest. These community patterns appear in single schools and in school districts; they appear in Texas and in California, Arizona, New Mexico, and Colorado. Chicano teachers are also segregated. Reports of the Commission on Civil Rights document these patterns in detail, noting also that Mexican American children tend to be segregated within southwestern urban areas as well as within rural districts. There are substantial differences in state patterns: in both Texas and New Mexico about two thirds of all Mexican children attend predominantly Mexican schools. Less than 30 percent of the Mexican American school children in California attend predominantly Chicano schools.

Ethnic segregation (or at least, ethnic imbalance) is pervasive throughout the Southwest. The Commission follows this conclusion by noting a gross underrepresentation of Chicano teachers: less than 4 percent of the teaching force in the Southwest is Mexican American although 17 percent of the students are Mexican. There is gross underrepresentation on yet another level—that of decision making. Very few Mexicans serve on school boards or on school administrative staffs.

In the past some educators rationalized school segregation for Mexican American children on the grounds that it spared them competition and allowed time to make up language deficiencies and other educational "handicaps." Although this rationale is now seldom used to defend segregation, it is still the basic reasoning behind *intra*school segregation, or "tracking." Like segregation, "tracking" has been found illegal as the result of litigation (*Hobson vs. Hansen*) but nevertheless there is very little doubt that it exists and that it especially affects Mexican Americans in the Southwest. The Civil Rights Commission found that some two thirds of the Southwest's schools have a form of "ability grouping"—that is, the placement of students in separate groups for instruction on the basis of ability. A much smaller percentage at the time of the survey (1969) admitted outright tracking or the placement of students in separate instructional groups for all their academic classes.[7] There is no doubt that Chicano students are disproportionately placed in low-ability groups. Twenty-six percent of the Anglos as compared to 14 percent of the Chicanos were placed in high-ability groups, according to the Commission. There is substantial evidence (despite widespread belief to the contrary) that ability grouping is not helpful in instruction.[8] Quite the contrary, it is now well known that, over time, ability grouping is a self-fulfilling prophecy: regardless of their potential, children placed in low-ability groups tend to perform poorly and *vice versa*. This "pygmalion" effect (children fulfill their teachers' expectations) has been specifically documented for Mexican American children.

The most extreme form of ability grouping (with a pernicious effect on Chicano children) is placement in classes for the mentally retarded.

7 *Toward Quality Education*, p. 21 ff.

8Warren G. Findley and Miriam M. Bryan, *Ability Grouping: 1970* (Athens: University of Georgia, Center for Educational Improvement), cited in Commission on Civil Rights, *Toward Quality Education*. An important article by Robert Brischetto and Tomás Arciniega, "Examining the Examiner: A Look at Educators' Perspectives on the Chicano Student" surveys the current views in *Chicanos and Native Americans: The Territorial Minorities*, ed. Rudolph O. de la Garza, Z. Anthony Kruszewski, and Tomás A. Arciniega (Englewood Cliffs, N.J.: Prentice-Hall, Inc., 1973).

Although there is little doubt that children who are functionally retarded get a more humane education in separate groups, there is also no doubt at all that many minority children placed in classes for the mentally retarded are *not* functionally retarded. Thus in California there are about twice as many Chicano students in "special education" classes as would be expected from school population ratios. Many of these students are what is called *"six-hour* retarded" children.[9] Essentially these are children who are functionally undifferentiated from other children during an 18-hour day. They play, perform household tasks, and interact with their environment in normal fashion during the day. But in school, as a result of the criteria used, they have been classified as "mentally retarded." Jane Mercer calls this process of classification "institutionalized Anglo-centrism."[10] The process involves the use of teacher judgment and of I.Q. tests. (As a result of concentrated scientific and legal attack, the use of I.Q. tests is declining.) This combination of criteria and especially the insensitivity of teachers to cultural cues is the unfortunate reason for the accuracy of the phrase "institutionalized Anglo-centrism." Much the same can be said for the placement of students in classes for the gifted. It is notable that Mexican American students (as, for example, in the Los Angeles system) are comparatively seldom placed in these programs, even when the system or schools have a relatively high proportion of Chicano pupils.

In addition to the use of ability grouping, there is another depressing phenomenon familiar to researchers in urban education. To overstate it slightly, the higher the percentage of Chicano students in any school, the lower the median scores on all standardized national tests, whether they are I.Q. or achievement tests. This pattern appears in Los Angeles as early as the third and fourth grades and continues through high school until the twelfth grade. This has some curious consequences. Specifically, one is aware that the median grade given to students in predominantly Mexican American schools reflects a very different level of actual performance on standardized tasks. Thus a B-plus student will probably show a much lower performance capacity on a standardized test

9 "The Six Hour Retarded Child," in *A Report on the Conference on Problems of Education of Children in the Inner City,* 1969, sponsored by the President's Commission on Mental Retardation and the Bureau of Education for the Handicapped, Office of Education, U.S. Department of Health, Education, and Welfare, as cited in Commission on Civil Rights, *Toward Quality Education.* See Jane Mercer, *Labeling the Mentally Retarded* (Los Angeles and Berkeley: University of California Press, 1973) for analysis of this process.

10 "Institutionalized Anglo-centrism": Labeling Mental Retardates in the Public Schools," in Peter Orleans and William Russell Ellis Jr., eds., *Race, Change, and Urban Society, Urban Affairs Annual Review,* 5 (Beverly Hills, Calif.: Sage Publications, 1971).

if he comes from a heavily Mexican school than if he comes from an Anglo middle-class school. Later, when Anglo and Mexican students meet competitively, as in college, the Chicano student will be seriously handicapped. The psychological effects of this competition can be serious because every school level aggregates students from increasingly larger areas —the final aggregation being that of colleges, and, of course, the job market.

In some schools in the Southwest, it has been the practice to use a form of grade retention. Students may be kept back to repeat either a full grade or a course. An alternative practice is "social promotion." The Commission on Civil Rights reports negatively on the practice of grade retention, although this sort of mechanism must be clearly distinguished from the other effects of lower performance on standardized tests.

A major technique for dealing with the language and culture of the "ethnic deviant" has been simple suppression. This is usually masked as a positive approach by an emphasis upon conformity to the "normal" means of instruction. Outright prohibition of the speaking of Spanish in the classroom is probably the most extreme example. Arguments for prohibiting Spanish are a mixture of the moral and the pedagogical. The moral arguments include such axioms as "English is the national language and must be used at all times." The pedagogical are such unsupported ideas as bilingualism is mentally confusing. The open acknowledgment that many Anglo teachers and Anglo pupils do not speak Spanish is also used as a reason for prohibiting Spanish because it is "impolite" to speak a language some people do not understand. Carter suggests that the real reason is that "the enemy is speaking in code." A Commission on Civil Rights survey showed that a third of the elementary and secondary schools discouraged the use of Spanish in the classroom. Most of these schools are in Texas. Such discouragement is rare in California.[11] Although none of the reporting schools admitted to more than mild punishment for the "persistent speakers of Spanish," there remains strong evidence that detention and even corporal punishment is still practiced in some of the schools in the Southwest.

Other cultural differences are often severely suppressed as well. Carter suggests that "the lower the social class level of the student body, the more rigidly the child is expected to conform to the educator's image of the perfect middle-class teenager." Secondary schools in Texas seemed particularly restrictive about dress and behavior. Dress styles are modified, first names are often changed for "convenience." (The name "Jesus," in

---

[11]U.S. Commission on Civil Rights, *The Excluded Student: Educational Practices Affecting Mexican Americans in the Southwest*, Mexican American Education Study Report no. 3, May 1972, pp. 15–16.

particular, seemed to disturb many teachers and was often changed to "Jesse.")

As late as 1970 both community and scholarly inquiries showed the nearly total exclusion of Chicano history and experiences from the curriculum of southwestern schools. This result meant that Mexican Americans had replaced the Blacks as the nation's "invisible men." But by 1971 the state of California appointed a number of minority persons to a task force to review proposed textbooks in social studies. The protests of this task force against the exclusion of Mexican American history had an immediate impact on the textbook industry because of the size of the California market for texts. But this impact is a new consequence of Mexican academic strength. Ten years ago the Chicano educators on this task force simply were not available.

But the essence of the classroom experience is the interaction between the teachers and the students. The quality of this interaction depends entirely upon the teacher; it is inevitable, therefore, that the most important cause of a high dropout rate of Mexican American students is the failure of teachers. Some recent legislation (the Stull bill in California) has attempted to establish a form of teacher "accountability" by requiring that teachers develop and reach certain learning goals in their classrooms or lose some benefits. Apparently the quality of this interaction between Chicano students and teachers is not high. One of the Commission on Civil Rights reports on the observation of a number of classrooms in the Southwest notes that one of its primary findings shows the "lack of involvement of Mexican children as active participants in the classroom. The teachers praise or encourage Anglo children 36 percent more often than Mexican Americans. They use, or build upon the contributions of Anglo pupils fully 40 percent more frequently than those of Chicano pupils . . . . The teachers respond positively to Anglos about 40 percent more than they do to Chicano students."[12] It is clear from these data that the Mexican American teachers are no more useful in these regards than are Anglo teachers, by and large. Under some circumstances, in fact, Chicanos are even more 'pro-Anglo' than are Anglo teachers. Although these findings may be distressing and certainly indicate that no quick solutions for Mexican American educational problems are in sight, they are not really very surprising. Like their colleagues, the Anglos, Mexican American teachers are the product of the social and educational system of the Southwest. In some ways it is not surprising that members of the subordinated minority will tend to reflect that status in their classroom

[12]U.S. Commission on Civil Rights, *Teachers and Students*, Report no. 5, March 1973.

behavior. Certainly one solution to this problem lies in the immediate pre-teaching experience given in schools of education. The Ryan Act, passed in California in 1970 (to become effective during the academic year 1974–1975), requires a "cross-cultural experience" during teacher training as a condition of teacher certification. California is the only state to recognize the importance of such experience. Increasingly, the large city school systems of the Southwest will reflect the immigration patterns and the differential birth rates of the Chicanos. Thus, for example, the Los Angeles unified school district student population is about 25 percent Mexican Americans. To this kind of demographic reality, the schools of education have been very unresponsive. The raw necessities of their future teaching problems have been outlined very sharply.[13] It will be interesting to watch the impact of the "cross-cultural experience" in California, as required by the Ryan Act. Heretofore a form of social essentialism (an effort to capture the essence of Mexican American life and to reduce it to simplicities) has been characteristic of most teacher-training approaches. Very often these simplicities become a mask for stereotypes. Above all, in this book we have tried to establish the extreme diversity of the Mexican American population. Such an approach is very rarely used in teacher education.

Only spasmodically has any effort been made to adapt schools to diverse local situations. This is clearly the case with teacher training as well. As only one example, the University of Southern California places a very large number of undergraduate students in local elementary schools which are very heavily Mexican (Joint Educational Program). Only recently has its school of education begun to relate to these experiences. But even now, the reactions of the students are only very dimly articulated into the core curriculum of the School of Education. This is even truer of any possible values of the involvement of teachers with local Mexican communities. Elsewhere in this book, we note the increasing sophistication of community groups. These groups have also begun to provide a "monitoring" system for the schools in their neighborhoods. Essentially the attention given educational deficiencies, the increasing number of Chicano teachers and teacher organizations, and the increasing participation of communtiy and parents provide a form of surveillance of the schools.[14] There is nothing in this change that differs from the "monitoring" system imposed upon middle-class schools by middle-class parents, but many educators are upset about "politicization" when it is

---

13 *Towards a Quality Education.*

14 Joan W. Moore and Armida Martinez, "The Grassroot Challenge to Educational Professionalism in East Los Angeles," in Alfredo Casteneda, et al., *Mexican Americans and Educational Change* (Riverside: University of California, 1971).

done by Mexican parents. The difference, of course, is that the children of Mexican American families are receiving an inadequate education and a "normal" interaction between parents and school is likely to be some form of protest. Middle-class Anglo involvement in the schools is likely to be a form of community support for an institution that appears to be adequate. Perhaps in no other way is the disparity between Anglo and Mexican relationships to southwestern schools so clearly seen.

There is a substantial degree of difference between states and localities in these matters. However the patterns of disadvantage are present even in the best school systems in the American Southwest. Contrary to the stereotypes of generations, there is no doubt whatever that most Mexican American children and their parents want formal education, including education after high school. There is no doubt whatever that they want access to the professions and skilled white-collar positions. There is also no doubt whatever that the schools of the Southwest must improve enormously before they can satisfy these aspirations.

MEXICAN AMERICANS
AND THE ROMAN CATHOLIC CHURCH

As institutions, churches can serve to socialize values in childhood, to maintain a form of social control over values and conduct in later life, and for minorities, to mediate between the minorities and other institutions of the dominant system. For most Chicanos, at least 90 percent, "churches" means the Roman Catholic church.[15]

Generally it is true that the Mexican identification with Catholicism acted to strengthen the already acute isolation of Mexicans from the predominantly Protestant Southwest (Chapter Three). But to assume that the Catholic church in the Southwest was a strong institution from the first days and strong enough to affect importantly the lives of the first great waves of Mexican immigrants is misleading. A study of the historical record of the archdioceses of Los Angeles and San Antonio back to the time of the first American settlement shows that, whatever its desires or intention, the church could do little to protect or help Mexicans.[16]

[15] Fr. Alberto Carillo argues that the Chicanos are less than nominal Catholics but are, in fact, basically alienated from the "institutional church" though faithful to Catholic values. Quoted in Patrick H. McNamara, "Catholicism and the Chicano: A Tentative Reassessment" (unpublished ms., 1972).

[16] Patrick Hayes McNamara, "Bishops, Priests and Prophecy: A Study in the Sociology of Religious Protest," (Ph.D. dissertation, University of California at Los Angeles, 1968), condensed in Grebler, et al., *The Mexican American People.* This study explores the history of the church generally in the Southwest, as well as in San Antonio and Los Angeles, and also utilizes survey data on Catholic practice from the two latter cities.

When the United States acquired the Southwest and its new "charter member" minority, the Catholic church in the region was very near collapse. The magnificent mission properties had been expropriated by the Spanish and Mexican governments and acquired by large Mexican and Anglo landowners. The residual fragments of the missions that were concerned with strictly religious activities became ordinary parochial churches, quite isolated one from the other in a vast territory, lacking either clergy or the means of supporting a clergy. The new American bishops were not much more than "padres on horseback."

They received some help from the priests of various religious orders, most of them from foreign countries. These included the Oblate Fathers from France, who appeared in 1847, Spanish Franciscans (once charged with service of the mission system), Spanish Claretians, Immaculate Heart Mission Fathers, Vincentian Fathers and Piarist Fathers. These men and a few native priests administered only the most essential religious services over a vast area. The burden was staggering for this small group of overworked and overextended clergy. We can pick a single year in the late nineteenth century (1890, in the archdiocese of Tucson) and find a lone parish priest trying to bring the basic sacraments of baptism, marriage, and burial to 1,052 Catholics spread over an average area of 7,000 square miles. In 1890 in the combined dioceses of San Antonio, Corpus Christi (including Brownsville), El Paso, Santa Fe, Tucson, and Los Angeles (including Monterey and San Diego) there were only 193 parish priests, and of this tiny number only 14 had Spanish surnames. (French, Irish, and even Spanish priests worked with the Mexicans. Mexican Americans have never been much attracted to the priesthood.)

It appears, in fact, that in these early years the bishops could at best hope for survival. The later mass immigrations from Mexico brought the Catholic church hundreds of thousands of new parishioners. The new immigrants were probably as unused to American Catholicism (with its heavy and rather ascetic Irish influence) as was the average Protestant. Moreover, many immigrants, fresh from the revolutionary church-baiting of Mexico, were anticlerical. The immigrants appear, indeed, to have come from precisely that population group in Mexico among whom Catholic influence was weakest. They were unaccustomed to parochial schools, financial support of the church, religious instruction, and regular attendance at Mass, all of which are important to American Catholics. Even the basic doctrines of Catholicism were so mixed with remnants of rural Indian paganism that the church, in summary, saw the new Mexican immigrants as likely "new converts" but not as true practicing Catholics. As McNamara says,

Contrary to the notion that the immigrant would seek out the Church for support and comfort, the Church had to reach out for the newcomer if it was to perform its function. This would have been difficult under the best of circumstances. The poor resources at the command of the Southwestern church made it an overwhelming task.[17]

Only very slowly was it possible for the church to move away from narrowly pastoral goals in the Southwest. In part, this advance was helped by substantial gifts from Catholic sources in the Midwest and East. The church began to interest itself more substantially in the building of parochial schools and in Americanization of the Mexican population. Both these motives were inspired, to a large extent, by the desire to defend Mexican Americans against Protestant missionaries and to keep Mexican youth from entering a public school system that was at least latently anti-Catholic and publicly devoted to strictly secular values. However, the available resources were never enough. Even the effort put forth by the Archdiocese of Los Angeles (the richest of the southwestern religious divisions) was extremely limited. Settlement houses appeared in Los Angeles in 1905, and a Bureau of Catholic Charities appeared in 1919 (there was none in San Antonio until 1941). Even a massive drive for a total system of parochial schools achieved only very limited success. By 1930 the combined archdiocese of San Diego and Los Angeles had 301,775 Catholics but only 79 schools. By comparison, Baltimore (with approximately the same number of Catholics) had 179 parochial schools in 1930. El Paso and Corpus Christi lagged then even more: El Paso had 12 schools for a Catholic population of 119,623 and Corpus Christi, 27 schools for 247,760 Catholics. Nearly all the Catholics in these Texas cities were Mexican Americans.

All these extensions beyond pastoral goals were characterized by a certain defensiveness in the public statements and publications of the hierarchy. This was particularly apparent in Los Angeles after the "zoot suit" riots of the early 1940s. Moreover, there had been no protests from the church during the Mexican repatriations of 1930 through 1933. When the Mexicans became a visible social problem during the Los Angeles riots, the church wanted to show Anglo citizens that the church was an institution determined to instill American ideals into the laity. These objectives included such diverse efforts in the Mexican community as citizenship instruction, classes in English, and youth activities of the type exemplified by the Catholic Youth Organization. Very often these socialization efforts were combined with anticommunist instruction.

[17] McNamara, in Grebler, et al., *The Mexican American People.*

After World War II the Los Angeles hierarchy began a massive program of parochial school construction in the Mexican areas of the city. Its completion by 1960 was, significantly, hailed by Catholic leaders as an important step in safeguarding the Catholic faith of Mexican Americans. This very expensive system of parochial schools might have served to maintain the cultural and social distinctiveness of Mexicans, as happened in other parts of the U.S. There is no evidence of any special effort to this end. McNamara sees the parochial system and the very limited sallies into social welfare as designed basically to defend the faith in a very narrow manner.

Social action designed to promote a more humane goal than defense of Roman Catholicism appeared in San Antonio as early as 1943 under the pressure of great poverty. In the words of Archbishop Lucey:

> A very general lack of labor organizations, the absence of good legislation and the greed of powerful employers have combined to create in Texas dreadful and widespread misery. The evil men who are driving tens of thousands of our people into a slow starvation will be held to strict accountability by the God of eternal justice.[18]

Archbiship Lucey's eloquence did not stir any action until 1945 when, ironically, practical help came not from the churches of the Southwest but from the American Board of Catholic Missions in Chicago, which set up a "Bishop's Committee for the Spanish-Speaking" to serve Chicano migrants. McNamara points out that the typical southwestern Catholic parish churches, locked into association with the dispossessed Mexicans and very poor, have been exceedingly vulnerable to economic pressure, particularly from Anglo Catholics. Thus when direct social action has appeared, it nearly always has been instigated by a group well outside the area of local pressure.

There are yet other reasons for lack of interest in social welfare among parish priests. Some San Antonio parish priests, interviewed only recently, felt their people were not yet ready for the social teachings of recent Popes; others simply lacked interest or training in the social doctrines of the Roman Catholic church.[19] Yet the need for social amelioration in San Antonio is so obvious that when the opportunity for obtaining federal money appeared in 1964 through the Office of Economic Opportunity, San Antonio church projects became the single most important devic. for funneling these funds into poverty areas in that city.

18 McNamara, in Grebler, et al., *The Mexican American People*; citing *The Spanish-speaking of the Southwest and West* (Washington, D.C.: National Catholic Welfare Conference, 1943), pp. 3–4.
    19 McNamara, in Grebler, et al., *The Mexican American People*.

Quite generally, the Roman Catholic church, whatever its intentions, has been quite unable to mediate between Mexicans and the Anglos in the larger society. Like the educators of the Southwest, the church has also suffered from misperceptions. Except perhaps in San Antonio which in 1970 proudly boasted the first "Chicano bishop," the ruling spirits of the Roman Catholic church have been reluctant to take the ideological lead in any of the important issues of past or present for Mexican Americans. Certainly they greatly overestimated the appeal of Communist organizers and underestimated the steady move of Mexican Americans to large urban areas. The strongest social actions of the church have always been in the agricultural areas, as with Cesar Chavez, and most of the unprecedented 1971 grant of the National Committee on Human Development also went to the rural poor.

Whatever the views of the church hierarchy from one decade to another, the church never involved Mexican Americans deeply in the institution itself. A dramatic series of what McNamara terms "lay protests" in 1969 and 1970 involved Chicano activists (*Católicos por la Raza*) and Anglo Catholics (Concerned Catholics) in Los Angeles. They culminated in several jail terms for the protesters as well as some publicity for their exclusion.[20] A group called PADRES, an organization of Spanish-speaking priests, was formed in 1969. It reflects a deep concern with the functioning of the church in urban as well as rural *barrios*. These moves are new; their significance remains to be tested.

CHICANOS AND THE CRIMINAL JUSTICE SYSTEM

Mexican Americans have had an extraordinarily bitter and consistently negative relationship with law enforcement agencies and other elements of the criminal justice system. It is probable that along with the public school system, this relationship has been critical in forming the attitudes of Chicanos toward the United States—and especially in sustaining the prevailing "culture of suspicion."[21]

The fact of exceptionally poor relations is treated in statistical detail both in such reports as that of the U.S. Commission on Civil Rights (*Mexican Americans and the Administration of Justice in the Southwest,* 1970) and also implicitly in the statistical reports of agencies that deal with the Mexican Americans such as local police jurisdictions, the Immi-

[20]McNamara, "Catholicism and the Chicano." See also Acosta, *Revolt of the Cockroach People* for a first-hand account.

[21] See for example, statements of panelists at the 1972 National Conference on the Administration of Justice and the Mexican American, reported in its *Conference Report* (San Francisco: Mexican American Legal Defense and Education Fund, 1974).

gration and Naturalization Service, and the like. Such special reports as those of the Commission on Civil Rights and, for example, the American Civil Liberties Union (*Law Enforcement: The Matter of Redress*, 1969) are meeting recurrent waves of outrage. There are endless stories of police harassment, periodically culminating in a death which is widely publicized within the Chicano communities of the Southwest but rarely captures the attention of the larger community. Thus in 1973 a Dallas policeman shot and killed a small boy while transporting the boy on a suspicion charge. The resulting storm of pressure caused a change of venue for the trial of the policeman. Every year has seen at least one similarly outrageous and widely protested event. Two cousins are shot and killed in a downtown Los Angeles hotel by visiting Fresno county law enforcement officers. The men understand no English; the officers understand no Spanish. A teenager chokes to death in a Corona, Calif., police lockup. In Riverside, Calif., a boy is shot to death while "resisting arrest." A coroner's jury in that case noted that the bullet entered the boy's back below the beltline and left the body at the front of the skull. Many Mexicans concluded that the boy had been helpless when shot, but as in many similar cases the jury returned a verdict of justifiable homicide, exonerating the police officer.

There is probably a true subculture of Chicano community attitudes toward the police based on a historically distinct treatment of people from those subcommunities. All available evidence that has been systematically analyzed shows such problems. Thus, an analysis of Los Angeles superior court records as far back as 1938 indicates dragnet arrests as a standard police mode of operation.[22] The same study shows that Anglos were put on probation three times more frequently than Mexican American offenders.

The 1970 Commission on Civil Rights Report concluded that "there is evidence of a widespread pattern of police misconduct, including incidents of excessive police violence, discriminatory treatment of juveniles, and excessive use of "arrests for investigation" and "stop and frisk." Both this report and that made by the American Civil Liberties Union detail the extreme difficulty of obtaining local remedies for police malpractice. Even the advice of Judge Donald Pachecho of Denver to people who

[22] The ratio of arrests to felony convictions was 5.3 to 1 for Mexican Americans as compared to a ratio of 2.7 to 1 for Anglos. The authors of this report conclude that prejudicial arrest procedures and treatment and the use of indiscriminate wholesale dragnet methods helped create the higher arrest to conviction ratio. Edwin M. Lemert and Judy Rosberg, "The Administration of Justice to Minority Groups in Los Angeles County," in *University of California Publications in Culture and Society*, II, ed. R. L. Beals, Leonard Bloom, and Franklin Fearing (Berkeley and Los Angeles: University of California Press, 1948), pp. 3, 12.

have been subjected to police excess ("You should start out, first of all, by suing the bastard.") is difficult: few attorneys, particular in smaller cities, are willing to sue the police on behalf of a poor Mexican American complainant.

Behind this problem of behavior and the difficulty of obtaining redress, of course, is about what one would expect—a considerable amount of direct prejudice on the part of the police. The southwestern law enforcement agencies tend to define the Mexican Americans as prone to crime and tend generally to attribute this to "racial" characteristics. Beginning with the investigation by Paul Taylor in 1931, we find reports of habitual police violence and disregard of civil rights in the Rio Grande valley in Texas, in Dallas, Denver, and in Los Angeles.[23] Sometimes the consequences are merely bizarre, as in the early 1940s when the Los Angeles police attributed the violence of the Pachucho (Zoot Suit) riots to the Indian blood of Mexican juveniles. (In fact, marauding sailors and other servicemen initiated and sustained the violence.) But more serious is the statement made before a federal commission in 1960 by Chief William H. Parker of the Los Angeles Police Department:

> The Latin population that came in here in great strength were here before us, and presented a great problem because I worked over on the East Side when men had to work in pairs—but that has evolved into assimilation— and it's because of some of these people being not too far removed from the wild tribes of the district of the inner mountains of Mexico. I don't think you can throw the genes out of the question when you discuss behavior patterns of people.[24]

But we must look to sources other than individual prejudice for an explanation of this prolonged and bitter relationship. The Mexican American population is distinctive in several ways that would tend to inflame its relationship with law enforcement agencies. First, there is the long history of the aftermath of conquest. One may depreciate this aftermath as "historical" and of no particular relevance—but then again, it is important to note that the Texas Rangers were founded in 1835 specifically to cope with the "Mexican problem" of the Texas Republic and that the Rangers survive to this day and are still involved with Mexican American communities in Texas. For example, the Rangers interfered in

---

[23]Paul S. Taylor, "Crime and the Foreign Born: The Problem of the Mexican," *National Commission on Law Observance and Enforcement, Report on Crime and the Foreign Born* (Washington, D.C.: Government Printing Office, 1931) and *National Commission on Law Observance and Enforcement, Lawlessness in Law Enforcement* (Washington, D.C.: Government Printing Office, 1931).

[24]*Hearings before the United States Commission on Civil Rights,* San Francisco, January 27, 1960 (Washington, D.C.: Government Printing Office, 1960).

Starr County in south Texas when Chavez' union attempted to organize the melon workers in the 1960s. Similarly they were present in Crystal City when this small Texas community was going through organizational and political changes that were entirely electoral.[25] The western tradition of vigilante law enforcement (and the chronic shortage of salaried peace officers) meant that in the nineteenth and early twentieth centuries the employers of Mexican labor could deputize men to serve their private interests. Arizona mine owners, Texas ranchers, and California fruit growers did this frequently in labor disputes with their Mexican laborers.[26] Thus there is something about the years after the conquest, the need to control Mexicans both as potentially autonomous and dangerous insurgents and as potentially disruptive to the labor supply. This is important in understanding the Chicano relationship with law enforcement agencies.

Recently law enforcement officers throughout the nation have been very concerned with "urban guerrillas" and "militants." It is perhaps too easy to see the linkage between the old revolutionaries from across the border and the "riot control" activities of urban police departments. But, in fact, this connection is made consistently by Chicano spokesmen. Armando Morales in his book *Ando Sangrando!* documents this history of law enforcement riot repression. He notes that in the late 1960s and early 1970s there were thirty-four Mexican American riots in the urban areas of the Southwest. Morales was unable to get his book published, yet it is a significant study of law enforcement and Mexican Americans.[27] In the most serious of the urban riots, that of August 1970 when Ruben Salazar of the *Los Angeles Times* was killed in Los Angeles, the aftermath was an outburst of extreme tension between city and county law enforcement officers and the Mexican minority. This history of bad relations and labor trouble is the first special condition under which Mexican Americans and the law enforcement establishment meet each other.

The second way in which Mexicans are distinctive is their foreignness to American society. Their very presence involves the work of the Immigration and Naturalization Service of the U.S. Justice Department—and this attention has been very significant. In its approximately fifty years of existence, the Border Patrol of the Service has acquired a reputation for ferocity among Mexican Americans. Their charge is not only

25 The best available account was done by John Shockley, *Chicano Revolt in a Texas Town* (Notre Dame, Ind.: University of Notre Dame Press, 1974).

26 Acuna, *Occupied America*, chap. 6. New Chicano historians are rapidly uncovering much new material about this conflict, particularly in labor.

27Armando Morales, *Ando Sangrando! I Am Bleeding* (Los Angeles: The Congress of Mexican American Unity, 1971).

to stop entry of illegal aliens and to apprehend deportable aliens but also to enforce all pertinent federal laws affecting the heavy traffic across the nation's borders, especially between the United States and Mexico. Thus a single patrol officer (representing the laws and regulations of some twenty federal agencies) can, for instance, stop a car carrying members of a Mexican family anywhere on a California highway. The officer's wide authority allows him not only to question the right of every member of this family to be present in the United States but, in addition, to enforce a wide range of federal laws. Thus *la Migra* (the Border Patrol), whether operating in Chicago or Denver, Los Angeles or Fresno, or at the border checkpoints, may appear to the ordinary Mexican American as the rude, dangerously arbitrary power of a hostile government. Moreover, local law enforcement agencies can always put considerable pressure on Chicanos by merely threatening to summon the Patrol. A California highway patrolman reported his contact as follows:

> 4–28 male, age 27. Packing house worker (Mexican national) cited for weaving in roadway. Subject was apprehensive but aware of violation. Negative toward questions, asserted ignorance, unable to understand or speak English. Subject was then asked to show passport, but still showed negative compliance. He was then informed that the Border Patrol would be contacted for assistance. Subject became more open, a little English spoken. He then presented a California drivers license.[28]

In addition to this exceptional scope of authority, the Patrol has a long history of periodically stepped-up raids on Mexican American communities. Thus the deportations of the 1930s (those in Los Angeles were done by the Los Angeles County Board of Supervisors) were preceded by a massive increase in Patrol raids. During Operation Wetback (1950–1955) the Border Patrol's vastly increased manpower was responsible for 3.8 million deportations. In recent years about a half million deportable Mexican nationals are located every year. Such raids sometimes erupt into violence during the interrogation of a group of brown faces and leave pervasive fear in the communities. Today in the normal pursuit of its duties the Border Patrol still swoops down on garment factories in East Los Angeles and packing sheds in Sacramento; neighborhood bars and bus stops in Chicago: the hired hands, the brown faces are lined up for a routine citizenship check. These raids and interrogations are concentrated in areas that employ large numbers of unskilled Mexican workers and in important transportation centers. Greyhound buses heading north have been routinely stopped and checked 50 miles from the border. In

28 Henry T. Levesque, "Ethnic Groups and the Police Officer" (unpublished ms.).

1973 the Patrol reports questioning more than one million bus riders, more than five million passengers in automobiles, and more than two million pedestrians. (Of course this figure includes persons questioned at border entry points as well as inside the U.S.)

It is true that the traffic in illegal aliens is lucrative, and increasing, and that smugglers are neither friends of aliens nor of the Chicano communities. (See Chapter Three.) Many abuses are discovered routinely; every few weeks one is spectacular enough to be reported in the newspapers. This traffic is increasing. In the decade 1964 to 1973 the number of smugglers apprehended jumped from about 500 to more than 6,000. It is also true that among law enforcement agencies, the Border Patrol is notably scrupulous about staying within its mandate to enforce certain federal laws. Nonetheless the reputation of the Patrol is still profoundly negative.

It is paradoxical that its reputation is so bad because in terms of economic gain, modern Mexican Americans owe something to the efficiency of the Patrol. Illegal aliens always supplied a reservoir of cheap labor that tended to undercut national gains in certain badly paid occupations. Illegal aliens are sometimes used to break strikes. In fact, in past years there is some reason to suspect that lobbying by some industrial and farm interests helped keep the Border Patrol short of money and manpower.[29] Yet the immigration experience is so recent for so many Chicanos that the memories of the watchdogs of the border remain. It is very likely that the current wave of illegal immigrants (see Chapter Three) will increase the bitterness, at least in certain subcommunities. Only the American Chinese share such an experience with a federal law enforcement agency.

There is an odd paradox in this bitterness about both the Border Patrol and the Texas Rangers. As a rule, local law enforcement agencies (police and sheriff) vary more widely in their customary treatment of Chicanos, depending of course on the local taste for discrimination. But they are also far less likely to be responsive to political pressure than are state or federal agencies. The paradox lies in the special effects of the Rangers and the Patrol, a state agency and a federal agency, on the Chicano population in the Southwest.

OTHER INSTITUTIONS

Mexican experience with other official institutions is much like the experience of immigrant groups—with exceptions.

[29]Ernesto Galarza, *Merchants of Labor: The Mexican Bracero Story* (San Jose, Calif.: Rosicrucian Press, 1965), p. 61.

Three important circumstances in particular affected Mexicans: the border was always very close; Mexican immigrants came in large numbers relatively recently; and the Southwest was peculiarly lacking in either political or ameliorative institutions. The historical events include most notably the use of social welfare agencies to channel Mexicans back to Mexico during the Great Depression. This lesson in practical cooperation between welfare agencies and the power structure of local communities was not lost on Mexicans. On the other side, the very success of these "repatriations" reinforced two important Anglo stereotypes about Mexicans. Mexicans are "foreign"; Mexicans are "passive."

Officials in public agencies almost always comment on the passive "hard-to-reach" character of the Mexican approach to public agencies. The exact word varies but the problem is the same: Mexicans are not responsive; they withdraw; they are uninterested; they lack aggressiveness. Various cultural explanations are advanced (sometimes by Mexican leaders); but it is clear that Mexican Americans are also simply distrustful and suspicious. Ultimately the activities of almost any public agency depends upon the coercive power of the state, and Mexicans are sensitive to this power.

Studies of health agencies in the 1960s concluded that Mexican Americans often avoid using them because of cultural conflicts in the definitions of health, causes of disease, and means of treating disease. From these studies have come some important training programs for reaching the Mexican community. But most of the studies also note, sometimes almost in passing, that the public health worker is greeted in the Mexican American home just as is any other government worker, as somebody coming to cause trouble.

However things are changing. More Chicano professionals enter public service and can at least "speak the language of bureaucracy." One legacy of the federal poverty programs, the community action group is adding more power to the growing Mexican political effort, particularly in the larger cities. This mechanism of self-determination is far from complete but very likely may succeed in changing the meaning of government for the poor.

Whatever their effect in ameliorating poverty, at least one important side effect of the poverty programs was a period of friction with Blacks. It is an unfortunate reality that both Chicanos and Blacks must compete for the same federal, state, and local monies in many communities. Generally federal grants tended to reward groups and communities that were fairly well organized. The Black community in most southwestern cities had a distinct edge over the Mexican community not only in internal organization but in well-established lines of communication to Anglo institutions. Thus in Los Angeles the Black community seemed always to have gotten a disproportionate share of grants and projects. This disparity was obvious and became an incentive to Mexican American organizations.

In general the tendency of federal poverty programs was to fit new programs into a network of existing agencies. As might be expected, this tended to slow down or stifle entirely any movement for social change that might occur outside of existing institutions. For Mexican Americans it may very well be that the greatest accomplishment of OEO was that of focusing attention on Mexican problems and the sources of their discontent. This tendency is well illustrated in the case of the single largest federal project to relieve Mexican unemployment, Operation SER. Funded in 1966 by OEO as "Plans for Progress, Inc.," this group used the existing organizational structure of the League of United Latin American Citizens and the American G.I. Forum (See Chapter Eight) to create a giant antipoverty project. Operation SER once guided twenty-three separate community projects in five states (Arizona, California, Colorado, New Mexico, Texas). There is no doubt that the primary purpose of the project to find jobs and training "slots" for the chronically unemployed, was quite successful. The projects used existing lines of leadership, competed with Black groups in every city for entry-level jobs in training programs and private industry, and in general, were most successful when they approached private and public groups as an instrument of tokenism.

Existing agencies (public school systems, employment services, and so forth) used by SER were often so resistant to change that, in effect, SER was forced to either establish duplicate facilities or even counsel its trainees in the techniques of avoiding discriminatory practices at the very agencies that received federal money to cooperate. Neither the OEO nor the Department of Labor did much to fight the limitations of existing bureaucracies.

But learning to "speak the language of bureaucracy" brought some benefits, particularly in 1972 when the very existence of SER was threatened as a consequence of revenue-sharing—the "New Federalism." The new approach would allow state and local governments to determine manpower needs locally. In fact, SER had some evidence that they would use this license to continue the traditional discrimination. Two years of intensive lobbying in Washington followed. It was partly successful and even at one point brought the nation's Puerto Ricans and Cubans into coalition for a short time. A compromise was facilitated by the Administration troubles with the Watergate scandal and in the Comprehensive Employment and Training Act of 1973, the SER program was given a special preference. Perhaps more important: a certain amount of federal and centralized control was retained over the funds. It appears at this time that the SER central technical staff will remain, advising local Chicano groups on effective manpower planning, techniques of negotiation, research, and implementation. Some of the complex of other related federal activities which grew up around the local SER projects may also be retained.

As a large and entirely Mexican institution, SER is interesting and important. It is efficient; it deals in Washington with a complex of executive and legislative groups; and it reaches throughout large Mexican communities nearly everywhere in this country. Not only does its strong local base demonstrate some of the possibilities of responsive federal institutions, but it trains continuously new crops of bureaucrats. For the Chicano community generally, this is a most important harvest. Former SER officials now hold a variety of public and private jobs, some of them critical in dealing directly with the endemic problems of Mexican Americans and Anglo institutions.

In recent years it has become plain to Chicano leaders in the smallest *barrios* that the reaction of American institutions is the most important single factor in their economic and social survival. Of course, a completely separate community offers a romantic ideal—and this notion still appears among both Chicanos and Blacks, particularly the young. But the idea has faded since the 1960s—why, nobody could know, but perhaps the new and quite intoxicating success of some community-based institutions may be the true reason. Self-determination may be even more desirable than separatism.

It is this rather obvious failure of the institutions that has generated some interesting speculation about "colonialism." These are some recent attempts to apply a model of the "internal colony" to Mexican life in the United States. This approach suggests that the Mexican situation resembles a post-colonial structure of dominance that is analogous to the relationship of an overseas colony to the "mother country," somewhat in the manner of Algeria and France in past years. Economic, cultural, and political exploitation and dependency are emphasized. A considerable amount of controversy is the result of this idea and in many ways, its candid and realistic description of the situation has been very helpful.[30] Among other virtues, it tends to direct attention to the failure of

30 See Joan Moore, "Colonialism: the case of the Mexican Americans," *Social Problems* 17 (Spring 1970): 463–472; Mario Barrera et al., "The Barrio as an Internal Colony," in *People and Politics in Urban Society*, ed. H. Hahn (Beverly Hills, Calif.: Sage Publications, 1972), and Guillermo V. Flores, "Race and Culture in the Internal Colony: Keeping the Chicano in His Place," in *Structures of Dependency*, ed. Frank Bonilla and Robert Girling (Palo Alto, Calif.: Bonilla and Gerling, 1973) for variations in this approach.

American institutions and to some of the consequences of institutional racism.

Probably nothing is more important to any American minority than the reaction of American institutions to their needs. These needs are usually not special nor even unreasonable. In fact, meeting these needs are the basic tasks of the institutions charged with such essentials as law enforcement, education, and vocational training. In the case of the Chicano population, the inescapable conclusion is that the response has been poor. It continues to be poor. Sometimes it is utterly destructive. On the other hand, measuring as carefully as possible some of the shifts in response from about 1950 to 1970, it is plain that important changes have been made. The direction and nature of the changes suggest the enormous adaptation to the future that will be needed by the institutions serving Mexican Americans.

It should be plain by now that Mexican Americans are a complex minority. They live in a wide variety of situations in a region of the United States that is changing with great speed. To be sure, they share with other minorities the problems of poverty and certain strains attendant upon a slow and painful emergence into participation in urban American life. At the same time they reflect some of the original diversity of the Southwest of an earlier age.

For example, many Mexicans still live in the uplands of the upper Rio Grande, in an isolation and bitterness that have enveloped them for a century. This atmosphere reached a point of tension strong enough in 1965 to produce a minor rebellion led by Reies Tijerina. (See Chapter Eight.) Moreover, many Mexicans still live in the small towns of borderland Texas, although many of the children are drifting away to the cities to earn a living. These traditional patterns also include hand labor by Mexicans who still leave their homes in Texas every spring to join the migrant farm workers in the fields of California and the Middle West.[1]

Thus it is that when "Mexican family life" or "Mexican community life" is discussed, we must capture and dissect something that is living, changing, and anything but unitary. It is diverse statistically, historically, and regionally. This diversity is not even

Family and Community: Stability and Change

a simple matter of generational change, as we shall see. In this chapter we take up the familiar forms of social differentiation: generation, social class, and community type. We will examine the varieties of meaning of each and the significance of each in general processes of change, particu-

---

[1] See Lyle and Magdaline Shannon, *Minority Migrants in the Urban Community: Mexican-American and Negro Adjustment to Industrial Society* (Beverly Hills, Calif.: Sage Publications, 1973) for a comparison of patterns of adaptation of Texas Mexicans and southern Negroes to life in Racine, Wisconsin; and the comparable set of studies conducted by Harvey Choldin and Grafton Trout of Mexican Americans settling in rural Michigan. (Harvey M. Choldin and Grafton D. Trout, *Mexican Americans in Transition: Migration and Employment in Michigan Cities* [East Lansing, Michigan: Rural Manpower Center, Agricultural Experiment Station, Michigan State University, July, 1969].) "Dropping out" of the migrant stream in these Midwestern communities is not a new phenomenon, but it is perhaps an increasingly important one. Wisconsin's permanent Chicano residents, many dropping out of the stream, are significant enough to have successfully demanded gubernatorial attention in 1971.

larly of change in the family. We will see that linear or straight-line change (for example, from first to third generation, from rural to urban setting, from lower-class to middle-class status) does not simply pertain to the Mexicans.

GENERATION: A QUESTION OF PLACE

Generation by generation, immigrant families and their descendants gradually acquire the values and enter into social relationships that make them indistinguishable from the larger society. Leaving aside the question of color, many Mexican Americans have acculturated over generations much as other immigrants have done and learned to live with their environment—although there are some important qualifications and exceptions.

The most important exception is the different rates at which generations change in different parts of the American Southwest. Thus the bigger cities tend to offer a more open milieu than smaller cities, but even here there is variation. A second generation Chicano in Los Angeles is generally more skilful in coping with his environment, of "surviving," than is a second-generation person in many Texas cities. As a consequence, generations of Mexican immigrants are difficult to compare from one city to another. The social milieu of some agricultural towns, on the other hand, is so repressive and offers so little opportunity for economic or social movement that change from one generation to another is almost imperceptible.

The second exception is a group of pre-conquest Spanish Americans who live in northern New Mexico and southern Colorado. They follow traditional occupations, speak English with difficulty, if at all, and appear to be more "Mexican" than even some of the new immigrants from Mexico. In this area generations have meant changes and adaptation, but this adaptation was not an adjustment to urban American values: these people adjusted first to a colonial society hard-pressed by hostile Indians, then to an isolated and alienated minority status under the first United States governments, and then to a set of changed economic circumstances that threatened their very livelihood. No great pressure for accommodation of urban American relationships and values has yet appeared among these people.[2]

2See Florence Rockwood Kluckhohn and Fred L. Strodbeck, *Variations in Value Orientations* (Evanston, Ill. and Elmsford, N.Y.: Row, Peterson and Company, 1961), for an account of traditional life in such a village. Note also Kluckhohn's account of the changes she observed in this village culture between her first research trip in the late 1930s and her later visit in the 1950s. Of these changes, she concludes (p. 257):

Any understanding of changes by generation must always be qualified by the milieu in which they are taking place. Accordingly, any intra-United States migration among Mexican Americans is of great importance. We will see later in this chapter that such geographical mobility, indeed, is taking place on a large scale. In effect, this mobility leads many of the more energetic and ambitious away from the small towns. As a result, the Anglo outsider would discern little or no change in the small cities and small towns of the Southwest. The local structure of these towns may seem unchanged, however, the *total* situation of this American minority may be radically changed. An analogous example is the American Black. The great exodus of Blacks from the South offers the outsider very little visible evidence of change in small southern towns. In reality, the movement has meant both important changes in small southern towns and drastic change for American Blacks on the whole.

Consequently the meaning of generations to Mexican Americans is very much a matter of geographical location. The significance of a boyhood in Kingsville, Texas, or El Paso strikes Mexicans at once. Third generation Chicanos from either of those towns are different from those reared in Los Angeles, as well as from each other. Among the Spanish Americans of New Mexico and Colorado, the consciousness of generational differences takes a different form. Here people can distinguish families that entered the Southwest with the *first* wave of Mexican immigration following the Oñate expedition of 1598 and the "late" waves of the seventeenth and eighteenth centuries. These distinctions are recorded,[3] memorized, and passed along from generation to generation. For a New Mexican, a name like Baca, Chávez, Roybal, Griego, Gallegos, Tafoya, or Montoya evokes a particular lineage, even if the family founder was hanged for thievery. On the other hand, to most outsiders such distinctions are obscured by the efforts of these charter-member *manitos* to distinguish themselves from the newer immigrants from Mexico, whom they called *surumatos,* in a clear-cut division by "generation."

Something of the Mexican interest in Mexican first families has been adopted by an Anglo society that in many areas is still short of a hundred

---

There can be no turning back by these people, given the fact that they are firmly held within the borders of the United States and are increasingly subjected to dominant Anglo American culture as one by one the small villages like Atrisco decay and the inhabitants of them move off to urban centers. . . . Two alternative end results appear possible. One is that of a greater acculturation of the group. . . . The other prospect is a fairly thorough-going disorganization. . . . At the moment the first of the two prospects seems the more likely.

[3] See Fray Angelico Chávez, *Origins of New Mexico Families* (Santa Fe: The Historical Society of New Mexico, 1954), for a compilation of family histories arranged by "wave."

years of settlement. It is part of the occasional local obeisance to "our Spanish heritage." Thus Santa Barbara, California (to name one of many such cities) still puts on an elaborate *fiesta* every year, which pays homage to the original "Spanish" settlers. Los Angeles is reverential to its del Valles, Ortegas, and descendants of the Dominguez-Watson family—only a few of the names in an elite group calling itself "First Century Families." In general, however, the California descendants of old families intermarried so heavily with Anglo Americans and newer Mexican arrivals that it is extremely difficult to find any "pure" descendants.

Another example of this attempt to establish old family lines is provided by the "Canary Islanders" of San Antonio, Texas. Shortly after San Antonio was founded in 1691 one group of settlers from the Canary Islands was given the equivalent of a patent of nobility and declared *hijos dalgo* (aristocrats) by the Spanish Crown.[4] Ever since, the Canary Islanders have distinguished themselves from the "Mexicans" around them, and today they are a significant segment of upper-status "Spanish" in San Antonio. The more general symbolic significance of this pattern of claiming old-line ancestry is indicated by the fact that during a household survey of San Antonio a very dark, very poor man proudly told the interviewer that he, too, was a "Canary Islander." Thus in many smaller cities as well, the actual or *soi-disant* descendants of such "old families" are among the elite, although they are also among the lower classes. But the lineages are so mixed that a "pure-blood" old-line group can scarcely be said to exist outside New Mexico and Colorado. Here the original population was large enough from the first years for marriage to be kept largely within the original group.

FAMILY AND CLASS
IN THE AGRICULTURAL TOWNS

In the small towns of south Texas, Arizona, central California, and other parts of the Southwest, visitors often express shock at the way Mexican Americans live. The standard Anglo apology, is, "Oh, you should see the way they live in old Mexico!" As noted in Chapter One, it is usually assumed that the benchmark for measuring Mexican American progress is Mexico. Anglos do not seem aware of the assumptions behind this comparison nor would it occur to them to compare Black homes with African huts.

[4] Sister Frances Jerome Woods, *Mexican Ethnic Leadership in San Antonio, Texas* (Washington, D.C.: Catholic University of America Press, 1949), p. 12. She gives an interesting historical analysis of the social structure of the Mexican American community of San Antonio.

In part, the appearance of the Mexican *barrios* or lower-class neighborhoods often helps along this southwestern double standard. The poor oftentimes live in shacks or adobe structures (depending on the area) that resemble those of old Mexico. Sometimes the yards are bare and sun-baked. Sometimes there are a few cacti and sometimes there is a profusion of flowers. The residents of these *barrios* are largely Spanish-speaking or speak a reasonably stable mixture of Spanish and English. The community depends upon a restricted range of jobs. There are typically a few storekeepers, gas station operators, priests, teachers, attorneys, and doctors (many living outside the *barrio*) who mediate between the laboring majority of the Mexican community and the larger Anglo system. Nearly always these towns look as if there had been no important changes since 1910. This date is not picked at random; the town of Roma in the lower Rio Grande valley of Texas, for example, was used as a site for the filming of the movie *Viva Zapata!* Presumably there had been very little change in Roma from the rural Mexico of Zapata's day. Although Roma now boasts an international bridge over the Rio Grande, not far downstream one can see little flat-bottom boats used to ferry people and freight across the river. And when the cities of Laredo and Nuevo Laredo, a bit further upstream, celebrate their annual *charro* day, horses are still swum across the river (in violation of custom regulations on the importation of animals) just as they swam in the time of General John J. Pershing.

These *barrio* areas of the small agricultural towns are among the poorest ethnic enclaves in the United States, but this is not as important as the fact that they also act to segregate the poorest Mexicans into visible communities: the more energetic move out; middle-class Mexican Americans (the only group that might act in some manner to modify the Anglo image of the *barrio*) move out into a less segregated part of the community as quickly and as permanently as possible. Others leave the town. (Several *barrios* in the Southwest have the name of "Sal Si Puedes" or "Get Out If You Can"—indicating the local opinion of such a traditional neighborhood.) Thus the Anglo stereotypes are perpetuated by the nature of the *barrio* itself.

The face of the *barrio* may remain substantially unchanged, but there is some internal change. There is some acculturation, although it comes very slowly. Some portion of the developing middle class may remain in the town, although such persons tend to move away. However, the most important change cannot be seen at all. This is the movement of the most energetic, most talented, and perhaps even the luckiest *barrio* residents to larger cities in the same area or to large cities in another area.

In this process the most traditional Mexicans tend to be left behind in the poorest areas. Here traditional pattterns are functional and instead of being surprised by their persistence, we should realize that if traditional life did not exist it would have to be invented. Faith healers are far cheaper than good medical service; priests cost less than an attorney; and it is easier for a migrant family who needs a loan to begin a season on the migrant worker stream to get it from a storekeeper than from a bank. However, it must be pointed out that all of these traditional features of Mexican American life that are taken as quaint or picturesque are associated in one way or another not only with Mexican Americans but with any ethnic group that lives in poverty. Formal resources, such as social workers, are scarce. In Texas, for example, social workers are few because the state of Texas allocates a pittance for social welfare programs. Even the immigration *notarios,* a notable feature of the Los Angeles Mexican "downtown," are almost missing in south Texas; most Mexicans in trouble with immigration authorities in south Texas simply cannot afford *notarios.*[5] In general then, there are few formal resources by which people can become adapted to life in a larger society.

From the existing ethnographic studies it appears that the family is the most important facet of life for Mexican Americans in south Texas as well as in other traditionalistic poverty enclaves. This is not only the immediate family of husband, wife, and children but the extended family of relatives on both sides. It is the main focus of obligations and also a source of emotional and economic support as well as recognition for accomplishment. According to these studies, family roles within the nuclear family unit are clear cut; the mother is seen ideally as an embodiment of the Holy Mother. Her daughters are expected to follow suit in their purity, their dedication to the welfare of the males in the family, and in the warmth of their relationship to each other. The woman is to be protected by the man, who must face the vicissitudes and hazards of the outside world. His masculinity (*machismo*) is of great importance; he demonstrates this by physical and sexual prowess, the latter even outside his marriage. His relations with the world outside the family are filtered through other close relationships with a group of friends. These are age peers who depend upon each other for work, pleasure, and various kinds of emotional support.

From this pool of friends the family will draw the godparents of its children. Godparentage (*compadrazgo*) in this sort of traditional sys-

---

[5] A *notario* is a lawyer in Mexico; in the United States, many notaries public upgrade their status in the eyes of their Mexican clientele by a simple and misleading translation. The small towns of south Texas figure in two reports on Hidalgo County: William Madsen's more general treatment in *Mexican Americans of South Texas* (New York: Holt, Rinehart and Winston, 1964), and Arthur Rubel's analysis of one town, *Across the Tracks* (Austin: University of Texas Press, 1966).

tem is a method of knitting the community together normatively and of formalizing the informal ties of friendship. The same system of godparentage is found in Mediterranean countries as well as Latin America.

A man and the godfather of his child become *compadres*. (The *compadre* relationship may also be a way of honoring a person superior in status: for example, a boss or *patrón*.) This formalization of the bonds of friendship into a pseudo-kinship relationship is a reliable indicator of the importance of kinship ties to the Mexican Americans. They can be so important that they form the prototype of all significant relationships. It is, in fact, more important as a tie between two age peers than it is as a religious belief or as a tie between godparent and godchild. (As a religious act, it symbolizes formally a promise by the godparent that the child will be brought up as a Christian should anything happen to the child's parents.)

Within the family there is a hierarchical allocation of responsibilities from the head of the household down through the males. Women are sheltered; it is felt that their most meaningful relationships should be within the family. Ideally, their social relationships and recreation should consist solely of visits to cousins and other relatives. They are expected to gossip, to cook the traditional dishes (many requiring a vast amount of hand labor), to look after many children of all ages, and to attend to the needs of their men.

In such communities relations with neighbors, however, can be fraught with hostility. The tight interdependence of the family does not encompass the neighbor, who may, in fact, wish you ill. The fear of witches is not unknown in traditional parts of Texas. It is more likely than not that the "witch" afflicting you with physical or emotional problems is a fairly close neighbor who may envy you (*envidia*). Warmth inside the family and hostility to those outside the family are almost elements of survival in a very crowded area. These are people who live in poverty. Things often go wrong; people get sick for no obvious reason. Houses in these communities are close together; there is often much less room than in the ordinary middle-class suburb. Small mischiefs—a man staring at a neighbor's wife, fruit stolen from a tree, dogs digging up the ground; these are the endless irritations that divide neighbors. But it is also true in the Mexican American *barrios* that many members of extended kin groups build homes next to one another, which might even be called "family compounds." They permit a man to surround himself and his family with people who are close and trustworthy.

Many of the same elements are found in Mexican middle-class life, especially in small, isolated Texas towns. This isolation continues to a remarkable degree. Although the middle-class Mexican in these towns visits the physician rather than the *curandera*, the attorney rather than the priest, and sends his children to a local college or to a state college some distance away, he remains in a basically traditional environment. He interacts little with Anglos—or even with Mexican Americans outside his own kinship and peer group. It is possible and not unusual for professional Mexican Americans in such towns to complete four years of college education at, for example, the University of Texas at Austin, or El Paso, without ever mingling socially with non–Chicanos. Although the existence of such separate social worlds often has been attributed solely to prejudice, there is also little doubt that it reflects a preference for what is seen as a distinctive style of sociability.

It is to some extent valid to describe this world as a caste system:[6] Mexicans and Anglos, sometimes living in the same yet different towns, each with a distinct and separate class system, dealing with each other through intermediaries in both ethnic groups, and with only a minimum of "off-the-job" social interaction. In many respects, in fact, the relationship of Mexican and Anglo in the many small agricultural communities of south Texas and other parts of the Southwest are like the relationship classically portrayed by Davis and Gardner between Negro and white in the Mississippi town described in *Deep South*.[7] There is even a rather frightening counterpart to the Ku Klux Klan. For decades the Texas Rangers terrorized the Mexican Americans of the Rio Grande valley,[8] and even today, although they are reduced in numbers, *los rinches* are still used to "handle" Mexicans. A recent use of the Texas Rangers was, appropriately, during a strike of Mexican melon workers near Rio Grande City.[9]

[6]The caste-like characteristics of small Mexican American *barrios* in agricultural towns have been explicitly noted by Walter Goldschmidt, in a study of a central California town, *As You Sow* (New York: Harcourt, Brace and World, 1947), as well as in several unpublished dissertations. Caste-like conditions in Corpus Christi in the 1920s are portrayed by Paul S. Taylor, *An American-Mexican Frontier* (Chapel Hill, University of North Carolina Press, 1934). The very special situation in New Mexico is analyzed by Donovan Senter, in terms reminiscent of the class-caste distinction, in "Acculturation among New Mexican Villagers in Comparison to Adjustment Patterns of other Spanish-Speaking Americans," *Rural Sociology* 10 (March 1945): 31–47.

[7] Allison Davis, Burleigh and Mary Gardner, *Deep South* (Chicago: University of Chicago Press, 1941). Rodolfo Alvarez develops the idea of caste in a more general way in "The Psycho-Historical and Socioeconomic Development of the Chicano Community in the United States," *Social Science Quarterly* 53 (March 1973): 920–942.

[8] Many of these stories of terrorization are given in Acuna, *Occupied America*.

[9] See Walter Prescott Webb, *The Texas Rangers* (Boston: Houghton Mifflin Company, 1935), for the story of the Rangers and their origins in border warfare. Even this account, which, though careful and objective, is generally something of a glorification of the group, recounts many stories of Ranger callousness and brutality toward Mexicans in the border areas. A state investigation of the Rangers, initiated by a Mexican American legislator, resulted in the reduction of the Rangers to a token force.

Thus it is in the Texas counties with the very large ranches that the analogy with southern Black-white life is most striking. Such a comparison is valid historically because the plantation model was the Texas ideal. It is not quite valid because of the position of upper-status Mexicans in some of the towns and because of the peculiar relationship sometimes found between upper-status Mexican Americans and upper-status Mexicans in Mexico. In many south Texas towns, middle-class Mexicans are indeed in much the same position as are middle-class, small-town southern Blacks. They maintain the middle-class style with fervor and with a conviction that it *is* a good life. But the towns of the Rio Grande valley are somewhat special. Here upper-class Mexican Americans sometimes intermarry with Mexican families across the river. Professional men sometimes keep memberships in Mexican country clubs. Thus the caste-like plantation system breaks down; as professionals or the descendants of original settlers, upper-status Mexican Americans can establish claims to prestige that are as valid in the Anglo system as among Chicanos. Further, in recent years south Texas has begun to send Mexican American legislators to the state legislature, as do many predominantly small town districts in New Mexico. One county in Colorado is known locally as "the Banana Republic," so great is the degree of Mexican political control there. The first Mexican American federal judge, Reynaldo Garza, comes from Raymondsville in south Texas. New Mexico has regularly returned Mexican senators to Washington: the well-known Dennis Chavez, and later, Joseph Montoya.

Thus the analogy between southern Blacks and whites and southwestern Mexicans and Anglos cannot be sustained. The Mexicans of south Texas are not all quite in the same subordinate positions as are the Blacks of Mississippi, although it should be recalled that in the Rio Grande valley of Texas it is the middle class rather than the total group that exerts a measure of political power and control in a few areas.

VARIATIONS ON A THEME: MEXICANS AND SMALL TOWNS

Even among the small traditional communities there are important differences. A few of these are almost entirely Mexican and control is in the hands of the Mexican middle class. A larger number are dominated by an Anglo power structure. The domination in these areas can be paternalistic or it can be suppressive; doubtless it is often a combination of the two. It is surprising to find some of these towns and small cities in the rich agricultural areas of California as well as the poverty pockets of rural Texas, but California's Imperial, Coachella, and San Joaquin valleys have many such towns.[10]

Many of these communities seem to have been completely bypassed by the enormous growth and expansion of California. Here the local elite are the large agricultural growers. Oddly and significantly, many of the growers are relative newcomers to the United States themselves. In Delano, the focus of a protracted and bitter agricultural strike, the growers are largely Slavic and Italian immigrants who are quite new to this kind of entrepreneurship.[11] But whatever their personal status, both the new and old large-scale employers of Mexican agricultural labor feel themselves embattled and threatened by César Chávez' attempts to organize agricultural workers, something which has never been successful in the past. Some employers attempt to play a paternal role and to help their laborers settle and accept some of the public opportunities available in California. But even more of them simply assume the present inferiority of their Mexican help. In this respect the power structure of these small communities (Delano is only one among them) is little changed from the California agricultural community of a generation ago or from today's small south Texas towns.

There are, however, two important changes, both of them in attitude. First, the climate of both the federal and the state governments for unlimited exploitation of Mexican labor is distinctly unfriendly. Second, Mexican labor itself has new leadership (most notably César Chávez), which is thoroughly familiar with some of the techniques of modern communications, with the climate of national opinion, and with methods of making use of potential political allies. These advantages in climate of opinion and in leadership were never before available to groups of Mexican American laboring men. The change is so crucial that it can be felt even in Texas. Thus, although Texas has a right-to-work law, some beginnings have been made in the unionization of Mexican agricultural labor, even in south Texas.

10 See Goldschmidt, *As You Sow*, for a Central Valley town in California; Margaret Clark, *Health in the Mexican American Culture* (Berkeley and Los Angeles: University of California Press, 1959), for a study of a very poor *barrio* in San Jose, which is within commuting distance of San Francisco. Recently, Theodore W. Parsons, Jr. completed a dissertation study of a small community close to Palo Alto, home of Stanford University, which is strikingly reminiscent of the south Texas towns ("Ethnic Cleavage in a California School" Ph.D. diss., Stanford University, 1965).

11 John Gregory Dunne, *Delano* (New York: Farrar, Straus & Giroux, 1967), presents an interesting journalistic account of the strike and the community. Ernesto Galarza, *Merchants of Labor* (San Jose, Calif.: Rosicrucian Press, 1965) presents a longer perspective on agricultural labor in California. Galarza was active in several efforts to form an agricultural workers' union, and his book is written from the point of view of a participant.

Of the smaller communities we know comparatively little. Much of what we "know" (like so much anthropological knowledge) concerns norms and beliefs: we know relatively little about actual day-to-day behavior and even less about the range of possible variation in this behavior. We do not know as simple and as important a thing as the most gross differences in the behavior of children reared in all-Mexican towns and in partly Mexican towns. It seems reasonable to expect there would be important differences in, for example, identity between the two groups. A poor Mexican child in an all-Mexican town would be lower class; in a predominantly Anglo town, he would also be a "Mex." We would also expect significant differences between the two groups in patterns of neighboring, degree of dependence on the kinship structure, and degree of dependence on other Mexican Americans. At this stage it is only possible to make reasonable guesses and to point out the complexities of Mexican American life even in small towns. The phrase "even in small towns" is appropriate because the complexities are even greater in large cities, where most Mexican Americans now live.

MEXICANS IN THE CITIES

We can see, for a beginning, that the degree of residential segregation of Mexican Americans throughout the largest cities of the Border States varies far more than it does for Blacks (Chapter Four). This variation in segregation has important social consequences. One of the indicators of assimilation of any immigrant group into American society is its degree of segregation. In general the new immigrants (from southern and eastern Europe) are more segregated than are old stock (from northern Europe).[12] The fact that patterns of Mexican American segregation vary among cities of the Southwest shows clearly that the usual paradigms of American assimilation of ethnic groups do not apply to this population; that is, segregation does not decline systematically with length of residence in the U.S. as with European ethnics, nor is it uniform as with Blacks.

[12] See Stanley Lieberson, *Ethnic Patterns in American Cities* (New York: Free Press, 1963) for an analysis of segregation patterns of various foreign stock populations. Mexican Americans are not included in his analysis, but their segregation in the Southwest is contrasted with Black-white segregation by Joan W. Moore and Frank G. Mittelbach. This material is condensed in Grebler, et al., *The Mexican American People.* Though there is no comprehensive ethnographic account of Mexican American life in the large cities of a generation ago, Carey McWilliams describes Mexican Americans in Los Angeles, in *North from Mexico* (Philadelphia: J. B. Lippincott Company, 1949). Ruth Tuck's fine study of San Bernardino, a citrus-growing community some 75 miles east of Los Angeles, was done during the same period. Interestingly, that large California city appears to be remarkably like a small Texas town in regard to Mexican American life. See *Not with the Fist* (New York: Harcourt, Brace and World, 1946).

Because of this extreme variation between cities, we can infer that the rate of change of segregation is different among cities for Mexican Americans. For example, Mexican Americans are escaping the *barrios* much more slowly in Odessa, Texas, than in Los Angeles. This rate of change is not itself a steady, even move toward acculturation or assimilation. As shown in Chapter Four it seems to depend not only upon changes inside the Mexican community but more importantly, upon changes in the larger community. Los Angeles has more people of Mexican descent than any other city in North America except Mexico City or (recently) Guadalajara. Los Angeles has grown enormously since the late 1920s when Mexicans first began to appear in large numbers. In the 40 years from 1928 to 1968, Los Angeles achieved strong economic as well as population growth. A regional trading city became an economic center of national and international importance. Slowly and with many setbacks Mexicans and other newcomers to the city were caught up in its expansion. (The setbacks peculiar to Los Angeles were the Mexican repatriations of the early Depression years and the serious and recurrent clashes with the police highlighted by the "zoot suit" riots of the early 1940s.) But even throughout the years of setback, Mexicans were carried along by the tide. Increasing numbers moved into the middle class and out of the *barrios*. Sometimes the movement was very much like the traditional invasion-succession cycles familiar to students of ethnic ecology in Eastern cities. Some *barrios* expanded at their periphery and filled in the non-Mexican spaces; and thus the new neighborhood became an expanded *barrio* with a scattered residue of non-Mexican residents and institutions. Again, as freeways cut through Mexican American areas in Los Angeles, whole neighborhoods appear to have been transplanted to other locations. More commonly, prosperous Mexican Americans would move into completely new housing developments as these new tracts began to fill the brushlands of Los Angeles county after World War II. Thus by 1965 almost no elementary school in the vast sprawl of Greater Los Angeles did not have at least some Mexican American children.[13]

Of course, this school distribution did not mean equal-status interaction. Moreover, even if Mexican Americans were dispersed throughout southern California, in 1965 there were still many thousands of Mexican Americans locked into, and moving into *barrios* as in south Texas. Consequently, in Los Angeles being "Mexican" can mean many different things.

The Mexican American who lives in a *barrio* is likely to be different from the individual who leaves an area of ethnic concentration to live permanently in Anglo areas. The terminology to describe the two kinds

---

[13] See California State Department of Education, *Racial and Ethnic Survey of California's Public Schools. Part One: Distribution of Pupils,* 1967.

of people comes from Alex Simirenko.[14] He uses the word "Frontier" for the predominantly non-ethnic areas and the term "Colony" for the predominantly ethnic areas. Simirenko studied Russian-Americans, and he noted that the Russian Colonists lived in the area immediately around the Russian Orthodox church; here remained most of the traditionalists. Choosing to remain in the Colony does not mean that an ethnic person is not occupationally mobile. Nor does choosing to live in the ethnic Frontier mean that one *is* mobile. Middle-class individuals may live in Colonies and poor people may live in Frontiers, although generally there is a close association, as one would expect, between poverty and the Colony and higher income and the Frontier. If we apply this idea to Chicanos in the mid-1960s, we see that the difference between Colonists and Frontiersmen is that the former is *more likely* to use other Mexican Americans as both a membership group and as a reference group. On the other hand, the Frontiersman is *more likely* to use Anglos. The value of the phrase "more likely" varies from city to city. The deciding factor apparently is the openness of the city to ethnic movement, as shown in Table 6–1. Here we list data for Los Angeles, Albuquerque, and San Antonio in approximate order of expected openness. We see that Mexican American adults and children living in Colonies in all three cities are far less likely than Frontiersmen to have predominantly Anglo friends and workmates, but the differences between cities are remarkable. Mexicans in the Colonies of Los Angeles are almost as likely as Mexicans in the Frontier of San Antonio to have Anglo friends and associates. Once again we can see how importantly assimilation depends upon the degree of acceptance in the larger society. General statements about Mexican American life in large cities must be based upon individual cities as a first step in dealing with this very complex pattern.

CLASS AND MOBILITY

The vast majority of Mexican immigrants were extremely poor, and although a large proportion of them remain poor, many have definitely been occupationally mobile, compared to their fathers. More mobility occurred (Chapter Four) where there was opportunity for education and where there were more and better jobs. How, then, has this change affected Mexican Americans in terms of social class?

[14] He used these terms in a study of second generation Russians in a Midwest city. See *Pilgrims, Colonists and Frontiersmen* (New York and London: Free Press and Collier-Macmillan, 1964). Paul Sheldon gives a portrait of Mexican American leaders of Los Angeles in "Community Participation and the Emerging Middle Class," in *La Raza: Forgotten Americans*, ed. Julian Samora (Notre Dame, Ind.: University of Notre Dame Press, 1966).

TABLE 6–1

PERCENTAGE OF MEXICAN AMERICAN RESPONDENTS HAVING PREDOMINANTLY
OR ALL ANGLO ASSOCIATES, FRONTIERSMEN AND COLONISTS,
LOS ANGELES, SAN ANTONIO AND ALBUQUERQUE, 1965–1967

| | City and Residental Area | | | | | | |
| | Los Angeles | | | San Antonio | | Albuquerque | |
	Frontier	Intermediate	Colony	Frontier	Colony	Frontier	Colony
Work associates	70%	47%	39%	41%	22%	55%	11%
Boss	84	81	73	73	29	54	11
Personal friends	29	11	7	12	1	59	23
Children's friends	66	35	12	34	6	20	0
Children's schoolmates	70	35	15	34	8	21	5
Total number (= 100%)	248	221	254	113	424	51	59

Source: Data for Los Angeles and San Antonio are derived from probability
samples of Mexican American households drawn by the Mexican American
Study Project, University of California at Los Angeles, and for Albuquerque by Operation SER, Los Angeles, California. We are grateful to both
organizations for making the data available.

To be "upper class" in the American Southwest always meant to be
"Spanish," even long before American settlers arrived. It is still true today
in Mexico and in any South American or Latin American country with
a large population of native Indians. (Thus the myth of "pure blood"
was not invented in the United States.) Mexicans of mixed Spanish-Indian
blood or of pure Indian ancestry have long suffered from discrimination
and exploitation in their own country. When the United States acquired
the southwestern territories the elite were "Spanish," and the Spanish-
surname settlers were almost entirely of *mestizo* (mixed Indian-Spanish)
stock. These were both *mestizos* from Mexico and persons who had become *mestizo* by intermarrying with Indians in the United States. The
new American settlers accepted the Mexican status system on its own
terms, and it matched their own biases. Most notably, they accepted the
"Spanish" as Spanish and as pure-blood persons entitled to superior
position. Thus before and after American sovereignty, socially mobile
individuals felt pressure to cease being "Mexican" and to become "Spanish." The distinction may appear to be absurd (often the color of the
"Spanish" person is notably far from white) but historically it has been
exceedingly important to Mexican Americans. (A thousand examples are
available. To cite just one: some Mexican restaurants in the Southwest
still attempt to legitimize themselves by advertising a "Spanish" cuisine.)

Because Spanish persons were acceptable, social class mobility was
possible even when there was strong race prejudice against Mexicans.

Once acceptable in a race-conscious society, the "Spanish" individuals did not hesitate to depreciate the claims of *arrivistes,* no matter how fictional their own claim to status. The establishment of such a "Spanish" upper-status group in new southwestern cities that had no firmly established elite group is a remarkable (and almost unnoticed) fiction of modern Mexican American life. In some cities this need for a fictitious "Spanish" mask for the middle class did not last long, yet it still persists in other cities, reflecting the status anxieties of the local Mexican American community and the prejudices of the Anglos. It may be that some combination of increased numbers and occupational security along with changes in the social climate makes it less necessary to deny Mexican ancestry. Now that some business firms and colleges try to recruit Chicanos, the status situation may be somewhat reversed in some cities.

It appears that in many parts of the Southwest (where rapid change has outpaced the evolution of a stable social class system with a clearly defined style of life) many Mexican Americans in middle-class occupations view the occupational system rather instrumentally. There seem, in fact, to be two different types of mobility.

The first is mobility as a means of obtaining enough money to establish higher material levels for the enjoyment of a manner of life that may reflect the ideals of one's childhood—that is, with Mexican associates, in a Mexican environment, and quite familistic. Status rewards are to be taken within a Mexican environment. Hence, such mobility might tend to expose the mobile person less to Anglos in work (even if it is middle-class work) and to less education (or possibly, to education inside the *barrio* context). Such people may, simply, not know how very much they resemble middle-class Anglo Americans in many values and attitudes. (The anxiety of such a Mexican American in a middle-class Anglo context cannot be ignored; he does not know the norms of sociability, and worries as much about proper behavior as a mobile person from any other ethnic group would.)

The second type of mobility is an experience that alienates Mexican Americans from other Mexican Americans. A typical pattern is that of dissociation from Mexican friends and schoolmates in high school in order to move increasingly in Anglo circles in high school, in college, and in work. It may end in anonymity and, perhaps, then a conscious decision for reidentification with Mexican Americans and even a conscious decision to enter or return to the *barrio.*

Intermarriage rates between Anglos and Mexican Americans give us some information on mobility (Table 6–2). Again, they emphasize the factors of time and place. From Table 6–2 it is evident that there was a slowly increasing rate of intermarriage through the 1960s. It is also probable that the more "open" environments show more intermarriage

TABLE 6–2

ENDOGAMY RATES: PERCENTAGE OF MEXICAN AMERICANS
MARRYING WITHIN THE GROUP

City and Date	Endogamy Rate [a]
Albuquerque, 1929–1940	92
Los Angeles, 1924–1933	91
San Antonio, 1940–1955	90
Los Angeles, 1963	75
Albuquerque, 1964	81
Albuquerque, 1971	87
San Antonio, 1971	76

	MA Grooms	MA Brides
Los Angeles, 1963: Mexican born	87	80
U.S. born of Mexican parents	77	74
U.S. born of U.S. parents	69	68
Los Angeles, 1963: high-status occupations	60	49
medium-status occupations	78	72
low-status occupations	79	80

Sources: Albuquerque, 1929–1940, derived from Carolyn Zeleny, "Relations
between the Spanish-Americans and the Anglo-Americans in New Mexico"
(Ph.D. diss., Yale University, 1944).
Los Angeles, 1924–1933, derived from Constantine Panunzio, "Intermar-
riage in Los Angeles, 1924–1933," *American Journal of Sociology*, 47 (1942):
690–701.
San Antonio, 1940–1955, derived from Benjamin S. Bradshaw, "Some
Demographic Aspects of Marriage" (Master's thesis, University of Texas,
1960).
Los Angeles, 1963, from Frank G. Mittelbach and Joan W. Moore, "Ethnic
Endogamy—the Case of Mexican Americans," *American Journal of So-
ciology* (July 1968): 50–62.
Albuquerque, 1964, derived from Nancie L. González, *The Spanish Ameri-
cans of New Mexico*, Advance Report 9 (University of California, Los
Angeles: Mexican-American Study Project, 1967).
Albuquerque and San Antonio, 1971 from Edward Murguía and Parker
Frisbie, "Trends in Mexican American Intermarriage: Recent Findings
in Perspective."
[a] Rates for *individuals*. If we had calculated rates on the base of marriages
rather than persons, a higher proportion of *marriages* involving Mexican
Americans would be exogamous, or with non-Mexicans.

at any given time. The Los Angeles material is presented in two ways:
first, to show that generation affects intermarriage. In Los Angeles of
1963 the Mexican-born were the least likely of all Mexican Americans
to marry Anglos. Children of Mexican parentage were the next most
likely, and Mexican Americans with parents born in the United States
were the most likely to marry Anglos. However, the Mexican born generation of Los Angeles is as likely as all Mexicans in San Antonio to
marry outside the community. Second, Table 6–2 shows that in Los

Angeles, persons with white collar occupations are far more likely to marry Anglos than are persons with lower-status occupations. White-collar Mexicans are, of course, the most likely to mingle with Anglos. Moreover, for some upwardly mobile Mexicans, to marry an Anglo apparently has a symbolic value. (This is not to say there is no love and affection between the pair: mobility is simply a factor.) Thus intermarriage data show that mobility may—or may not—mean assimilation. In a city like Los Angeles a mobile Mexican American can make a choice.

People with lower-status occupations also have options, though fewer than the middle class. Their situation also shows that change inside the Mexican American community is not a single process. In the cities many lower-class Mexicans also have residential options; but of course, in the cities more lower-class Mexicans than middle-class Mexicans live in the *barrios*. As shown in Chapter Four, their social profile is much like that of the poor of any ethnic group. Many are unemployed, and many depend on welfare and pension payments. Many are older people; many are foreign-born and poorly educated. Often households are headed by women, and even if not, family solidarity may not be enough to compensate for an endlessly unrewarding life. But the poor can show at least one kind of social mobility: they can change their circumstances by moving physically.

Geographical mobility is one of the two kinds of social mobility among Mexicans. If the social class system is considered as a set of ranks, the ethnic system can also be considered a set of ranks. It is mobility both to move into the middle class and to move inside the ranks of the ethnic system. It is social mobility as well as geographical mobility to move from Texas to Los Angeles, whatever a person's social class. That is, such a move changes the social conditions of life. Accordingly, mobility from the country to the city or from one state to another state is more important for Mexican Americans than even for Blacks. It may be meaningful even for those Mexicans who have accomplished nothing very substantial in the occupational world by the move. Even the occupationally unsuccessful know that such a move gives children much greater chances for occupational and income gains.

A move from one part of the Southwest to another is never easy. It is usually accomplished only after careful and long consideration, often by use of a network of kinship relations and acquaintances. It can occur in youth as a sort of exploration of the world, or it can occur later with a family. Many of the movers return home: some miss the close relationships of the small town; others are badly trained and recognize their deficiencies in a more demanding area. (A college education can be of doubtful interchangeability in the Southwest: some colleges are of poor quality as are certain southern Black colleges.) However, it should be noted that this radical shift in structures of opportunity can be accomplished by Mexican Americans without leaving the Southwest.

This availability of opportunity in different parts of the Southwest, particularly in southern California, plus the probable presence of friends and relatives in the new city may be the reason why so few Mexican Americans do leave the Southwest. A Mexican who leaves rural Texas for Los Angeles is spanning nearly all the full range of opportunity available in this society.

CITIES AND CHANGING FAMILY

Familism seems to be declining in the big cities of the Southwest. Here again, the burden of certain family responsibilities is greatly diminished by public services available in the city. The city offers more jobs, temporary and permanent. Availability of welfare services diminishes the obligation to support an indigent relative. If a widowed or deserted wife does not *choose* to live with her relatives, she may do otherwise. Her choice may involve the personal degradation of bureaucratized Anglo charity, but it is still an option. That there are many who take such options is shown by the very few extended-family households in Los Angeles and San Antonio: very few Mexican Americans in these two cities will "double up" families even if so doing is supposed to be the "norm" of Mexican culture. Nearly all families in these two cities live in single-family households.[15]

In general, family roles change to meet changing circumstances. For urban Mexican American families it appears there has been more shift in the male role and role expectations than in the female role. (One sign of this lack of change in the female role is that female juvenile delinquency is notably lower than among other ethnic groups.)[16] Women still find their major role and validation in their families, as wives and especially as mothers. Higher education and careers are stereotypically considered alien for many Mexican American women, even though a growing feminist movement among Chicanas vehemently challenges such statements.[17] The feminists also challenge what they conceive to be the false glorification by Chicano activists of that aspect of Mexican culture

15 See Grebler, et al., *The Mexican American People*, for data on generalizations made in this section.

16Joseph Eaton and Kenneth Polk, *Measuring Delinquency* (Pittsburgh: University of Pittsburgh Press, 1961) gives rates of delinquency by sex for Los Angeles juveniles of several ethnic groups.

17See for example Anna Nieto Gomez in *Encuentro Feminil* 1, no. 1 (1974).

which degrades women. As Francisca Flores remarks, "Women who do not accept this philosophy are charged with betrayal to 'our culture and heritage.' Our culture, hell!"[18] Although there may be controversy on differing versions of Mexican cultural values (or on which is most conducive to either personal or collective growth) there is little doubt that the actual behavior of men and women alike deviates from the traditional stereotypes. Increasingly, survey data show that Mexican American men are inclined to share both important family decisions and to work with their wives.[19] The data suggest that a milieu offering more life-style options and opportunities (Los Angeles as compared with San Antonio and Albuquerque) is conducive to a lower need for men to have a subservient, servant-like or child-like wife. Changes in role behavior in the Chicano family probably occur as the result of a complex interaction of forces—models provided by the mass media, the increased visibility of a variety of styles of intra-family relationships in larger and more complex urban environments and increased geographical mobility, even within an urban area. Husband and wife interaction patterns are, of course, also related to other patterns of sociability both within and outside of the kinship groups. Data on Mexican Americans agree with more general findings about the effects of urbanization on kinship—that is, the husband and wife pairing tends to become more significant as the interaction between the wife and her female relatives and the husband and his male friends becomes less significant.

Middle-class norms remain the parental ideal for many Mexican American children. These may be Mexican middle-class norms, with emphasis on respect and deference to elders; American middle-class norms with emphasis on getting along with other people and on getting ahead in the world, or some combination of the two. Although children are important and highly valued in the Mexican American family, an increasing proportion of Chicanos use and approve of birth control devices, including abortion.

Extended family functions have declined, and with them there appears to have been a decline in *compadrazgo* in the cities. Nonetheless, *compadrazgo*-like friendship and mutual support groups persist, among the poor and the middle class alike. Valle refers to such groups as *"amistad-compadrazgo* webworks," and reports that the groups he studied in Houston and San Antonio largely exclude both formal ritual kin (*comadres* and *compadres*) and organized groups of non-kin. Valle finds that

---

18 In *Regeneracion* 1, no. 1 (1971).
19 Grebler, et al., *The Mexican American People.*

among the poor these *amistad* groups supported the utilization of mental health and other community services.[20] Among other subgroups in the community, such as political and civic activists, the formal *compadrazgo* is often used to cement chains of obligation and mutual support. Mexican American politicians thus may often have what one could facetiously term a ritualized form fo ethnic solidarity.

[20] Juan Ramon Valle, "*Amistad-Compadrazgo* as an Indigenous Webwork Compared to the Urban Mental Health Network" (Ph.D. diss. University of Southern California, 1974).

Everybody in the Southwest thinks he knows something about the natural inclinations and habits of Mexican Americans. This overlay of preconceptions and stereotypes is the primary difficulty in understanding and even in studying Mexican American culture.

Ideally the professional training of the social scientist gives him the ability to see and to describe a matrix of culture without preconception, though this ideal is realized only now and then. The less disciplined observer, Anglo or Mexican, often sees what he wants to see, or generalizes wrongly from correct observation. He may be limited to what he sees in his job as social worker, teacher, or citrus grower; or the Mexican may be restricted by what he must tell the Anglo community in order to retain his status as spokesman and extract favors for the *barrio*. Thus Anglos and Mexicans in southwestern communities (and a certain amount of the scholarly literature) continue to perpetuate clearly formulated but often inconsistent and weakly substantiated ideas about Mexican American culture. Social and even personal values are rarely far below the surface. Sometimes the values are obvious and glaring.

Language and Culture

We must say flatly at the beginning of this chapter that there is very little firm systematic knowledge about what exists, none about why it exists; and any speculation about what *ought* to be is out of place here. We have some solid information about the persistence of Spanish and good evidence that certain patterns of behavior and values do hold up (but rather inconsistently) across the variety of Mexican ethnic communities in the Southwest. Accordingly we will consider only those aspects of Mexican American culture on which some systematic and objective data are available: in regard to language, distinctive patterns of behavior and values, and the question of ethnic cohesiveness. Even so, the data are limited.

THE NATIVE LANGUAGE

No foreign language has been so persistently retained and is as likely to survive in this country as Spanish. A 1969 national survey showed that 53 percent of the Americans who speak some language other than English in the home speak Spanish.[1] This remarkable "language loyalty," or persistence, is attributable primarily to the Mexican Americans, according to an extensive survey of language loyalty in the United States.[2] Surveys show that most Mexican Americans in Los Angeles, San Antonio, and Albuquerque are bilingual in Spanish and English. Some speak no English, and a small proportion speak no Spanish. This pattern is "normal" for American ethnic groups. Most of those speaking Spanish in Los Angeles and San Antonio were either Mexican-born or have Mexican-born parents. In the nation as a whole, about half of the Mexican Americans report that they usually speak Spanish in the home.[3] The special loyalty of Mexican Americans, however, appears when we see what a large proportion of Spanish speakers there are among New Mexican descendants of seventeenth century settlers and among third or more generation Mexicans in the border towns and in the more isolated areas of the other states. Chicanos speak Spanish not only to communicate with foreign-born relatives but also habitually and as a matter of tradition through many generations. Why is this so?

Part of the answer lies in the special history of the isolated Mexican Americans of these special areas. Even today a visitor entering a small town in south Texas (Presidio, Rio Grande City, etc.) or a village in northern New Mexico or southern Colorado (Truchas, Tres Piedras) will hear Spanish rather than English as the normal language in the streets and shops. The few Anglos in many such towns are oftentimes also bilingual. Learning Spanish in these places is essential for social and economic survival, just as learning English is essential for Mexicans nearly anywhere else in the United States. In the previous generation all-Mexican work crews throughout the Southwest were supervised in Spanish—even in the large cities. Anglo bosses learned enough simple Spanish to handle the work situation. Thus Mexican families speaking only Spanish could go on living in a completely Spanish-speaking environment. This degree of isolation has fallen off sharply in most larger cities but it still may be found in, for example, the Los Angeles garment shops that employ recent immigrants as laborers. But it is very common in many rural areas of the Southwest and few except for those in school and perhaps young men who enter the Army need to speak any language except Spanish.

When Mexicans leave these villages and rural areas for the large cities they bring with them their language patterns. Thus the new arrival

---

[1] U.S. Department of Commerce, "Persons of Spanish Origin in the U.S.: November 1969," *Current Population Reports*, Series P-20, no. 213, February 1971, p. 15.

[2] Joshua Fishman, ed., *Language Loyalty in the United States* (The Hague: Mouton and Company, 1966).

[3] *Current Population Reports*, Series P-20, no. 213, p. 14.

coming to Albuquerque from the northern part of New Mexico is as handicapped in English as the "greenhorn" fresh from Tijuana. Most southwestern cities have such a steady influx of Spanish-speaking new arrivals. If the new arrivals choose to live in the *barrio* they will find retail stores, gas stations, and banks with clerks who speak Spanish by preference. There are Spanish-language movie theaters, religious services (both Catholic and Protestant), and Spanish radio and television.[4] There are politicians and social workers ready to speak Spanish—for whom, in fact, an ability to speak Spanish can be an important part of their career.

Just as with some other ethnic groups in transition, the use of Spanish carries great symbolic meaning. This symbolism began from the time of the earliest contacts between Mexicans and Anglos. It is today widely believed that the right of Mexican Americans to use Spanish is guaranteed by the Treaty of Guadalupe Hidalgo. This is not true. It *is* true, however, that the constitution of the state of New Mexico, drawn up in 1912, guarantees that "the right of any citizen of the state to vote, hold office, or sit upon juries, shall never be restricted, abridged, or impaired on account of . . . inability to speak, read, or write in English or Spanish languages."[5] For years the state legislature of New Mexico was officially bilingual, with, of course, a certain liberty in translation adding to the political spice of the proceedings.

Thus the right to speak Spanish meant, symbolically, a certain inalienable right guaranteed to a conquered people. This symbol has gained in significance because the right to speak Spanish had been so suppressed by the public school system. In many parts of the Southwest (see Chapter Six) an anomalous situation has been perpetuated: the use of Spanish in informal relationships persists along with the enforced use of English in formal situations.

Whatever the pedagogic reasons, the prohibition of the use of Spanish in school has been a symbol of cultural suppression. Educational professions have, for a very long time, defined language problems as the major source of Chicano troubles in school. Just as did their counterparts in the schools of the East generations ago, they often have used strong measures to bring about the desired change from Spanish to English. However, in the Southwest, these measures appear to have been largely ineffectual in an environment where work, street life, and leisure all were

---

[4] In 1960, 66 percent of the total American foreign-language broadcasting and 86 percent of the foreign-language broadcasting in the West was in Spanish. Mary Ellen Warshauer, "Foreign Language Broadcasting," in Fishman, *Language Loyalty in the United States*, p. 80.

[5] State Constitution of New Mexico, New Mexico Bluebook, 1921, Article VIII, Section 3, p. 21.

dominated by the use of Spanish. Much of this environment is now changing as Spanish-speaking parents slowly begin to interact more substantially with Anglo American society. A recent survey of school districts in California with a large proportion of Mexican American children showed that only 20 percent of those children needed an "English as a second language" program. (These included many small agricultural areas.)[6] In seven counties of south Texas, however, a huge 69 percent of the Spanish-surname students spoke little or no English when they entered school.[7] School principals surveyed in 1969 estimated the proportion of Chicano first graders who "did not speak English as well as the average Anglo first grader." Estimates ranged from 27 percent in Colorado to 62 percent in Texas.[8]

Even more disturbing to traditional Mexican American intellectuals than the loss of Spanish through English-speaking schools is their awareness that the historical suppression of Spanish has tended to degrade the quality of the Spanish. Many of the immigrants to the United States were illiterate agricultural workers who spoke a variety of rural Spanish. Years of exposure to American society meant that English words were adapted to Spanish syntax. Thus there are neologisms (*pochismos*) such as *el troque* (the truck), *la ganga* (the gang) and *huachale* (Watch it!). In parts of Mexico near the border people often find themselves eating in *loncherias*, or in Los Angeles, perhaps at a "Mexicatessen."

These words may amuse the Anglo but they are a source of deep embarrassment to many Mexican Americans, especially in their relationship with educated Mexican nationals. Spanish-language radio and television stations in the United States go to Latin American countries to recruit announcers. As one Texas radio station owner remarked, "I have tried to acquire the services of our local youth as Spanish announcers, but have found them to be unqualified to speak correctly the language left to them through heritage. It has been necessary for my station to import announcers."[9] However, the Chicano movement has tended to

---

6 Statement of Eugene Gonzáles, Assistant Superintendent of Public Instruction, California State Department of Education, in hearings before the Special Subcommittee on Bilingual Education of the Committee on Labor and Public Welfare, U.S. Senate, 90th Congress, First Session, Part 2 (Washington, D.C.: Government Printing Office, 1967), p. 473.

7Statement of Harold R. Dooley, Director, Valley Association for Superior Education, in *ibid.*, Part 1, May 29, 1967, p. 275.

8U.S. Commission on Civil Rights, *The Excluded Student: Educational Practices Affecting Mexican Americans in the Southwest*, Mexican American Education Study Report no. 3, May 1972, p. 14.

9 Statement of Arthur Thomas, Vice President and General Manager, Radio Station KUNO, Corpus Christi, Texas, in hearings before the Special Subcommittee on Bilingual Education of the Committee on Labor and Public Welfare, U.S. Senate, 90th Congress, First Session, Part 2 (Washington, D.C.: Government Printing Office, 1967), p. 259.

glorify the slang that is both inventive and unique to the Chicano *barrio*. In some colleges, courses are taught in *caló*, which has a vocabulary and sentence structure forming a distinctive style of communication.

Pochismos are not only an indication of shift in a language but also an indication that Spanish is giving way to English. As one Mexican American lawyer in south Texas commented:

> I am sad to see the Spanish language fading in the United States, southwestern part. I can see it fading everywhere in the homes, particularly in the higher bracket homes of lawyers and doctors and well-to-do businessmen and other professional people. I mean in formerly Spanish speaking homes . . . I think it's a deterioration of a language and I think it is a mistake. These kids simply are being reared today where they cannot speak Spanish. The problem there is that they cannot speak Spanish, not that they cannot speak English. That's no problem whatever. Now it is still a problem with the lower income brackets. English is still a problem, there. You have got to teach them English.[10]

Stories symbolizing the depreciation of the language are common. Mexican American intellectuals who know and love Spanish-language classics and the vital contemporary literature resent what they perceive to be the American preoccupation with French and German as the only "cultured" foreign languages. A frequent theme is that this "liability" of Mexicans should be turned into a national asset so that the United States will always have diplomatic and other personnel to serve in the eighteen Spanish-speaking countries of Latin America and South America. But as far as integration into practical job-seeking America is concerned, speaking Spanish continues to be a handicap. In recent years there have been increasing numbers of challenges to the once universal practice of written tests in union apprenticeship programs, civil service jobs, and training for law enforcement agencies. Challenges to the use of English in school I.Q. tests have been widespread.

The crucial role of language among Mexican Americans cannot be overestimated. As a man from Texas remarked, "In Texas the teacher beats you for using Spanish in school to remind you that you are an American. Your friends beat you after school to remind you that you are a Mexican." Thus the language used has far more than a "technical" or instrumental significance for Chicanos. Similarly, there have been generations of attempts to evaluate the significance of Spanish made by Anglos and Chicanos alike. No matter the particular rationale used by the evaluator, it is very difficult for him to be dispassionate. There are passionate denunciations; very few southwestern papers fail to print at least

---

[10] Statement of Robert P. Sanchez, Attorney at Law, McAllen, Texas, in *Hearings on Bilingual Education*, Part 1, p. 288.

once a year a denunciation of "people who refuse to learn the language of our country." There is equally passionate advocacy by most Chicano spokesmen and especially by Mexican educators.

There are many factors that will determine whether the use of the Spanish language will persist, grow, or decline. At this writing, the continued flood of Mexican nationals into the Southwest rather clearly suggests an increased use. On the other hand, the declining isolation of Mexican *barrios* suggests increased circulation and probably a less consistent use of Spanish. Policy will have an impact, as well as demographic and ecological circumstances; the efforts to develop bilingual and bicultural educational programs may affect language usage. It is probable that the Chicano movement's great emphasis on ethnic self-awareness will contribute to a greater interest in Spanish. Yet in spite of these forces and counterforces, it is probable that the greater involvement of Mexican Americans in occupational and educational worlds outside the *barrio* will tend to diminish the use of Spanish. In a sense, therefore, some of the "natural" social processes sustaining the use of Spanish may be losing their force.

BEHAVIOR AND VALUES

Even to begin to discuss the touchy and value-loaded subject of Mexican American culture we must recognize that it is really two different things. There is first the highly visible surface of "Mexican culture": the artifacts that can be seen by any visitor. But beneath the surface there are behavior patterns and values that many social scientists believe to be far more important. The existence and pervasiveness of some though not of all, are in great controversy. All are in some way empirically measurable.

The visible surface of Mexican American culture includes a great range of oddities. In Los Angeles, visitors are shown the shops of Olvera Street; the famous Plaza, a popular tourist center, and a huge baroque church in downtown Los Angeles that is much used by Mexicans. There are distinctive modes of dress and hairstyles although these modes are often marks of specifically lower-class Mexicans. Occasionally a visitor may see a *curandera* (faith healer), and there are shops selling a variety of esoteric herbs for medicine. There are many foods peculiar to Mexicans and to Mexican restaurants. A special kind of music is played endlessly on southwestern Mexican radio stations. These are the interesting touches that a casual visitor can accept as "Mexican culture." They are a little touching, a little quaint, and often kept alive for commercial purposes in such tourist centers as Disneyland because they make money and please visitors.

This visible surface does not contradict the impressions gained from the rather restricted range of Mexican life available to the average Anglo's observation, because this range of Mexican life is structured by both social class and age. Thus, contact between Mexican Americans and Anglos may be at a maximum in youth, when both are in school. However, even this limited contact is likely to be structured by social class. The Anglo child who goes to a predominantly Mexican American school is likely to be relatively lower class. The Mexican going to a predominantly Anglo school is likely to be middle class. But given the proportions of each group in most southwestern cities, *most* Anglos probably will have little opportunity to interact extensively with Mexicans even in a school setting. This lack of opportunity would hold solely on the basis of probabilities, even if there were no other mechanisms of ethnic exclusiveness.

For adults, it is likely that most interethnic contacts between middle-class Anglos and Mexicans occur within an institutional context in which most Mexicans are likely to be lower class. Thus the Anglo professional working in public health, schools, welfare, probation, law enforcement and similar agencies "knows Mexicans" only when they are very young or in trouble. This fact may affect the general middle-class Anglo perception of the ingredients of Mexican culture, and may be as important as the fact that Mexicans are, of course, frequently seen in clearly lower-class occupations.

This skewed nature of Mexican American and Anglo contact is almost surely an important influence on mutual perception. We can possibly summarize this off-balance perception by noting that most middle-class Mexicans are probably familiar with middle-class Anglos. Most middle-class Anglos don't know middle-class Mexicans. This lack of contact obviously can affect middle-class perception of the ingredients of Mexican culture.

Some of the cultural misunderstandings arising from institutional contacts have resulted in a special literature about Mexican Americans. In public health practice, to name one institutional area, the apparent difficulty of getting Mexican American cooperation has prompted considerable systematic research in areas beyond overt behavior. Some such studies into Mexican folk beliefs about the causes of illness are important and interesting. We note, for example, that several conditions Mexican Americans define as illness are not known or recognized by modern medicine. (Conversely, modern medical practice diagnoses certain conditions in a fashion totally discordant with folk beliefs.) One folk belief, in *susto* (fright), is closely related to the belief in Mexico that a soul can be jarred out of the body by terror, and illness will ensue. Another folk belief is that poor health may result from a mixture of a "hot" food (white beans, rice, fish, peppers) and a "cold" food (red beans, beef, cucumbers).[11] In New Mexico considerable research into such folk beliefs and folk diagnoses has led to a series of manuals for public health workers who may be called upon to deal with the folk diseases and diagnoses.

Whatever the degree of "superstition" or folk theory about illness, the observers are struck by the pragmatic quality with which illnesses are acted upon by Mexican Americans in remote areas. A visit to a folk healer may delay a visit to a doctor. Sometimes this places a seriously ill patient in danger, but at other times a minor ailment is cured at very low cost. Along with the folk healer and the herbalist, the poor make use of the supply of patent medicine in the local drugstore and the local public health clinic as well. Different levels of belief and of usage may exist in the same household. The mix of beliefs gets even more complex in metropolitan areas where the range of resources increases and the behavior of neighbors and friends about health becomes more varied. Perhaps more important, the local network of social relations and controls that accompanies a close group of neighbors and friends in a city permits more "strangers" to enter the system. Thus an individual may behave in "deviant" fashion and go unpunished, or unobserved.

The decline of these "Mexican" health practices does much to illustrate the fate of some visible features of this special culture. In general, practices detrimental to welfare tend to disappear in a quite pragmatic fashion in urban areas. Some usages persist, perhaps because they are pleasant and quite harmless as, for example, the use of herbal teas. But in the past many mobile Mexican Americans felt it necessary to discard all such behavior. Some now prefer the drugstore patent medicines to "superstitions." It is increasingly likely that various levels of medical practices co-exist among the poor of less isolated areas.

Many visible cultural features that were rejected by generations of Mexican Americans who wanted to be "accepted" by becoming inconspicuous are being revived as symbols of identity with the Chicano movement. Styles are reminiscent (and sometimes based on) the omnipresent posters of Mexican revolutionaries—Villa and Zapata. Mexican artistic traditions are proudly displayed in homes and offices. Mexican dance

[11]Good discussions of folk medicine appear in Margaret Clark, *Health in the Mexican American Culture* (Berkeley and Los Angeles: University of California Press, 1959), and Lyle Shannon, *Cultural Differences and Medical Care: The Case of the Spanish Speaking People of the Southwest* (New York: Russell Sage Foundation, 1954), as well as several of the community studies cited elsewhere in this book.

groups based on the famous *folklóricos* of Mexico are created in high schools and colleges throughout the Southwest. *Teatros* or folk theaters of the type that became so well known with the Chavez farmworkers (*Teatro Campesino*) have urban counterparts in the *Teatro del Barrio*. Colleges and *barrios* alike have seen a cultural flowering.

But apart from the visible aspects of Mexicanism, we must be concerned with those values and norms of life that are generally called "culture." This is an area of doubt, controversy, and ideology—these issues excite more argument than even the questions of language and bilingualism.

There are some sound reasons for this controversy. As we saw in the chapter on institutions (Chapter Five), "Mexican culture" has been blamed for a wide range of troubles which are just as easily treated as problems of function of American institutions. Often the blame is put on Mexican culture in terms of stereotypes. But often it is cast in scholarly fashion, with expensive surveys supporting a type of institutional racism operating under the best academic auspices. Social psychology becomes a sophisticated substitute for old genetic explanations—thus the "innate propensity to violence" is replaced by data on "differential values" which may accurately reflect the response of Chicanos to a questionnaire but do not in any manner reflect the realities of the Chicano situation.[12] It is also becoming increasingly difficult to analyze Mexican values inside the Mexican community without a great deal of ideological friction. It is assumed for some reason that a description of the values placed on assimilation, acculturation, and social interaction implies an ideological stance. Since many researchers have fixed ideological positions, almost any data are sure to arouse controversy.

There are at least three issues involved in any discussion of Mexican American values. There is a description of the extent to which Chicanos and Anglos may differ and the extent to which Chicanos differ among themselves. Second, implications can be drawn from differences in values to differences in behavior (school achievement as an example) from which useful conclusions might be drawn. Third, implications of desirable or undesirable effects might be drawn—and this, of course, depends entirely on what the word "desirable" means to the researcher. The result, of

---

[12] For critiques, see Miguel Montiel, "The Social Science Myth of the Mexican American Family," *El Grito* 3 (Summer 1970): 56–63; Amado Padilla, "Psychological Research and the Mexican American," in *Mexican Americans in the United States*, ed. J. Burma (Cambridge: Schenkman Publishing Company, 1970); Octavio I. Romano-V., "The Anthropology and Sociology of the Mexican Americans," *El Grito* 2 (Fall 1968): 1,13–26; Nick Vaca, "The Mexican American in the Social Sciences," *El Grito* 3 (Fall 1970): 17–52. Some of these have been reprinted in Octavio I. Romano-V., ed., *Voices* (Berkeley: Quinto Sol Publications, 1971).

course, is so much controversy in value research that it is tempting to consider leaving the whole question to the ideologues.

But cultural "explanations" of Chicano behavior are so popular in American professional schools and among lay people generally that the question cannot be avoided. Accordingly, we will deal with three distinct areas: first, values relating to familism; second, values relating to traditional views of fatalism and the like; and third, values relating to "clannishness." As elsewhere in this book, we will attempt to describe some data, to note some interpretations made of these data but to avoid drawing conclusions about what is "desirable."

On familism, Chicanos are seen by both Anglos and by themselves as particularly familistic. That is, they tend to place more value on family relationships and obligations than do most Anglo Americans. In Chapter Six we suggested that familism might serve some important functions in an economy of destitution. But there are also arguments that familism may inhibit certain kinds of mobility for Chicanos in American society. It may inhibit geographical mobility and some kinds of educational or occupational mobility. On a more general level, a number of social theorists or philosophers argue that a society totally dominated by familism would be a society seriously handicapped in the twentieth century with its emphasis on "rational" bureaucratic forms of organizational action. Others argue that even such rational forms as, for example, large bureaucracies are not really very rational at all and that the apparent American cultural emphasis on "individualism" (the cultural antonym for familism) is just a facade, a tenet of America's "civic religion" and more honored in the breach than in the observance.

In Table 7-1 we show some survey data on what samples of Chicanos said they felt about two aspects of the familism/individualism dilemma; the first question is relevant to geographic mobility and the second question concerns occupational values. We see immediately from the table that these Chicanos in Los Angeles, San Antonio, and Albuquerque are far from uniform in either value. There are differences between cities and within cities between social classes or income groups. On the first question (if a person should find a job close to his parents even if it means losing a good job opportunity) only a minority in any city or in any income level agree that the family should be given priority. Although this response clearly contradicts a stereotype, it should be recalled that a very high proportion of Mexican Americans have either moved themselves or are the children of persons who moved from smaller towns and rural areas or from Mexico to one of these urban areas. Thus the discovery that they (implicitly) value job opportunity over family closeness should not be surprising.

TABLE 7–1

PERCENTAGE OF MEXICAN AMERICAN SURVEY RESPONDENTS
HOLDING FAMILISTIC VALUES, BY INCOME, LOS ANGELES,
SAN ANTONIO AND ALBUQUERQUE, 1965–1967

Value	Percent Agreeing with Item					

1. Los Angeles

	High Income		Medium Income		Low Income	
	Per-cent	Total N (=100%)	Per-cent	Total N (=100%)	Per-cent	Total N (=100%)
A. Immobility a	7	344	15	292	26	277
B. Nepotism b	22	353	36	292	41	272

2. San Antonio

	Medium Income		Low Income	
	Per-cent	Total N (=100%)	Per-cent	Total N (=100%)
A. Immobility a	15	317	35	239
B. Nepotism b	29	291	58	228

3. Albuquerque

	High Income		Medium Income		Low Income	
	Per-cent	Total N (=100%)	Per-cent	Total N (=100%)	Per-cent	Total N (=100%)
A. Immobility a	4	22	2	50	28	39
B. Nepotism b	4	22	6	50	28	39

Data for Los Angeles and San Antonio were provided courtesy the Mexican-American Study Project, University of California at Los Angeles, and for Albuquerque by Operation SER, Los Angeles, California. All three surveys used probability samples of Mexican-American households. Income levels vary greatly among the three cities, and, accordingly, different definitions of "high," "medium," and "low" have been applied, though each refers to approximately comparable levels of living. *Source for wording of items:* Joseph A. Kahl, "Some Measures of Achievement Orientation," *American Journal of Sociology* 70 (May 1965): 680–681.

a "When looking for a job, a person ought to find a position in a place located near his parents, even if that means losing a good opportunity elsewhere."

b "If you have the chance to hire an assistant in your work, it is always better to hire a relative than a stranger."

The findings about "nepotism" are different. Still, except for the poor in San Antonio, most respondents disapprove of the practice in flat contradiction to the stereotype. Second, the more prosperous in each city are far less likely to approve of this value. This suggests that persons who are doing reasonably well in the job market are indeed more likely to agree with the stated values of American society about nepotism. They are probably more likely to hold jobs in firms that promote competitive values quite explicitly. They are less likely to be in "dead end" jobs where promotions are rare and where job mobility is accomplished through a network of friends and relatives.[13] Third, the differences between the cities is clear. This probably reflects differences in opportunity structures or opportunities to become involved with others in a truly competitive rather than discriminatory job market.

Our second concern is with the complex of values that we can describe as "traditional." This complex includes the ideas that Chicanos emphasize the present rather than the future, intangible gratifications rather than material rewards, and enjoyment rather than (as one Anglo respondent phrased it) the "run-run-run" of other Americans. The Mexican is pictured as a serene rather than anxious person, perhaps just a bit improvident in planning for the future, but his pleasure in life and living more than compensates.

At this point it is worth asking the source of this complex of values: is it the "noble savage" of romantic myth? Is it possibly some kind of variation of the counterculture of the 1960s? Or is it an accurate statement of the archetypal value system of Mexico? Even a casual examination of the ideas of *Chicanismo* (Chapter Eight) shows that they are at least as close to the counterculture as they are to traditional Mexican values.[14] And how close is it to archetypal Mexican values? Certainly neither at the level of empirical research (Oscar Lewis, Joseph Kahl, and Rogelio Diaz-Guerrero) nor at the level of philosophical analysis (Octavio Paz or Samuel Ramos) does any observer of Mexico develop such a version of Mexican culture. In actual fact, it appears that this version of "tradition" is found most clearly in the works of Florence Kluckhohn and her associate in their studies of a small village in New Mexico.[15]

The impact of this study has been phenomenal, despite the obvious limitations of such a milieu. Kluckhohn has been cited, quoted, and used as *the* authority on the traditional values of Chicanos to an extraordinary

[13]See Paul Bullock, *Aspiration vs. Opportunity: "Careers" in the Inner City* (Ann Arbor, Mich.: Institute of Labor and Industrial Relations, 1973), for an account of the job-finding practices of the poor in Los Angeles.

[14] We must also recognize that some proponents of *Chicanismo* as a cultural movement emphasize some of these traditional values. Thus, for example, Tomas Martinez, "Chicanismo," *Epoca* 1 (1972):35–38, defines "Chicanismo as a philosophy of living seen as an alternative to the values persisting in Anglo American society. The major concepts involved are spiritualism, honest self-examination, complete love of life and a consciousness for here and now." This description comes from Elizabeth Martinez Smith, "A Chicana Bibliography," in *New Directions in Education: Estudios Femeniles de la Chicana* (UCLA: University Extension, n.d.)

[15] See Florence R. Kluckhohn and Fred L. Strodtbeck, *Variations in Value Orientations* (Evanston, Ill. and Elmsford, N.Y.: Row, Peterson and Company, 1961).

degree, despite both the unusual nature of the place she studied and her own comments that the culture of this small village was in the process of substantial change. It is unfortunate that not enough attention was given her prediction that the culture of the village would undoubtedly change as it became more integrated into the institutions of the larger American society, particularly those concerned with economic life.

In fact, Kluckhohn's analysis of the culture of this village is an analysis of the adaptability of values to a local situation, rather than an attempt to derive an archetype of Mexican culture. Her work has been badly distorted. The pace of change of society and technology is very slow in a remote village. The slow change of seasons and the natural risks of an agricultural society may mean that American urban values would be dysfunctional in a small New Mexican village. And of course, a present-time orientation is not the only alternative to a future-time orientation. One can venerate the past (as is done in New Mexico) and *still* plan for the future. Subjugation to nature is not the only alternative to mastery over nature; one can feel in harmony with natural forces rather than at their mercy. But to plan meaningfully for the future in a small mountain village with a primitive technology might mean a kind of insanity or even an alienation so complete that such an individual could not cope with the realities of the environment and would ulti-mately emigrate. In fact, there *is* a great deal of emigration—enough to leave some of these villages nearly depopulated. Whatever these specu-lations, one can argue in retrospect that traditional values, at least at a time in the past, may very well have been of adaptive value to Mexican American communities.[16]

But to return to our main task—the presentation of empirical data. Although the data are limited, Table 7–2 gives results from the three major cities of Los Angeles, San Antonio, and Albuquerque. The data show the strong relationship between reactions to traditional values and the income of the individual. The poor in all three cities are far more traditional. *Most* poor Chicanos see comparatively little virtue in plan-ning because "plans are hard to fulfill." *Most* poor Mexican Americans try to "be content with what comes their way," rather than "expecting too much out of life." But, interestingly, comparatively few at any income

---

[16] A similar kind of analysis of time perspective is made by Dorothy Nelkin, "Unpredictability and Life Style in a Migrant Labor Camp," *Social Problems* 17 (Spring 1970): 472–487. As the Shannons sum it up, "the sense of causality, the relation between effort and return, is perceived in terms of an environment which may be neither predicted nor controlled," Lyle and Magdaline Shannon, *Minority Migrants in the Urban Community: Mexican-American and Negro Adjustment to Industrial Society* (Beverly Hills: Sage Publications, 1973), p. 225.

TABLE 7–2

PERCENTAGE OF MEXICAN AMERICAN SURVEY RESPONDENTS
HOLDING TRADITIONAL VALUES, BY INCOME
LOS ANGELES, SAN ANTONIO AND ALBUQUERQUE, 1965–1967

Value   Percent Agreeing with Item

1. Los Angeles

	High Income		Medium Income		Low Income	
	Per-cent	Total N (= 100%)	Per-cent	Total N (= 100%)	Per-cent	Total N (= 100%)
a. Don't plan a	35	359	49	285	63	268
b. Think present b	26	354	24	290	35	261
c. Be content c	56	359	73	290	80	271

2. San Antonio

	Medium Income		Low Income	
	Per-cent	Total N (= 100%)	Per-cent	Total N (= 100%)
a. Don't plan a	46	316	58	242
b. Think present b	17	307	38	248
c. Be content c	59	312	69	245

3. Albuquerque

	High Income		Medium Income		Low Income	
	Per-cent	Total N (= 100%)	Per-cent	Total N (= 100%)	Per-cent	Total N (= 100%)
a. Don't plan a	14	22	36	50	62	39
b. Think present b	14	22	18	50	49	39
c. Be content c	32	22	69	50	69	39

See Table 7–1 for sources of data.

Source for wording of items: Joseph A. Kahl, "Some Measures of Achievement Orientation," *American Journal of Sociology* 70 (May 1965): 680–681.

a "Making plans only brings unhappiness because the plans are hard to fulfill."

b "With things as they are today, an intelligent person ought to think only about the present, without worrying about what is going to happen tomorrow."

c "The secret of happiness is not expecting too much out of life, and being content with what comes your way."

level are wholeheartedly in favor of "thinking only about the present, without worrying about what is going to happen tomorrow." Apparently, even if you distrust planning for the future, it is wise at least to *worry* about the future. When we look for differences among the three cities we see (as with familism) that the middle-class Spanish Americans of Albuquerque are the most "acculturated" about these values.

We may also note here that a 1960 study of Chicano, Black and Anglo migrants to Racine, Wisconsin, using almost identical questions, reports a rather similar pattern. Most devastating for the notion of a unique Mexican value pattern is the Shannons' finding that Mexican American and Black migrants into this midwestern industrial city have a very similar world view, and it is dramatically different from the world view of Anglo Americans. This is true even when income is controlled. It suggests that the minority experience may be at least as significant in affecting values as is the particular cultural heritage.[17]

In general, the data given in Tables 7–1 and 7–2 suggest that cultural value patterns are highly responsive to the demands of a situation. This agrees with the Kluckhohn interpretation and with any reasonable belief that human beings show a very considerable ability to adjust to their circumstances, when these circumstances change. And yet, for some reason the notion of a cultural archetype, of a single value system persists. Somehow there is a need for a single and simple cultural explanation, despite a growing literature that is critical of cultural interpretations on a theoretical or ideological level. There must be a profound need to find some explanation of the problems of Chicanos within Chicanos themselves, and this need is distorting reality.

But to return to a third major consideration. Mexican Americans are reputed to be clannish. It is said, "They stick together. They don't want anything to do with other Americans." From available historical material (Chapter Two) we know that such clannishness in the past was often imposed upon Mexicans by their strict isolation from American society. Such isolation occurred because of settlement patterns and work patterns and was retained or reinforced by many Anglo institutions. Isolation is hardly avoidable in a town where Mexicans must attend segregated schools, work in segregated industries, and live in segregated residential areas. Thus "clannishness" was inevitable and oftentimes it would be exacerbated by open prejudice, discrimination, and in some cases, the state of open conflict between Mexican nationals and the United States.

Clannishness is an important defense for a poor and unskilled population in a demanding, indifferent, or hostile environment. Some of this attitude is a natural consequence of Mexican familism: a network of obligations was extremely important in the past among Mexican Americans and is important even today. In some ways the ethnic collectivity,

17 Shannon and Shannon, *Minority Migrants*, p. 230.

that is, all Mexicans, functions as a more elaborate extension of the family. One is born into being Mexican and cannot escape the collective fate of all Mexicans. From this sense of group identification comes the term "ethclass," coined by Milton Gordon to describe the notion that an American is defined in social terms largely by a combination of his social class and his ethnicity or religious heritage. It assumes that the American Catholic, Jew, Black, Puerto Rican, or Mexican American (and even the WASP) will generally prefer and/or be forced into social and occupational associations with fellow ethnics of his own class level.[18] In our discussion of social class (Chapter Six) we suggest that the extent of ethnic exclusiveness at various class levels varies with the nature of the local milieu. We used the terms "Frontier" and "Colony" to refer respectively to the more assimilationist and the more ethnically exclusive Mexican Americans. The proportion of Frontiersmen and Colonists varies from class to class and from city to city, depending upon a variety of factors. That the ethnically exclusive Colonists are more visible to the non-ethnic than are the Frontiersmen or assimilationists should not blind us to the fact that *both* types of adaptation exist.

For some ethnic groups there have appeared in-group terms referring to ethnic solidarity. The terms describe the sense of peoplehood, of a common history, of a sharing of common perceptions and preferences about the social world. There are many such terms for Blacks. For Chicanos a major term is *la raza*. The word can be narrowly translated as "race," but its implications are far more complex than that among Mexican Americans and indeed among Latin Americans generally. Originally it referred to the creation of *la raza* in the fusion of the Spanish and the indigenous peoples of the New World. In fact, throughout Latin America Columbus Day is called *"El dia de la Raza"*—the day of *la raza*. Used among Mexican Americans, however, it appears to be restricted to fellow Mexican Americans. (This appears to be the case among all except the militant and others concerned with other forms of national political solidarity among Latin groups—especially, Puerto Ricans and Chicanos.) A man accepting a federal appointment may state that, among other things, his new position will give him the opportunity to "do something for" (or he is accused by others of not doing something for) *la raza*. "The community" is yet another phrase implied by *la raza*.

We would not expect loyalty to *la raza* to decline in the modern social world of the United States, and there is no evidence that it has done so. Appeals to such obligations are fully legitimate: there are very

[18] See Milton M. Gordon, *Assimilation in American Life* (New York: Oxford University Press, 1964).

few people inside or outside the group who can comfortably sneer at such a form of clannishness, at least if it is on behalf of Mexican Americans. On the other hand, we find that ethnic exclusiveness in social relations is becoming far more variable. As noted in Chapter Six, intermarriage is increasing in Los Angeles, and this increase reflects the general growth in effective interaction with individuals outside the ordinary circle of Mexican Americans in work and friendship. Figure 7–1 presents data on how closely Mexican Americans in three important cities confined

FIGURE 7–1

PERCENTAGE OF MEXICAN AMERICANS HAVING
ALL MEXICAN AMERICAN ASSOCIATES, 1965–1967

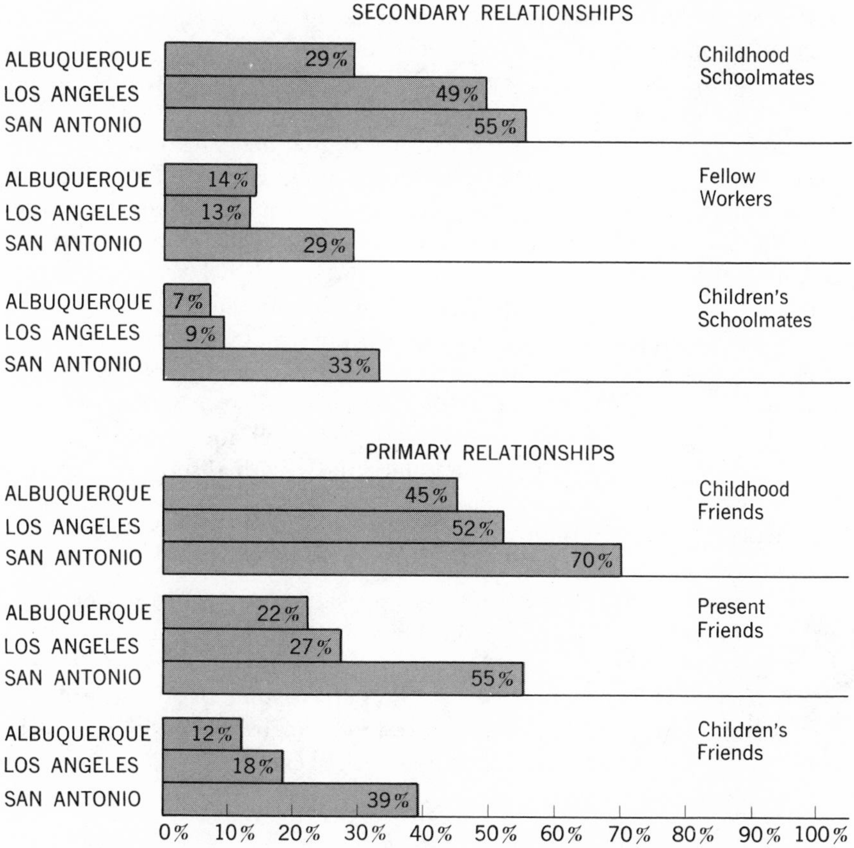

SECONDARY RELATIONSHIPS

ALBUQUERQUE	29%	Childhood Schoolmates
LOS ANGELES	49%	
SAN ANTONIO	55%	
ALBUQUERQUE	14%	Fellow Workers
LOS ANGELES	13%	
SAN ANTONIO	29%	
ALBUQUERQUE	7%	Children's Schoolmates
LOS ANGELES	9%	
SAN ANTONIO	33%	

PRIMARY RELATIONSHIPS

ALBUQUERQUE	45%	Childhood Friends
LOS ANGELES	52%	
SAN ANTONIO	70%	
ALBUQUERQUE	22%	Present Friends
LOS ANGELES	27%	
SAN ANTONIO	55%	
ALBUQUERQUE	12%	Children's Friends
LOS ANGELES	18%	
SAN ANTONIO	39%	

0%   10%   20%   30%   40%   50%   60%   70%   80%   90%   100%

Data from Los Angeles and San Antonio were provided by Mexican-American Study Project, University of California, Los Angeles. Data from Albuquerque provided by Operation SER, Santa Monica, California.

themselves to work and friendship with other Chicanos. There are striking differences between the three cities, and also between age groups with, for example, 70 percent of the San Antonians and 55 percent of the Angelenos over 50 reporting that *all* their childhood schoolmates were Mexican, whereas 50 percent of the San Antonians and 42 percent of the Angelenos under 30 reported such ethnic exclusiveness in their childhood.

Even more interesting than the age differences, however, are what we might call generational differences. Figure 7–1 shows data for three cities for a mid-1960s study in which the respondents were asked how "Mexican" were their social relations during their childhoods, in the present, and for their own children. One respondent thus gives us a look at three generations. The graph also distinguishes between "primary" relationships—friendships—and "secondary" relationships, those at school and at work. Of course, the city differences are of major importance but even in such a segregated city as San Antonio the degree of "Mexican exclusiveness" generally declines from one generation to the next.

However, it is important to note that leaving the fairly narrow circle of ethnic exclusiveness does not mean assimilation, and as a matter of fact, in some circles the word assimilation itself has become pejorative. It means, simply, that Mexican Americans have more options, less compulsion to confine relationships to fellow Mexican Americans either because of Anglo hostility or because of pressure from the ethnic community. One can help one's fellow Mexicans and retain full loyalty to ethnic traditions without total exclusiveness in social relations. To project a bit, it seems that the Mexican Americans living in ethnic frontiers appear to have made this decision for themselves. A few, but only a few, reject the name "Mexican Americans," preferring to be called simply "Americans." It also appears that some kind of "dualism" is emerging, to borrow a term common among Blacks at the turn of the century. Applied to Mexican Americans it expresses the idea that "we Mexicans are Americans but we also share the fate of all Mexicans."

This dualism has been slow to appear. Many Mexican Americans believe themselves to be far more Mexican than American, a belief that is shaken by the disrespect and displacement they experience while visiting Mexico. Sometimes this belief is also helped along by Mexican American leaders and spokesmen who can reinforce their own position, that is, their basis of support, their "clientele," as Mexican American.

Until recently Mexican Americans were stereotyped as politically apathetic, political nonparticipants, and in general, as people who had contributed little if anything to the political processes of the Southwest. Some evidence for this viewpoint was the disproportionate underrepresentation of Chicano officials at the federal, state, and local levels. A further supposed proof of Mexican disinterest in politics came from the reported lack of development of ethnic political organizations and the low electoral participation rates. Servin states the essence of this perspective:

> . . . it is difficult to understand the political failure of the Mexicans. With a population of some 3.5 million in the Southwest, the Mexican American outnumbers the Negro but has not capitalized on the opportunities in this area where mediocrity is far from a disadvantage.[1]

Politics and the Mexican American Experience

The explanations for this "failure" included the idea that the native "Mexican" or "Latin" culture was responsible for the Mexican lack of political success. In the face of Mexican American activism in the 1960s and 1970s this argument has lost much of its credibility. Yet the idea that Mexican Americans were not active politically in the Southwest until the 1960s still persists and is still widely believed. This chapter will examine the reasons for the development of this stereotype. It also will examine the factors that have worked against Mexican American political success. Then contemporary Mexican American political activity will be reviewed and the current "politics of ethnicity" assessed.

THE DEVELOPMENT OF A STEREOTYPE

Let us first examine the idea that cultural predispositions keep Mexicans from participating in political activity to further ethnic group

---

[1]Manuel Servín, "The Post-World War II Mexican-American, 1925–1965: A Non-Achieving Minority," in *The Mexican Americans: An Awakening Minority* (Beverly Hills, Calif.: Glencoe Press, 1970), pp. 143–159.

This chapter is written by Harry Pachon, Assistant Professor in the Department of Urban and Metropolitan Studies at Michigan State University, East Lansing, Michigan.

goals. As with so many other stereotypical characteristics about Mexican Americans, this particular image probably grew from a number of factors. The first of these is a confusion between ethnic characteristics and class characteristics. In fact, we know now that many of these characteristics of political apathy and nonparticipation are really class linked—in particular, they are poverty linked characteristics. The poor lack the opportunities and resources (such as money and prestige) requisite to successful political participation. Moreover, class biases inherent in this system also inhibit participation. We know, for example, that residency requirements and periodic voter disqualification procedures both contribute to the political passivity and political nonparticipation of the poor.[2] Given the incidence of poverty among the Mexicans (see Chapter Four) and the likelihood that this poverty was greater in the past, there is good reason to accept Cassavantes' statement that reseachers on the Mexican American have "in a confounding manner described the characteristics and attributes of individuals living in . . . poverty."[3] The poverty of a substantial segment of the Mexican American population must be considered a major factor.

But there is yet another confusion that has helped create this stereotypical image. Many Mexican Americans are foreign-born or recent immigrants. And further, the presence of both legal and illegal aliens is often overlooked. Consider for example the conclusion that may be drawn from Table 8–1. At first glance the conventional wisdom about low Mexican American electoral participation is confirmed. Yet these figures fail to show the importance of recent arrival and noncitizenship. In many areas, a significant proportion of the persons of Spanish origin are recent immigrants. Census figures for 1970 show that 30.8 percent of East Los Angeles' Mexican population were foreign-born; 11.5 percent of those

TABLE 8–1

REGISTRATION AND VOTING IN THE 1972 ELECTION BY ETHNICITY

Ethnic Origin	Total	Percentage Registered	Percentage Voted
Mexican	3,219,000	45%	37.5%
Black	12,467,000	67.5	54.1
Irish	9,683,000	76.7	66.6

Source: U.S. Census.

[2] See William Gamson, "Stable Unrepresentation in American Society," *American Behavioral Scientist* 12 (November/December 1968): 808–832, and for the many requirements that serve as obstacles to the poor, Peter Kimball, *The Disconnected* (New York: Columbia University Press, 1972).

[3] Edward Cassavantes, *A New Look at the Attributes of the Mexican American* (Albuquerque, N.M.: Southwestern Cooperative Educational Laboratory, 1969), p. 11.

in Texas; 22.9 percent in California; and only 3.8 percent in New Mexico. Therefore, because so many Mexican Americans are not eligible because of noncitizenship, the only reasonable way to compare these three ethnic groups is on the basis of those who voted as a percentage of those registered to vote. These results are quite different. A remarkable 81.5 percent of the registered Mexican Americans voted in 1972; whereas only 80 percent of the Black Americans voted and 86 percent of the Irish. In fact, voting participation among Mexican Americans is slightly higher than that of Black Americans—an ethnic group considered highly politicized. The higher Irish American vote may be explained by class differences.

Although the presence of many Mexican Americans who are not citizens must always be remembered, many descriptions of Mexican American politics fail to consider this.[4] Recentness of arrival and a foreign-born status may be even more important when we consider that recently arrived immigrants, even full citizens, are not as active politically as the general population. Among Mexican immigrants of the early 1900s this tendency toward nonparticipation in the political system may have been reinforced by a disillusionment with politics suffered in revolutionary Mexico. Tirado argues that the reluctance of Mexican Americans (of this period) to label organizational activity as "political" stems from their past experiences in Mexico. Furthermore he concludes that this abhorrence of the political was so strong that it was transmitted to their children.[5] While the latter factor probably does not affect more recent immigrants, the constant influx and presence of recently arrived individuals significantly affects the political characteristics of the entire group. It is this high proportion of new arrivals that distinguishes Mexicans from most other ethnic groups in the United States today.

Recentness of arrival, noncitizenship, and a low socioeconomic standing are important, but there are other factors greatly affecting the image of political nonparticipation that surrounds the Mexican American. These factors were not brought to their new home by Mexican immigrants; they were present in the institutions affecting the new residents. (They also affected Mexicans already living in this country before conquest.) The first of these "exogenous" factors—the nature of Mexican interaction with the larger society after the Anglo American conquest—

---

[4]The neglect of this important variable ranges from V.O. Key, *Southern Politics* (New York: Vintage Books, 1949) to contemporary works such as Mark Levy and Michael Kramer, *The Ethnic Factor: How America's Minorities Decide Elections* (New York: Simon and Schuster, 1972).

[5] Michael David Tirado, "The Mexican American Minority Participation in Voluntary Political Associations" (Ph.D. Diss., Claremont Graduate School, 1970), p. 11.

has been overlooked by a previous generation of scholars. It is said that "history is written by the victors," and this is particularly true of Mexican American history. As noted in Chapter Two, the idea that Mexicans were peacefully assimilated into American society simply is not true. Social banditry and rebellions swept the native Mexican population in the 1850s and later. The Cortina uprising in Texas, the Salt War of 1877, and the formation of Las Gorras Blancas in New Mexico have not been examined as political responses of a minority to domination.[6] Instead these incidents have been dismissed as being insignificant, or merely the acts of individuals.

But there have been further oversights by scholars who have failed to notice the institutionalized obstacles which hindered ethnic political participation in the Southwest. Such devices as the discriminatory poll tax, the White Man's Union in Texas (which existed until 1944) gerrymandering, and the overt suppression of political activity by threats, economic sanctions, subterfuge, and violence affected both Mexican Americans and Black Americans.[7] Furthermore, there have been other obstacles in such requirements as the English literacy tests which disenfranchised Mexican Americans in all states except New Mexico after the 1890s. Voter residency periods have disenfranchised most of the migrant labor population.

The failure to see Mexican American "resistance" and the failure to see Anglo American "repression" shows the great gaps in our studies of Mexican American participation in traditional politics. Other gaps exist in that there simply is very little knowledge about how the Mexican American minority in the Southwest accommodated itself organizationally to the Anglo American system. There is a gradually increasing record of formal organization, some overtly political and some latently political. Some of these studies point out how upper-class elements of Hispanos and Mexicanos in the Southwest slipped successfully into Anglo American society. Thus in California Mexican Americans were influential in southern California. They were active at the State Constitutional Convention. In New Mexico Hispano political power was an acknowledged factor from the first days of Anglo American rule. Other studies show that Mexican Americans were very active in the trade union movement of the 1930s. The earliest attempts to unionize California

6 Robert J. Rosenbaum, "Las Gorras Blancas of San Miguel County, 1889–1890," in *Chicano: The Evolution of a People*, ed. Renato Rosaldo et al. (Minneapolis: Winston Press, 1973), pp. 128–136.

7 On external conditions affecting Mexican Americans specifically see Mario Barrera, Carlos Munoz, and Charles Ornelas, "The Barrio as an Internal Colony," in *People and Politics in Urban Society, Urban Affairs Annual Review*, vol. 6, ed. Harlan H. Hahn (Beverly Hills, Calif.: Sage Publications, 1972), pp. 465–499.

agricultural workers came about through the *Confederacion de Uniones Obreras Mexicanas* and the mutualista societies, e.g., the *Sociedad Mutualista Benito Juarez* of El Centro (established 1919) and the *Sociedad Mutualista Hidalgo* of Brawley (established 1921).[8]

A possible reason for these oversights is the tendency of scholars to assess many political organizations in the Mexican American community by using models of Anglo American political organizations. Tirado notes that many observers were unable to detect political organizations because they could not see that many such groups were multifunctional and undifferentiated. He notes that the pattern for Mexican Americans appears to have been to "establish undifferentiated multipurpose organizations which not only served his political needs but also his economic, social and cultural ones as well."[9] Illustrative of this multifunctionality is the *Alianza Hispano Americana* whose functions over a 60-year period ranged from providing insurance benefits to pursuing advocacy programs in civil rights during the 1950s.[10] Numerous "traditional" organizations such as *Sociedad Liga Protectora Mexican, La Sociedad Progresta Mexicana, Comite de Beneficencia Mexicana,* and the *Soceida Union Cultural Mexicana* appeared in the communities. But not until recently have they been seen as vehicles for political purposes.

Another reason for the Mexican American stereotype is the comparison of Mexican political efforts with Blacks and those of European ethnics of the late 1800s and early 1900s. The inevitable result is a negative evaluation. Both analogies are misleading. Mexican American political efforts have existed in entirely different milieux. European ethnics did not suffer such a heavy burden of differentiation by race. Nor were they associated with a conquered subordinate population. Racial differentiation and a subordinate status made it easier for the dominant-subordinate relationships to be institutionalized. Further distinctions between Europeans and Mexicans can be made if one considers that European ethnics immediately met institutions favoring their political participation. In particular, the political machine of urban America in the nineteenth and early twentieth century depended heavily upon the successive waves of European ethnics. The political machine which gave the new immigrant both physical and psychic resources in return for his vote also politicized the immigrant. It established avenues of upward mobility in the political sphere. The advantage given to previous

[8]Charles Wollenberg, "Huelga, 1928 Style: The Imperial Valley Cantaloupe Workers' Strike," *Pacific Historical Review* 38 (1969): 45–58.

[9]Tirado, "Minority Participation," p. 37.

[10] Kaye Briegel, "The Alianza Hispano Americana" (Ph.D. Diss., University of Southern California, 1974).

waves of immigrants (who were often voting within a short time of their arrival) was not available for the Mexican American in many of the urban centers of the Southwest.[11] In some states, notably California, political institutions were "reformed" by the Progressives to eliminate the possibilities of machine rule. This "reform" negated the one advantage of low-income ethnic populations—that is, their basic vote power. In states characterized by a political machine form of government, Mexican Americans were able to take some political advantage of their numbers, as in El Paso, Texas, and in New Mexico.

If Mexican American political efforts are not comparable to those of European ethnics, neither are they comparable to Black Americans. While both groups share racial distinctiveness, Mexican Americans are not so distinctive. As a result, Chicano communities experienced selective assimilation and political cooperation to a much higher degree than Blacks.[12] Differential patterns of discrimination (depending on such variables as the darkness of skin, socioeconomic status, and the local "taste for discrimination") inhibited the feelings of ethnic group solidarity so strong in the Black community. One further differentiation between Black Americans and Mexican Americans appears in the relative size of these groups. There are more than twenty million Black Americans. They are significantly concentrated in most states of the United States. Mexican Americans are concentrated in five states and number less than seven million. This low national visibility, particularly on the East Coast, helps explain why such groups as labor, the Democratic party, liberal groups, educational institutions, and the large foundations did not champion Mexican American causes before the 1960s as they did Black causes. Rowan aptly quotes a Chicano college professor who said, "For the Mexican American, there are no liberals."[13]

Many factors thus account for the political stereotype of the Mexican American. But the underlying truth is that a variety of endogenous and exogenous factors did actually affect Mexican American political efforts. There were factors present within the group such as high poverty levels, many recent immigrants, and intra-ethnic racial differences. These

11 For the role that the political machine played in European immigrant ethnic politics, see Oscar Handlin, *The Uprooted* (Boston: Little, Brown and Company, 1951). See also Elmer Cornwell, "Bosses, Machines, and Ethnic Politics," in *Ethnic Group Politics*, ed. Harry Bailey and Ellis Katz (Columbus: Charles Merrill Publishing Company, 1969), pp. 190–206.

12 Jose Villareal, "Mexican Americans in Upheaval," in *Readings on La Raza*, Matt Meier and Feliciana Rivero (New York: Hill and Wang, 1974), pp. 213–217.

13 Helen Rowan, "The Minority Nobody Knows," *Atlantic* 219 (June 1967): 47–52.

were all obstacles hindering successful political efforts. Conversely, there were outside or "exogenous" factors. These include societal hostility, the absence of political institutions receptive to ethnic minorities, and the bias of scholars. But this is no excuse for the lazy development of a stereotypical image of Mexican American political efforts. Fortunately a critical body of literature is now emerging. A reevaluation of the Mexican American experience is well under way. This reevaluation (and the ethnic political activity in Mexican American communities during the 1960s and 1970s) should rapidly eliminate the image of Chicano passivity. An understanding of the range and the variety of contemporary Mexican political activity is best gained by examining some significant historical antecedents.

MEXICAN AMERICAN POLITICS
BEFORE WORLD WAR II

Before World War II the impact of Mexican political organizations had been limited indeed. Before the 1900s, ethnic organizations were subjected either to overt oppression (as in Texas) or they were limited in their impact largely because of the very few Mexican Americans actually living in the Southwest (only New Mexico had any substantial population). When heavy immigration began later, the ethnic organizations that did arise, such as the *mutualista*, were limited by their immigrant membership and the primary nature of their mutual aid orientations. Other organizations such as the *Orden des Hijos de America* and the League of Latin American Citizens (LULAC) were not hindered by an immigrant membership because they limited themselves to the middle class. Because they were explicitly assimilationist in orientation, lower-class Mexicans were excluded. Contemporary writers are now quick to criticize these organizations for assimilationist ideologies, but it must be remembered that in their time the obstacles to assimilation were not clearly perceived. Furthermore, the "middle class" was the only element of the Mexican American community that "tended to be American citizens anyway." Other political efforts during the 1920s and 1930s, such as those of the Catholic church and the Communist party and others, including *El Congreso de Pueblos de Habla Espanola* and the Mexican American Movement (MAM), were hampered by Anglo hostility. These were the years of the xenophobic activities of the Ku Klux Klan in Texas, the national "Red Scare," and the forced repatriations of Mexican Americans. But World War II changed this atmosphere drastically.

ACCOMMODATIONIST POLITICS

World War II was an event of unparalleled significance in the history of the Mexican American. The War profoundly affected Mexicans because: (1) Mexican Americans who served in the armed forces were exposed to social climates quite different from conditions in the Southwest—namely, the novel experience of not being treated as second-class citizens; (2) the war itself created an expanding economy in the Southwest which drew Mexican Americans much more rapidly into urban centers and into industrial employment; (3) the rhetoric of the national war effort, and (4) the attempts of the federal government to project a positive image of Latin Americans. (Ironically it was during the war years that the zoot suit riots overtly demonstrated the nature of prejudice faced by Mexican Americans.) The sacrifices and contributions of Mexican Americans to the war effort gave increased legitimacy to their political activism during and following the war.[14] The LULAC group caught this mood and expanded its constitution in 1944 to include the following goals: "eradication of discrimination . . . seek equal protection under the law . . . political unification . . . (and) participate in all local, state and national political contests." With the end of the war and the return of the Chicano veterans, this stage of political activism developed even further. With the aid and assistance of such organizations as the Race Relations Council and the Industrial Areas Foundation, newly formed groups that included the Community Service Organization (CSO) and the Unity Leagues of Southern California emphasized voter registration drives and articulation of community needs. These organizations were different. They were less oriented toward middle-class interests; they were less interested in assimilationist goals. More important, the stress on the articulation of *barrio* needs marks the first politicization of the lower socioeconomic strata of the community.[15] These organizations taught needed skills. A remarkable number of present-day Mexican American leaders (including Congressman Edward Roybal and Cesar Chavez) were at one time associated with organizations like the CSO.

This new activism is perhaps best demonstrated by the American

---

[14] Ethnic groups are disproportionately represented in combat units and therefore suffer disproportionate losses. In Vietnam 20.5 percent of the casualties of soldiers from the Southwest were Spanish surnames. Mexican Americans served in the armed forces with exceptional distinction because 37 percent of all Medals of Honor given during World War II went to Spanish surnamed soldiers.

[15] Ralph Guzman, "Politics and Policies of the Mexican American Community," in *California Politics and Policies*, ed. Eugene Dvorin and Arthur Misner (Reading, Penn.: Addison Wesley Publishing Company, 1966).

G.I. Forum. The Forum appeared as the direct result of an incident in Three Rivers, Texas, in the late 1940s. When private cemeteries and mortuaries refused to handle the body of a Mexican American soldier, Mexican American veterans protested this action and national attention was focused on the discriminatory conditions of Mexican American life in Texas. As a result of this incident and because he realized the necessity of continued activity, the G.I. Forum was organized in 1948 by Dr. Hector Garcia. It is still now in existence in over twenty-three states with a membership of over 20,000. The Forum was officially nonpartisan but it urged members to participate in politics, and it lobbied for Mexican American appointments at the local and state levels. In common with CSO, the Forum was not as fully committed to assimilationist goals as were the pre-War organizations.

In the late 1940s and 1950s, there was continuous effort to develop political power. The G.I. Forum conducted fact-finding investigations of the segregated school system in Texas and lobbied for changes. While national attention was centered on Black Americans, Mexican Americans also had to contend with segregated public facilities, segregated schools, and discriminatory jury selection procedures. A study conducted in the west Texas city of Ozona, showed for example, that the city's drugstores were closed to Mexicans until the 1940s. Restaurants and movie theaters were not desegregated until 1958. Even today the Chicano residents of Ozona still complain about segregation practices in the city's bowling alleys, cemeteries, and swimming pools.[16] The G.I. Forum and other Mexican American organizations were active in the struggle for change, conducting fact-finding surveys and in some cases bringing court suits. More direct political activity continued in the 1950s but at a low profile. It is probable that this reduction in activity was a consequence not only of the repressive atmosphere of McCarthyism but of the overt hostility shown Mexican Americans during Operation Wetback in 1954.

Toward the end of the 1950s a different type of political organization appeared. The Mexican American Political Association (MAPA) was created in 1959 after the defeat of Mexican American candidates in a California election. MAPA marks yet another stage in Mexican American political activism. In California (as in other states of the Southwest) it was paradoxical that although Mexican Americans had developed potential bloc voting strength, the established parties (particularly the Democrats) were not actively integrating Mexican Americans into party positions. The formation of MAPA, which was seen by many as a "rad-

---

[16] "Project Report: De Jure Segregation of Chicanos in Texas Schools," *Harvard Civil Rights-Civil Liberties Law Review* 7 (March 1972): 307–390.

ical" organization, was a direct response to this frustration. MAPA was clearly an ethnic organization with clearly stated ethnic goals. From the inclusion of the word "Mexican" in the name, to the active endorsement of Mexican American political candidates, MAPA was a new departure from the older sociopolitical organizations.

The formation of MAPA was closely followed by an event of special significance to the community. The *Viva Kennedy* campaigns were designed expressly to bring out the Latin vote for John Kennedy in the 1960 presidential election. These campaigns drew together Mexican Americans from different states and different organizations. Because the Mexican American vote was crucial to Kennedy in carrying such states as Texas (where his margin of victory was a slight 50,000 votes and Mexican Americans voted for him, 9 to 1) Mexican Americans received political aid and patronage positions in the early 1960s. In California MAPA's increased prestige helped elect two assemblymen, one congressman, and various judges. In Texas a counterpart organization to MAPA appeared with an identical name. However, the growth of the *Viva Kennedy* clubs and the desire to have a more inclusive ethnic label on the Texas organization resulted in the Political Association of Spanish Speaking Organizations (PASSO). PASSO attempted a branch in Arizona but regional interests prevailed and the American Coordinating Council for Political Education (ACCPE) became the counterpart for both MAPA and PASSO in Arizona. Like their MAPA counterpart, both PASSO and ACCPE won initial victories at local levels. In Arizona ACCPE was successful in electing various city councilmen. In Texas PASSO worked with the Teamsters to elect in 1963 a slate of Mexican Americans to the city council of Crystal City.

Even though it was not apparent to the larger society, by the early 1960s Mexican Americans had established themselves to a degree as an ethnic political power in the Southwest. It is true that their effective political power was not commensurate with their numbers. It might be said, however, that Mexican Americans were following the path of other ethnic political minorities such as the Irish and Italians who also first developed power at the local level and were courted during national presidential campaigns. Yet the traditional route followed by European minorities in the past was no longer as rewarding for an ethnic minority in the early 1960s. The primary reason for this was that the level of local government where ethnics such as Mexican Americans could theoretically have the most impact was the level which has become most limited in influence since the 1900s. In earlier years the control of local politics inevitably meant control of governmental appointments. By the 1960s most governmental bureaucracies were protected from political control by such institutions as the Civil Service. Not only were positions in the bureaucracy politically immune to some degree, but the control of policy in bureaucracies by local government was limited by both state and federal guidelines. This new insulation of governmental bureaucracies denied contemporary ethnic groups the job-rich and upwardly mobile opportunities traditionally given ethnics by government.

A further limitation to traditional ethnic group politics was the focus of Mexican organizations in gaining legal and political equality without their leaders realizing that the problems of Mexican Americans also encompassed economic and social inequalities. By definition, these inequalities had been termed "nonpolitical." The development of a sophisticated awareness of the problems facing modern ethnic minority groups influences both traditional and militant ethnic politics in the Mexican American community.

MEXICAN AMERICAN POLITICS
AFTER 1965

From the vantage point of the 1970s it appears that various events accelerated the realization among Mexican Americans that the traditional styles of ethnic politics would not accomplish the needed changes. Among the most significant of these events were the Black Civil Rights movement and the Black Power movement of the 1960s. The impact of the Black movement was threefold. First, the movement revealed that civil equality was not sufficient in itself to achieve meaningful social change. Second, the Black Power movement legitimized an ideology that rejected assimilation and fixed blame on the larger society for the deprivation of Black Americans. Mexican Americans were occupying a similar socioeconomic position and they could see the relevance of such terms as "institutional racism." Third, and most important, was the effect of the Black riots on the Mexican American community's view of government. Federal, state, and local governments responded to the Black riots with pledges of massive amounts of aid. This reaction jolted and politicized all elements of the Mexican community. One question epitomizes Mexican feelings during this time: "Do we have to riot in order to receive attention?" Many Mexican Americans felt that problems facing Mexican Americans in the Southwest were as severe (if not worse) than those of the Black community. Consequently, when the federal antipoverty programs of the War on Poverty and Model Cities were started, Mexican Americans began demanding a "fair share" of these.

In addition to the Black movement, such events as the Vietnam antiwar effort and the whole "counter-culture" movement provided alternative ideologies and models of political action to which Mexican Americans and especially young Mexicans could adapt. Inside the community itself, the emergence of ethnic leaders into national prominence gave further legitimacy to unconventional ethnic political efforts.

It is the emergence of ethnic political leaders like Cesar Chavez, Reis Tijerina, and Rodolfo (Corky) Gonzalez that brings full realization of the multiple factors behind the variegated nature of the Mexican American movement today. Each of these three individuals represent to some extent a different factor in the history of the struggle behind the Mexican American emergence into a nationally recognized ethnic minority. All three individuals were active in Mexican American community affairs prior to the middle 1960s. Cesar Chavez was a community organizer for CSO during the 1950s and moved to Delano in 1962 to begin organizational efforts for the Mexican and Filipino farm workers. Reis Tijerina was active in New Mexico attempting to regain the lands lost during the Anglo American conquest. In 1963, for example, Tijerina journeyed to Mexico City to seek support from the Mexican national government in attempting to regain these lands. Gonzalez was active in the *Viva Kennedy* movement during the early 1960s and in the antipoverty programs in Denver. All three individuals emerged at different times as leaders. But all three leaders contributed to the new ethnic militancy that captured national attention.

ETHNIC MILITANCY
AND THE CHICANO MOVEMENT

This new militancy began sometime in the mid-1960s. Cesar Chavez began the strike effort of *"La Huelga"* in 1965. Also in 1965 Corky Gonzales resigned from the Denver poverty program boards and founded *La Crusada Para La Justicia*, which later was to support high school strikes, demonstrate against police brutality, and advocate mass actions against the Vietnam war. In 1966, the National Farm Workers Association began a highly publicized march in California and Texas to dramatize the conditions of the Mexican farm workers. And in 1966 Mexican American leaders began demanding that Mexicans be included as target populations for federal antipoverty programs. In March 1966, Mexican Americans walked out of an Equal Employment Opportunity Commission conference in Albuquerque, New Mexico. This group petitioned the Johnson administration for a special conference, demanded more federal jobs, and threatened to picket a White House conference if their demands were not met. But the actions of this group were quickly eclipsed by Reis Tijerina and his supporters who occupied the Kit Carson national forest to publicize claims of the *Alianza Federal de Mercedes* to these New Mexican lands. The next year the lieutenant governor of New Mexico was forced to call out the National Guard and the State Police (with two tanks and a helicopter) after a spectacular "raid" on the courthouse at Tierra Amarilla. These events almost immediately held the sympathy of a significant segment of the Mexican American community. In particular, it excited and attracted young people.

Many young Chicanos (it was now possible to identify throughout the Southwest as part of a regional "Movimiento") met at a La Raza Conference held in October 1967. This meeting provided an opportunity and a forum for the young to articulate their frustrations and anger at the traditional style of politics. Armando Rendon captures this anger when he quotes one participant saying, "The young Chicanos see this conference as the last chance you older Chicanos have to come through. If nothing happens from this you'll have to step aside—or we'll walk over you."[17] The United Mexican American Students (UMAS), the Mexican American Youth Organization (MAYO), and the Brown Berets were all organized in the same year (1967). Common to all three organizations was an active rejection of traditional styles of political action.

These specific events and their conjunction with the Black Power movement (and the antiwar effort) provided the genesis of the Chicano movement. Today the word "Chicano" is synonymous with Mexican American, perhaps as "Black" means Black American but the term in the mid-1960s was something new for the Mexican American community. Originally the word "Chicano" was used almost exclusively by poor, lower-class Mexicans but now began to represent an ethnic viewpoint. Chicano ideology or "Chicanismo" was most actively (but not exclusively) promulgated by Mexican American student and youth organizations. These included UMAS, the Mexican American Student Association (MASA), the Mexican American Student Confederation (MASC), the Movimiento Estudiantil Chicano de Aztlan (MECHA), and MAYO.

In its essence, *Chicanismo* is an eclectic ideology that at times has drawn inspiration from the Black experience, the Latin American revolutionary experience, and the Mexican revolutionary tradition.[18] A full range of possible political actions is encompassed by different factions of the Chicano movement. Many Chicanos feel that the traditional forms of political participation are the least effective, especially

[17] Armando Rendon, "La Raza—Today Not Mañana," in *Mexican Americans in the United States*, ed. John Burma (Cambridge: Schenkman Publishing Company, 1970), pp. 307–326.

[18] A full and interesting account of *Chicanismo* of the late 1960s is given by Alfredo Cuellar in "Perspective on Politics" in the first edition of this book.

participation in the two party system. Others favor confrontation-type tactics of mass demonstrations and "walk-outs." A minority endorses the active self-defense tactics of the Brown Berets, and a smaller number sympathized with the revolutionary activities of the Chicano Liberation Front.

Chicanismo sees Chicanos as basically a conquered people—a people who were stripped of their land, their history and their culture as the result of Anglo exploitation. The Chicanos in the American economy are victims of an exploitative relationship. Chicanos have been used as a source of cheap labor for the economy of the Southwest but they have received little economic reward. Deculturization means that Chicanos are ashamed of their Mexican Indian heritage. Chicanos should have pride in their cultural heritage and in their unique adaptation to Anglo American society. Meanwhile, the process of deculturization continues in schools that fail to teach Chicano children their bilingual-bicultural heritage. *Chicanismo* emphasizes the concept of *la raza*—and it rejects materialistic standards of individualistic self-achievement. Rather, collective orientations based on *la raza* are more valuable standards.

The new ideology profoundly affected the Mexican American community, particularly the youth and the college students. The impact may have been greatest in the politics of education. Here increased demands for ethnic studies programs, ethnic heritage classes, and ethnic personnel reflected the ideological precepts of *Chicanismo*. The high school "blow-outs" (walk-outs) that swept throughout the Southwest indicate the strong appeal of Chicanismo in the community.

But the general course of ethnic militancy after 1968 followed old issues that had long been important to everyone. Many of the issues that were important rallying points in the Chicano movement—protests against police brutality, protests against miseducation, demands for more political voice—were always active issues in the community. But young Chicanos articulated these issues in ways that were both unconventional and grasped the attention of all American society. Consider, as an example, activism in school reform. Efforts by Mexican Americans to reform southwestern school systems reach back into the 1930s. (See Chapter Five.) The new Chicano approaches were marked by "blow-outs" and protest demonstrations. These appeared in California (1968), Texas (1969), and Colorado (1969). They were watched with interest by the general community, bringing as they did the inevitable police reprisals and reviving old tensions.[19] Colleges and universities felt Chicano protests for the first time,

[19]Dial B. Torgerson, " 'Brown Power' Unity Seen Behind School Disorders," in *Mexican Americans*, ed. Burma, pp. 279–288 and Carlos Munoz, "The Politics of Educational Change in East Los Angeles," in *Mexican Americans and Educational Change* (Collected Papers from a symposium at the University of California, Riverside, May 21–22, 1971) .

reflecting the greater number of Mexican Americans entering these institutions.

But there were some issues peculiar to the 1960s that emerged from the Chicano movement. The National Chicano Moratorium Committee organized demonstrations against the Vietnam war in 1969 and 1970. The protest in August, 1970 in East Los Angeles resulted in large-scale violence between the police and the demonstrators. In a terrifying manner it brought to national consciousness the anger and the frustration always latent in the *barrios*. (A noted Mexican American journalist was shot to death by the police, and a great deal of property damage done.) The antiwar issue rapidly lost momentum, but the question of police behavior continued to be a problem that Chicano activists used to generate community support.

In addition to this articulation of long-standing grievances and certain new issues, the most highly publicized aspect of ethnic militancy in the Mexican American community was the formation and development of a separatist third party effort—La Raza Unida Party (LRU). LRU may be seen as a response by Chicanos to the insensitivity of the American political system. Thus just as MAPA was an ethnic response in the 1950s, the new party was an ethnic militant separatist reaction in the late 1960s and early 1970s. The concept of the third party was developed by Jose Angel Gutierrez, a cofounder of MAYO and the leading spirit of the LRU in Texas. It was actively supported by Corky Gonzalez, who once described the two major parties as "an animal with two heads eating out of the same trough." The rationales for an ethnic party are numerous: third party organizations have access to media during elections; third party campaigns need not compromise with either of the established parties and thus can allow clear articulation of Chicano goals. Tactically, Chicano third party efforts in areas where Chicanos are a majority present opportunities for Mexicans to gain control of their own communities. An additional advantage is that by running candidates in general elections (even where there is little, if any, chance to win) the potential for a Chicano bloc vote is further developed.

Since its birth in 1970 in Texas, *La Raza Unida* has had some noteworthy successes. The most notable of these was in Crystal City, Texas. Here LRU candidates gained control of the city council and board of education in the 1970 elections. Since then "el partido" has been successful in such other Texas towns as Cotulla and Carrizo Springs. Even in its defeats, *La Raza Unida* has made its presence felt. In the Texas state elections of 1972, the LRU candidate for governor, Ramsey Muñiz, captured close to 6 percent of the vote. At present the LRU has official party standing in Texas and is seeking official status in California and Colorado. In New Mexico, *La Raza Unida* has not made significant inroads because of the ethnic representation that has existed historically in the major parties.[20] *La Raza Unida* is perhaps the most representative vehicle of the new militancy. It is comprised mostly of younger community people and has adopted radical or left-of-center positions on most issues—even to the point of splitting with Cesar Chavez for his endorsement of George McGovern in 1972. At the present time there appears to be a schism in the party between the Colorado faction (Corky Gonzalez) and the Texas faction (Jose Angel Gutierrez) on whether the right priorities are local level organizational efforts and the winning of elections (the Texas position) or building a vanguard type of party designed to politicize the Mexican American community (the Colorado position).[21]

Yet for all the excitement, its electoral showing in states other than Texas has not been strong. In California and Colorado no LRU candidates have been elected. In 1974 only 20,000 LRU voters were registered in California. In addition to its poor electoral showing in states other than Texas, there are several obstacles on the way to a viable political organization for Chicano interests. Mexican Americans are a minority in all five southwestern states. Mexicans do not reach a majority in most urban centers of the Southwest. Chicano control of cities or counties is not possible outside towns and counties in southern Texas or possibly New Mexico. (The victory in Crystal City heartened many Mexican Americans but the total population of Zavala County around Crystal City is 74.4 percent Spanish surname. Thus the uniqueness of Crystal City indicates certain limitations on LRU strategy.)

The second obstacle appears when the major parties run Mexican American candidates. *La Raza Unida* candidates splinter the Chicano vote and defeat both the Mexican candidates. Thus LRU candidacies resulted in the defeats of Joe Bernal in Texas and Richard Alatorre in California. It is not possible to assume (considering the diversity of political outlook among Mexican Americans) that Democratic or Republican candidates are not "true" representatives. Quite possibly "ethnic solidarity" may not be present in the Mexican American community now or ever, any more than it is present in Black communities. In the case of Crystal City, the new party was able to capture political power through a unique set of circumstances: the socioeconomic characteristics of the community included a large number of migrant workers who were more easily mobilized and the disproportionate number of Chicano voters in the community.[22] In the long run, therefore, appeals

---

[20] Statement from F. C. Garcia, Assistant Professor of Political Science, University of New Mexico, Albuquerque.

[21] "A Position Paper on the Status of La Raza Unida Party in Califas, Aztlan," August 21, 1972 (mimeographed).

[22] John Shockley, *Chicano Revolt in a Texas Town* (Notre Dame, Ind.: University of Notre Dame Press, 1974).

based solely on ethnicity may be of limited usefulness. La Raza Unida now has existed for more than four years and the pressure to win elections and to get candidates into offices appears to be building slowly but strongly. The 1976 elections (especially in Texas) may be crucial in determining the continued growth and viability of this ethnic third party.

It may appear at first glance that the impact and the actual gains of the Chicano movement are minimal. To say the least, *La Raza Unida* has not made extensive gains. Many militant organizations such as the Brown Berets have come and gone; ethnic militancy, in fact, appears to be on the wane. Yet in retrospect, Chicano militancy has had tremendous impact on the Mexican community. In the American political system protest activity must always be considered a potential political resource.[23] The protest activities and the new awarenesses brought by the Chicano movement have served at the very least as political resources that have benefited other political groups in the Mexican community.

THE NEW ETHNIC POLITICS

While the Chicano militants were expressing anger and frustration at a political system that was unresponsive to Mexican American needs, the system itself was undergoing certain changes that will continue to have a significant impact on Mexican American politics.

The first of these changes is the increased awareness by both parties of Mexican Americans as a "swing" group that can affect elections. As an example, the Mexican American vote probably cost the Democrats the governorship in Texas in 1966. In 1968 the Mexican vote carried Texas for Hubert Humphrey in a victory of only 39,000 votes. Also in Texas the nearly 200,000 votes given to a Chicano *La Raza Unida* candidate in 1972 clearly indicated the possibly disastrous consequences for the Democratic party if Mexican Americans were to vote either Republican or for the LRU. In fact, both parties made highly publicized advances to the Mexican American community. During the 1968 and 1972 campaigns both presidential candidates addressed themselves to actual problems of the Chicano community, rather than the customary stock speeches on the "contributions" of the Mexican American people to the history of the Southwest.[24] More importantly, both parties began sup-

[23] Michael Lipsky, "Protest as a Political Resource," *American Political Science Review* 62 (December 1968): 1144–1158.

[24] Unfortunately, much of the rhetoric in presidential campaigns is simply rhetoric. In attempting to win Chicano votes in Texas, Spiro Agnew promised a special conference on Chicano problems with most of the major foundations in attendance. The conference was scheduled in 1969, but cancelled because most of the foundations did not attend. On the symbolic recognition so common in American politics, see Ray-

porting Mexican American candidates. And more Mexican Americans are being elected to public offices, below the federal level, aided somewhat by the elimination of some of the traditional obstacles. (See Table 8–2.) The increased representation, of course, also increases belief in the viability of traditional electoral politics.[25] The 24th Amendment to the United States Constitution eliminated the poll tax which had disenfranchised Mexicans in Texas for a very long time. In California the legal case of *Castro vs. California* eliminated the requirement of literacy based solely on the English language, thus enfranchising thousands of Spanish-speaking Mexican Americans. While support of ethnic candidates is a traditional means of the American political system of appeasing ethnic constituencies, ethnic elected officials can serve some very needed functions.

Elected ethnic officials can articulate ethnic issues at a level where significant outcomes in public policy may occur. A relatively small group of elected ethnic officials in a state legislature, as in California, have the potential for developing a bloc vote. Increased Chicano representation in the California legislature has seen this body handle such issues as

TABLE 8–2

SPANISH SURNAMED STATE LEGISLATORS

Year	Arizona	California	Colorado	New Mexico	Texas
1950	0	0	0	20	0
1960	4	0	1	20	7
1965	6	0	1	22	6
1973	11	6 a	4	32	10

Numbers were determined by consulting the *Book of the States*, Supplement I, *State Elected Officials and the Legislatures* (Chicago: Council of State Governments, 1950, 1960, 1965, and 1973). Figures for these years are approximate and involve the author's determination of Spanish surnamed legislators by name.

a A Chicano State Senator was elected in 1974.

---

mond Wolfinger, "Some Consequences of the Ethnic in Politics," in *The Electoral Process*, ed. Kent Jennings and L. Harmon Ziegler (Englewood Cliffs, N.J.: Prentice-Hall, 1966).

25 A recent survey in East Los Angeles found a very high proportion of the residents favoring elections of public officers, (90 percent) and the traditional parties (67 percent) as a proper solution for community problems. Only 43 percent favored a separate political party for persons of Mexican background. Biliana C. Ambrecht and Harry Pachon, "Ethnic Political Mobilization in a Mexican American Community," *Western Political Quarterly* (Fall 1974). These findings were substantiated by a survey taken by the Committee to Re-elect the President (CREEP) at approximately the same time. This survey found a substantial percentage of Chicano respondents approving of traditional electoral politics.

demands for bilingual-bicultural education, placing bilingual personnel in state agencies, and certain issues relevant to the farm workers. In addition, skilled ethnic politicians can enhance their political power beyond mere numbers by invoking an image of ethnic militancy. Consider in this respect Congressman Edward Roybal's testimony during the establishment of the Cabinet Committee on the Spanish Speaking People:

> The students are asking questions. The militants in our community are on our backs almost every moment of the day. And the question that is being asked of me, members of the Congress, and other elected officials is . . . "Is it necessary for us to burn a town before the government looks at our problems objectively."[26]

Further recognition of Mexican Americans on a national level appeared in the creation of the Inter-Agency Committee on Mexican American Affairs (IACMAA) by President Johnson in June, 1967. This was in direct response to Chicano demands for such recognition by the federal government. Its goal was to advise federal agencies on the needs and special problems of the Mexican Americans in federal programs. In 1969 IACMAA was given official congressional standing and renamed the "Cabinet Committee on Opportunities for Spanish Speaking People." The history of this Committee is almost a classic case study of the symbolic appeasement that so often is the response of the American political system to ethnic demands. Not until 1970 was a director appointed by the president—and even then, it coincided with a drive by the administration to court Latin and Mexican American votes for the 1972 election. The belated appointment of the cabinet committee director, a highly publicized appointment of Romana Banuelos as U.S. Treasurer, and the announcement of a 16 Point Program to hire Spanish speaking persons in the federal government might be considered positive responses to Chicano demands. But no substantial change in governmental policy was involved. After two years the much-heralded program increased Mexican American and Latin federal employment only 0.3 percent to a total of 3.1 percent. More recent studies show that fourteen out of twenty agencies in the executive office had no Spanish-speaking representation whatever.[27] The Cabinet Committee was never adequately funded. More importantly, some leaders of the Committee were so active in the 1972

[26] Hearings before the Committee on Government Operations on Establishing the Cabinet Committee on Opportunities for Spanish-speaking People, 91st Congress, 1st Sess., November 25, 26, 1969, p. 18.

[27] Hearings before the Committee on Government Operations on the Activities of the Cabinet Committee on Opportunities for Spanish-speaking People, 93rd Congress, 1st Sess., July 23 and September 12, 1973, p. 42.

presidential campaign that they were charged as being more interested in the reelection of President Nixon than in furthering the interests of the Mexican American population. These rather ineffectual efforts opened the entire concept to charges of tokenism and probably contributed to the abolition of the Cabinet Committee in 1974.

But real political gains have been made at other levels. In local and state activity, Mexican Americans have become deeply involved in bureaucratic politics. This politicization and awareness is a direct result of the expansion of federal antipoverty programs and Model Cities programs of the early 1960s. Such programs as Head Start, the Concentrated Employment Program, Model Cities (and the satellite support programs) opened up thousands of bureaucratic positions which not only hired middle-class Mexicans but drew in *barrio* people in paraprofessional jobs. But this was not all. Many of these programs placed great emphasis on citizen participation through such groups as "citizen advisory boards" and resulted in further political access points. The participation of *barrio* residents has developed the political skills of a great many people who can now manipulate political resources to influence governmental bureaucracies.[28] Both established Chicano groups and new functional groups have begun to seek this type of access in order to influence public policy. Health care, drug abuse programs, social welfare programs, and educational programs—many varieties of *barrio* programs— are now sensitive to community opinion and influence. Generally the results are that many persons in the Mexican American community feel they are indeed able to influence and to alter the shape of governmental policy.[29] The consequences of this feeling of participation may be very great in the future.

Ethnic militancy has captured the attention of the nation, and it has great appeal for many young Chicanos. But militancy is only one aspect of the political development of the Mexican community. There are many styles to this development. We have outlined the shape and meaning of some of these styles. They will continue in all their diversity but it can be said that the Mexican American people have established their presence in American politics as a significant ethnic group.

[28] An excellent study of the effects of Mexican participation in citizen advisory boards was done by Biliana C. S. Ambrecht in "Politicization as a Legacy of the War on Poverty: A Study of Advisory Council Members in a Mexican American Community," (Ph.D. Diss., University of California, Los Angeles, 1973).

[29] For a case study see Joan W. Moore, "LUCHA in Agencyland: Chicano Self-Help Organization Meets the Establishment," *Growth and Change* (Summer 1972).

Epilogue

Social scientists are always being warned about the dangers of over-generalization. In turn, they warn their students about the dangers of stereotyping. The situation of this nation's Chicano citizens rather sharply illustrates both the futility and the injustice of overgeneralization and stereotyping. There can never be too many warnings.

Historically, many Mexican Americans were reluctant to call themselves a minority. By contrast, and by ironic accident, those Chicanos who do consider themselves a minority find so little recognition from the rest of American society that they are profoundly frustrated. It is disappointing to be "invisible" and a "second minority" and yet to suffer deep and unyielding problems that are lost in the national preoccupation with Blacks. In a strange way, the Mexican reluctance to accept any single generality as their position in American society is only one of a series of contradictions. ·

Mexicans have been very nearly as long in this country as the Indians, and yet they are also the newest minority. Mexican immigrants settled in the upper Rio Grande valley of New Mexico a full generation before the Plymouth Colony in New England. Descendants of those first colonists never left New Mexico. On the other hand, no other group has entered the United States in such massive numbers since 1930—and still enters both legally and illegally at such a rate.

Mexican Americans are remarkable not only for their uncomplaining acceptance of their conditions of life in this country but also for a consistent record of military assaults upon the American government. While American Blacks are constantly discovering a lost and forgotten intransigence, the Chicano historical record has passed quickly from border warfare to a great range of civil violence in the cities of the Southwest, much of it not known beyond a local area. And in June of 1967 a band of more than fifty Mexican Americans assaulted the Rio Arriba County Courthouse in Tierra Amarilla, New Mexico. Yet the masses of Mexican Americans in the large cities of the Southwest are politically inert. The very model of Mexican leadership has been the "quiet fighter," who does not create any public difficulties. Until the arrival of Cesar Chavez in 1965, the dramatic agricultural strikes in the

159

San Joaquin Valley in California and in the Rio Grande valley in Texas, the "Mexican way" was quiet and private negotiation.

Mexicans have no very clear consensus on whether they are a racial group, a cultural group, or even if they are white or nonwhite. Yet the idea of *la raza* permeates the Mexican American population. *"La Raza"* does not refer to "race" at all, but to a vague sense of ethnic identity, a compelling feeling of belonging—but to *what* is left relatively unconceptualized. For their part, Anglos long thought of Mexicans as a racial group, but the Mexicans themselves have always shown much ambivalence in their attitudes toward the predominantly *mestizo* strain. Spanish blood was always carefully distinguished from the Indian stock. The confusion is not confined to the Mexicans. Although there were never miscegenation statutes or other legal discrimination, as there were against Filipinos and Blacks for example, segregation has been widespread and pervasive, and discrimination equally so. Only very slowly has the consciousness of discrimination become legitimated among Mexican American spokesmen: only very slowly have they been willing to define the Mexican Americans as a minority and to risk the pejorative implications of such a definition.

The minority includes peons—but also aristocrats. Some Mexican Americans, for example the Canary Islanders of San Antonio, are aristocrats who consider themselves such, and are accepted as such by white Americans. But they and even the small (but growing) middle class are overshadowed by the desperately poor, an underclass exemplified by thousands of stricken families in the large cities of the Southwest and by the migrant farm laborers, who still perform agricultural tasks throughout the Southwest.

Mexicans include both the assimilated and the unassimilated. Full acceptance into American life is available for many. In Los Angeles the middle-class, third generation young people intermarry with native Anglos to a large degree. On the other hand there are still large Mexican enclaves, particularly in certain counties in Colorado, New Mexico, and Texas, where ethnic exclusiveness is almost complete—even among middle-class individuals who have lived for many generations in the United States.

It is precisely these contradictions that create special dilemmas for Mexican immigrants and their children who can usually see both alternatives at once. In terms of models, the young Chicano has many. He can very nearly disappear into "white America." He can remain very Mexican, returning frequently to Mexico. He can become a tough young militant on the black power model. He can even withdraw completely from any form of collective action; he can be a Colonist or a Frontiersman.

It is this diversity that makes any characterization of Chicanos so extremely difficult. Generalizations about the total population must always be taken with a grain of suspicion. Unfortunately, most Americans can think about America's Mexican minority in only two ways. One is in terms of the classic and seemingly inevitable merger of the immigrant into the mainstream of American life. The other is the familiar situation of the Black American. But neither of these ways of thinking describes the Mexican American in the United States. Both ways tend to obscure much of the single hardest problem in American society which is probably that of the great reluctance of American institutions to change fast enough to meet the needs of Mexican Americans. Much of the future history of the Chicano minority will depend on the speed and the shape of this change.

But again, even this generalization must be considered carefully. There are always the contradictory realities of the nation's second largest minority which, after all, is even more fascinating because of its challenge to modern social scientists and makers of social policy.

Index

Texas (*cont.*)
agriculture, 14, 26
border cities, population, 34
border conflicts, 23
Chicano Movement, 152
Cortina War, 142
demand for cheap labor, 13, 14
as destination for immigrants, 45
development of white collar class, 22–23
disenfranchisement, 24
drug programs, 77
economy, 13
education, 35, 66–69, 73, 75, 84, 124
Emigrant Agent Law, 22
Great Depression, 26
housing, 72
income, 34, 63
land shifts, 13
language, 122
law enforcement 93–94
migration from, 29, 52
Operation SER, 98
Operation Wetback, 43
patterns of original Mexican settlement, 13
patterns of settlement, 2, 55–57
political activity, 34, 109, 142, 147, 148, 153, 154, 155, 156
Political Association of Spanish Speaking Organizations, 148
population, 13, 34, 55
population in 19th century, 12
Populist Party, 24n
racial minorities, 35
religious organizations, 88, 89
right-to-work law, 110
social diversity, 34, 109–10
social welfare programs, 106
Texas Rangers, 33–34, 93–94, 96, 108
Texas Revolution, 3, 4, 11
Thomas, Arthur, 124n
Tijerina, Reies, 101, 150, 151
Tirado, Michael David, 141, 143
Tracking, 82
Trout, Grafton, 101n
Tuck, Ruth, 111n

U.S. Bureau of Census, 1n, 12n, 54
U.S. Civil Rights Commission, 72, 73, 80–82, 85, 91, 92
U.S. Immigration and Naturalization Service (*see* Immigration)

United States-Mexico Border:
conflicts, 23–24, 37, 38
control, 39–44, 50–51
geography, 36–37, 37–38
German intervention, 23
origin of, 37–38
U.S. Supreme Court, 73, 75
Urbanization (*see also* Albuquerque; Los Angeles; San Antonio), 25, 26, 27, 32–33, 57–58, 77, 119

Vaca, Nick, 127n
Valle, Juan Ramon, 119–20
Value differences (*see also* Culture, Mexican), 129
clannishness, 135–38
familism, 130–32
future orientation, 132–35
New Mexican village, study of, 132–33, 135
traditional views, 130–33
Vasquez, Richard, 9
Vietnam War, 146n, 149–50, 153
Vigilante tradition (*see* Law enforcement)
Villa, Francisco (Pancho), 24
Villasenor, Edmund, 9

Warshauer, Mary Ellen, 123
Waters, Lawrence Leslie, 21n
Webb, Walter Prescott, 108n
Weiss, Gertrude, 1n
Wetbacks (*see* Immigration)
Winnie, William W. Jr., 20n
Wolfinger, Raymond, 156n
Wollenberg, Charles, 143n
Woods, Sister Frances Jerome, 104n
World War I, 23, 25
World War II, 146–47
broadened experience for Mexican Americans, 29
Wyse, Ronald, 46n, 48n

Yo Soy Joaquin (Gonzalez), 9

Zeleny, Carolyn, 116n
"Zoot suit" riots, 28–29, 77, 89, 93, 112, 144

60,761